No Fixed Address

JON EVANS

NO FIXED ADDRESS

SIX CONTINENTS, SIXTEEN
YEARS, SIXTY-SIX NATIONS

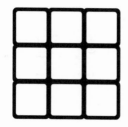

The Porcupine's Quill

Library and Archives Canada Cataloguing in Publication

Evans, Jon, 1973–, author
    No fixed address : six continents, sixteen years, sixty-six nations
/ Jon Evans.

ISBN 978-0-88984-387-5 (paperback)

    1. Evans, Jon, 1973– —Travel. 2. Authors, Canadian (English)—
Travel. 3. Journalists—Travel. 4. Voyages around the world. I. Title.

PS8609.V337Z85 2015   910.4'1   C2015-907076-7

1   2   3   •   17   16   15

Published by The Porcupine's Quill, 68 Main Street, PO Box 160,
Erin, Ontario NOB 1TO. http://porcupinesquill.ca

Edited for the press by Chandra Wohleber.
The quotation on page 135–136 is from Graham Greene's *The Comedians*
(published by Vintage) and is used with permission.

Represented in Canada by Canadian Manda Group.
Trade orders are available from University of Toronto Press.

We acknowledge the support of the Ontario Arts Council and the Canada
Council for the Arts for our publishing program. The financial support of the
Government of Canada through the Canada Book Fund and the Government
of Ontario through the Ontario Media Development Corporation is also
gratefully acknowledged.

To my father and mother
for lighting the way

Contents

❖

In Search of a Lonely Planet

One implication of the phrase 'no fixed address' is that its subject is, in some sense, lost.

In Filipino, or so I'm assured by Alex Garland in his superb novel *The Tesseract*, the word for 'unhappy' is the same as the word for 'lonely'. If so, in the future we need never be unhappy again—because we will never be alone. We will always be connected, even underground, even out in the middle of nowhere; and that connection will worm its way closer and closer to the core of our being. First desktops, then laptops, then phones, then wearables, then implants? The Internet will become as omnipresent as air, and to many, very nearly as necessary. We will never be lonely—and we will never be lost. We will always be able to know exactly where we are and exactly what is nearby.

Many people view this as a good or even wonderful thing. I am not one of them. I have spent a considerable portion of my life seeking out new and interesting places in which to be lost and alone, and I think I'm a much better person for it. I think people who have never been truly alone will never truly be able to be self-reliant and independent, and those who have never known the intoxicating terror of being lost will be far less able to deal with the new, the uncertain, and the inevitable transience of everything in life. Eliminating 'lonely' and 'lost' may sound good on paper, but it strikes me as akin to settling into a very comfortable chair rather than learning how to run.

❂

I. AFRICA

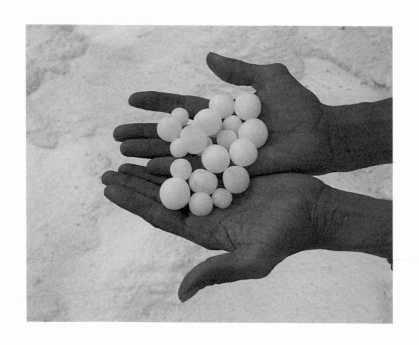

⊞⊞⊞⊞⊞⊞⊞⊞⊞⊞⊞⊞⊞⊞⊞⊞⊞⊞⊞⊞⊞⊞⊞⊞⊞⊞⊞⊞⊞⊞

In 1998 I joined an overland truck tour that was supposed to drive from London to Kenya via Morocco, Mauritania, the West African coast, Congo, and Uganda. Civil war and group dynamics had different ideas, and the trip disintegrated in Cameroon—but subsequently became the basis for my first published novel, *Dark Places*.

After that I was hooked. In 2005 I spent three months roaming from Nairobi to Cape Town as research for another novel. I returned for a few weeks in 2011 and again in 2014 mostly because I couldn't resist.

By 'Africa' I almost invariably mean 'the Sahara and south'. That epic desert divides cultures far more decisively than any mere ocean. Even that reduced region is, obviously, immense and diverse: I've spent almost a year of my life wandering around it, and I feel like I've only scratched its surface. People who say 'it's a small world' generally haven't seen much of it.

Africa has become a byword for blood and bullets, thanks to media reports of tragedy and silence in the face of progress, but it is the continent that most richly rewards the time and effort invested in travel. Especially overland travel. The distances are vast—my relatives who grew up there refer wryly to 'MMBA', or 'Miles and Miles of Bloody Africa'—but the more effort you put into African travel, the greater the rewards. If you only have one epic journey left in you, make it an overland trip from Cairo (or at least Nairobi) to Cape Town, or from Marrakesh to Lagos. Nothing else in this world compares.

October 2005: To Penetrate the Impenetrable
Lake Bunyonyi, Uganda
I have been to the middle of nowhere, and it is not the Bwindi Impenetrable Forest. It is, rather, where you go when your teenage taxi driver takes a wrong turn en route to said impenetrability and continues for half an hour unawares.

I was first made aware of our misdirection when the top of my head smacked into the roof of our car. I'd splashed out on a private ('special hire') taxi to Bwindi, public transit being chancy-to-unavailable except on market day, and somehow contrived to fall asleep despite the humped, fissured, rocky dirt road that winds along ridgetops and steep hillsides, past glorious views of the Western Rift Valley, and the cloud-shrouded Ruwenzori and the Virunga volcanoes, along terraced fields and stands of eucalyptus forest, during the (theoretically) three-hour journey. But when I woke, the road was no longer dirt. It wasn't even, really, a road. Barely even the idea of a road: more of a wide grass walking trail, very uneven—hence the wake-up bump—segregating raw jungle from small semi-cultivated fields and banana plantations.

I gently suggested to Isaac-the-driver that this couldn't be right. (Thinking: *I know they call it impenetrable and all, but this is ridiculous.*) Isaac bridled but eventually, with universal male reluctance, agreed to stop and ask directions. *Of whom?* I thought, but indeed, round the next bend, next to a small igloo-like structure made of mud and strips of bark, there they were: a woman and five children, dressed in colour-drained rags, staring at us amazed.

Information was exchanged. A clearing was found, a little ways on, in which to turn around. We drove past the (now more amused than amazed) family and rattled back up a road I wouldn't have taken a 4WD down, much less a battered Corolla. It was vertiginously steep, narrow, twisted, uneven, and incredibly bumpy. As I offered silent prayers of thanks to Toyota engineers, two parallel strips of dirt emerged from the grass; then the grass meridian vanished; and finally, thirty minutes' drive and maybe twelve kilometres after turning around, we were back on the proper route to Bwindi.

To give Isaac credit, he did drive with ferocious skill. If only his navigational abilities were commensurate. Or his negotiating skills. I later learned that he'd severely undercharged me, which may explain his failure to turn up today for the agreed-upon return leg.

The nearest town to Bwindi is called Butogota, and even more than most small African towns, it's like something out of the Wild West. A single wide street of blasted dirt runs between two rows of storefronts, concrete blocks with tin awnings. The store I entered sold big sacks of wheat and beans; bags of salt, sugar and tea; soap (in long unwrapped bars), candles, baking soda, matches, toilet paper, paraffin—and that was it. No chocolate, no sweets, no biscuits, no baby food, no Vaseline, no lotions or powders—none of the other usual array of colourful disposables found in most African shop-stalls.

The bottle shop next door sold beer, Coke, and water. There was a post office; a police station; a gas station with hand-cranked pumps; an immigration post (the town is right on the border of the Democratic Republic of the Congo); a hotel/bar with a pool table; a few dry-goods-type stores, J. Nkrumah and Sons and such by name, with shadowed, indeterminate contents; and, in the town's one concession to the twenty-first century, an MTN mobile-phone airtime-voucher stall. There were two secondary schools, one Muslim and one Christian, and a bunch of one-room primary schools. There were fewer than a dozen vehicles. But for the vehicles, the MTN store, and the banana-tree backdrop, we could have been at the Texas–Mexico border a hundred years ago.

The Bwindi Impenetrable Forest is a national park in remote southwest Uganda, on the Congo border. It is best known for being home to half of the world's mountain gorillas (the other half are fifty kilometres south, in the Virunga range of volanoes that straddle the Uganda–Rwanda–Congo borders). *Bwindi* means 'dark'. The Dark Impenetrable Forest—it's like something out of a fantasy novel, isn't it? I mean, Mirkwood's got nothing on this place.

Where even the epiphytes have epiphytes
Bwindi is rainforest, not jungle. Rainforest is dominated by enormous canopy trees, fifty metres high, that soak up almost all the sunlight—hence 'dark'—and means the undergrowth, though still extremely profuse, is push-your-way-through rather than hack-your-way-through, though Bwindi verged on the latter in many places—hence 'impenetrable'—far more so than other African montane rainforest I've seen. (Mount Afi, on the Nigeria–Cameroon border, and the Vumba in eastern Zimbabwe.)

From the park gate, you can see the forest rising high across a steep ravine. It is an incredible wall of thick, tangled green, interrupted only by the thin pale strips of canopy tree trunks. Only trees are visible, a vast, looming, endless mass of them: no trails, no clearings, no landscape features; only this utterly opaque arboreal shield.

Within, the forest is so violently, densely fecund that even the greenery has greenery. Roots and branches are covered by moss; vines hang on vines; the very stones look like verdant hillocks. Clouds of pure white butterflies scatter as you walk. Birds hoot, monkeys ook, water burbles. It's beautiful.

On the way in, en route to the first three-hour hike, the sky was bright blue. Mindful that they don't call it rainforest for nothing, I asked at the park gate if it might rain later. 'No,' the guard assured me, 'I guarantee.' I decided not to double back to the village of lodges and curio shops just outside the park for my raincoat, and pressed on. Naturally a massive tropical downpour commenced two hours later.

I was assigned a guide and two guards with Kalashnikovs. Overkill, for a maybe-seven-kilometre walk, you'd think—but in 1999, forty tourists were kidnapped here, and eight murdered, by members of one of the Congo's innumerable warlord-led militias. Since then security has been high. *Lonely Planet* calls the Uganda military presence here 'invisible', but it sure didn't look that way to me when we passed a troop going into the forest. 'To find snares set by poachers,' my guide helpfully explained. I smiled, nodded, looked at the dozen soldiers' light machine guns and bulbous RPGs, and disbelieved.

In perhaps-not-entirely-unrelated news, the Ugandan papers have of late been full of reports that the Lord's Resistance Army, a rebel group of eye-popping barbarity that has terrorized northern Uganda for two decades, has just moved its base from the Sudan to eastern Congo, although they are believed to be hundreds of miles north of Bwindi. (As of 2014, the LRA has allegedly moved to the Central African Republic, although eastern Congo remains, at best, an unsettled and violent land.)

The main trail, where we passed the soldiers, runs straight through the forest to a market at the Congo border, some two hours' walk. I asked if I could go see the market, but only local villagers are allowed to pass through the park to the market, and I'm sure my guards weren't keen on escorting an unpredictable *mzungu* there, and that was all a moot point because the government had ordered the market closed this week to contain a cholera outbreak. Instead we hiked up through the surreal density of the Impenetrable Forest proper, until the rain began; then we fled, soaked to the skin, back to the lodge.

Cholera, machine guns, gorillas, a divinely inspired army of atrocity, the Dark Impenetrable Forest—I mean, if I can't get story material out of this place, I ought to hang up my thriller-writer keyboard now, no?

October 2005: Gorillas, in the Midst
Gisenyi, Rwanda

'Get ready for the experience of a lifetime' says *Lonely Planet East Africa*, with respect to preparations for tracking wild mountain gorillas in the Virungas. The Bradt *Guide to Rwanda* concurs: 'In 15 years of African travel, we have yet to encounter anyone who had gone gorilla-tracking and regretted the physical or financial expense.'

Well, then. Let me be the first. The silverback has no clothes!

Okay, yes, it was a pretty cool experience. There was indeed a faint alien-species first-contact *frisson*. The gorillas were cute or majestic or occasionally both. The setting, a bamboo forest straight out of *Crouching Tiger, Hidden Dragon*, was stunning, all vertical lines enclouded by leaves, which also formed a soft brown carpet. (Apparently young bamboo shoots are like gorilla chocolate.) The gorillas played together, climbed trees, groomed, wandered, ate, hooted, and growled. (No chest beating though.) These gorillas, despite being wild, are habituated to human contact, which means they almost entirely ignored us. One, a mother with a tiny baby riding on her shoulder, actually brushed past me. (In theory you're supposed to keep a seven-metre distance, but in practice the guards only enforce two metres, and more to the point, nobody ever sent the gorillas the memo.) Another mother left her child behind, and it ran after her, mewling and weeping piteously, before catching up and leaping onto her back as she walked. The silverbacks strolled past us in the forest like lords of the jungle. The hour passed in a flash, and yes, $400 is a lot to pay for an hour, but it's what you'd pay for the same amount of time with a hotshot lawyer, and the apes are a lot more photogenic.

But oh, the opportunity cost. Because, you see, the gorillas are found in one of the most stunning landscapes on the planet, the green, stark-jutting Virunga range of volcanoes, and for that same $400 you could spend five days climbing up and down a couple of those volcanoes, visiting gorgeous crater lakes, wandering nature trails, viewing golden monkeys, and seeing the Dian Fossey memorial. All of which would cumulatively be far more beautiful and rewarding, I'm sure—but nobody does. Instead they pony up the hundreds, hang with the gorillas for an hour, and flee. And now, having spent the money, and not having the time to take the five-day hike, I've done the same damn thing. It's a terrible shame.

Also, I have what I believe to be gorilla dung smeared on my jeans. I swear I'll never wash them again!

October 2005: In the Shadow of Doom
Goma, Democratic Republic of the Congo

This place is *crazy*.

Can whole cities be cursed? Because it seems that's what happened to Goma. As if being situated in eastern Congo, the farthest-flung province of a nation ransacked by three decades of kleptocracy, wasn't bad enough, ten years ago things started to get *really* bad.

In 1994, more than one million refugees fleeing the rebel army invading Rwanda from Uganda (and putting an end to the genocide there) came to rest in Goma. Tens of thousands died of cholera before the UN constructed the world's largest refugee camp. But many of these 'refugees', fed and sheltered and medicated by the UN for a million dollars a day, were in fact members of the militia who planned and carried out the Rwandan genocide. These *interahamwe* ruled the camps with iron fists, and, unwittingly supplied by the UN, used them as bases for a continuing low-level war with Rwanda for some years, until finally, in 1998, Rwanda invaded and repatriated the refugees.

That was just the start of Goma's problems. The Rwandan invasion was part of a Congolese civil war that quickly grew to involve seven nations and innumerable rebel armies, factions, and militias. The resulting war dragged on for years and is believed to have killed some three million people. Then, a couple of years ago, a deal was struck, UN peacekeepers moved in, things began to settle down—and that's when Mount Doom blew its top. Mount Nyiragongo, some twenty kilometres north of the town, erupted in January 2002, and half-mile-wide rivers of red-hot lava flowed straight through the city centre into Lake Kivu. Hundreds died; half a million more fled their homes.

City on the edge of never

Today, as I type, an ever-present plume of smoke drifts from the mountain, a looming flat-topped darkness visible from most of the city, like the CN Tower in Toronto. On a clear night the volcano's murky red glow can be seen for miles. The word on the street is that a volcanologist recently told the governor that the volcano will almost certainly erupt again in the next two years (it did not) and that all of Goma should be

18

immediately relocated—but the governor quashed the report. Not that relocation would help. A gargantuan inversion layer of methane gas and carbon dioxide is believed to be festering beneath the surface of Lake Kivu, and further volcanic activity might cause it all to be released at once, possibly suffocating to death the two million people who live around the lake. Experts believe they may be able to give as much as eight minutes' warning.

A cataract of black lava runs straight through the city, dotted by the jumbled, rusted carcasses of cars and a few burnt skeletons of buildings. Goma's cathedral took the full brunt of the flow and only its walls remain, beneath an ashen crucifix, surrounded by a glistening field of solid lava, patterned in huge whorls, like the fingerprints of titans. The main market was immolated. The city was cut in two.

And the Congolese have responded with typical—well, either indomitable tenacity or bewildering optimism, depending on your point of view. Much of the lava that, as in Tolkien's *Return of the King*, 'cooled and lay in twisted dragon-shapes', has been put to use: heaps of lava gravel and orderly piles of watermelon-sized stones wait to be mortared into huge lava walls that will surround newly built properties on the newly vacant real estate, and, hopefully, will divert any future 'red rivers' that flow from the mountain. Children in blue-and-white uniforms play on the enormous jagged field of dark lava that starts just outside the doors to the biggest local school. Nearby, brand-new homes, unprotected by perimeter walls, sit brightly on the jet-black rubble. The streets seethe with noise, chaos, colour: Congolese are far more exuberant, in both attitude and dress, than the reserved Rwandans. The city is very much alive.

And it's a crazy kind of life. This is the Wild East. According to the map, I'm in the Congo, but in practice, the Congolese government does not function here at all. Eastern Congo is a crazy-quilt patchwork of shifting territories controlled by various armed groups: Congo troops; Rwandan troops; *interahamwe* remnants; rebel forces with connections to one or more of Rwanda, Uganda, Zimbabwe, Angola, and Namibia; independent warlords; the feared Mai Mai cannibal rebel army; and the Lord's Resistance Army—more factions than you can shake a Kalashnikov at. The UN force here (MONUC, some 17,000 troops, which sounds like a lot, but remember that this country is the size of Western Europe) maintains an uneasy and regularly broken stability.

MONUC costs a billion dollars a year, and its staffers live in a world parallel to that inhabited by most of the Congolese, riding around in gleaming white armoured personnel carriers, passenger trucks, and oil tankers, most of which live behind razor-wired lava-rubble walls down by Lake Kivu. The troops here are Indian (from Bihar, incidentally, India's poorest and most corrupt state). The hordes of NGOs— Médecins Sans Frontières, Save the Children, UNICEF, UNHCR, etc., etc.—live the same satellite-dishes-and-4wDs-behind-high-walls-and-guards existence. The local bar, Doga, is frequented by expats, NGO workers, the haggard-looking volcanologist, and a supporting cast of shady characters from God knows where, most of whom are very good pool players. The place serves good pizza and burgers, even though they don't really need to. Doga is the only bar in town.

You don't really get any tourists. I'm the first unofficial visitor my NGO-worker quasi-hosts here have ever had. As I walked through the thriving, colourful market yesterday, people stared at me amazed, and there was a constant refrain of '*mzungu mzungu mzungu*'; there are plenty of white people in town, but they don't wander around on foot much. (Several kids independently shouted, 'Zidane!' at me, in blatant and highly successful attempts to flatter me by implying I resembled the incomparable French midfield maestro.) The other guests at my (quite nice, US$50) hotel are all Congolese or NGO people here temporarily.

Sample overheard snippet of conversation, in French, from a nearby breakfast table one morning: 'I assure you, the money is ready!'

Both of my plans here have been torpedoed. Due to bad timing/logistics, I just missed out on joining a few British medical students' expedition to climb Mount Nyiragongo, which is kind of a shame, 'cause I was thinking of dropping in my Iron Ring to see what would happen, but maybe it's better for the world that I didn't. I'm a little bummed about this (and starting to wonder if I'll ever climb a volcano again), especially since I passed up the opportunity in part so I could take a boat across Lake Kivu to Bukavu, another Congo city, tomorrow morning. But I have discovered that, in traditional African style, tomorrow's boat is definitely not running, and Saturday's boat may or may not run. Sigh. I might just go back to Rwanda *demain*. Which is, amazingly, less than a mile away as I type, but feels like a whole other world.

What's left in *this* world, after MONUC and the NGOs, is somewhere between a libertarian paradise and terrifying anarchy. Start with the economy. The local currency is a bizarre hybrid of cash US dollars with Congolese francs instead of small change. (And the dollars can be wrinkled, grubby, and brown, but God help you if there's even the smallest tear.) No credit cards, no traveller's cheques, but one of the local banks does do Western Union. No gas stations either: instead, gangs by the side of the road sell gasoline from yellow twenty-litre jerry cans, siphoning it into empty water bottles.

Let's explore that a little further. Because there is no government here, there is no tax. And so this gas, which is mostly trucked in from Kenya via Uganda, sells for half the price in Congo that it does in Uganda due to that nation's taxes; there is a thriving business in smuggling jerry cans and two-hundred-litre drums of gasoline *back* into Uganda and selling it for a huge profit. The rest of the Congo's extraordinary natural resources—oil, gold, diamonds, emeralds, manganese, cobalt, copper, coltan, mahogany, all here for the taking in vast amounts—follow similar shady routes to enormous profits ... for someone.

Meanwhile, airplanes and helicopters zoom in and out of Goma's lava-shortened airstrip at all hours, going to and from other Congo cities, courtesy of companies with names like Hewa Boru Airlines and Wimbu Diwa Airways. You have to fly, you see; no roads connect

Congo's provinces. There are hilariously frightening tales of drunken Ukrainian pilots and of radio chatter that goes like this: 'Hello, Goma? I'm trying to land! Is there anyone there? Is there anyone at the tower? Goma, do you read? I'm trying to—oh, hell. I'm just going to go ahead and land. Okay, I'm landing now. Hello? Is anyone there?'

The aircraft are limping Antonov jets or prop planes—hence the Ukrainian pilots—carrying rebel leaders, mining prospectors (within five minutes of my arrival in Congo, a guy named Chi-Chi tried to talk me into investing in a local manganese mine), aid workers, NGO employees, smuggler-barons, and God knows who else. For a twenty-dollar *doucement*, they'll put anyone's name on your plane ticket. At this very Internet café, the printer beside me just churned out a CERTIFICAT DE NAVIGABILITÉ for an Antonov. I'm sure that's *entirely* on the up-and-up.

At least communication is easy. And amazingly cheap. Mobile-phone companies have towers all over the hills that dot this rugged landscape. For $3 I bought a SIM card that came with a dollar's worth of talk time, and ten free text messages a month for a year. (Talk ain't cheap at 30 cents/minute but Internet is at 75 cents/hour.) Every intersection has a booth selling air-time cards. Eastern Congo is theoretically part of the Democratic Republic of the Congo, but it doesn't have any governance in the traditional sense. But it's not quite anarchy either; it's this weird distributed economic community, built around doubtful airstrips and mobile-phone antennas, connected by a bad intra-province road network guarded by the roadblocks of maybe a dozen armed factions, some of whom play nice, some of whom will kill you on sight. It's utter madness. I kind of like it.

October 2005: One Day in Dar
Dar es Salaam, Tanzania
9:00 Arrive ferry terminal. Wander through dusty, cavernous customs hall to gauntlet of taxi drivers. Bargain half-heartedly with a couple of them, determine that taxi prices have doubled from when my guidebook was printed. Employ none of said drivers and stop at nearby French bakery. No bread—curious—but good coffee, served with steaming-hot milk.
9:30 Continue through downtown streets. The sidewalks tend to be pillared arcades to provide shade for pedestrians. The buildings are

mostly 1960s monstrosities or cheaply-thrown-up concrete shells, but
there are a couple of nice old colonial buildings. Everything permanent—
walls, roads, signs—is faded, shabby, cracked, peeling, crumbling, dusty,
mottled with sun and water damage, drained of colour. Men dress in
drab slacks and short-sleeved shirts, women in colourful wraps. They
pour past me in a slow-walking stream. Stores sell stationery, tools,
textbooks, clothes, dry goods; street hawkers sell shoeshines, Cokes,
sunglasses, used books, newspapers. Taxi drivers and would-be
moneychangers call for my attention. Generators whir on both sides of
the street. I see a headline: DAR PLUNGED INTO DARKNESS. It isn't
until then that I realize none of the buildings around me have power.
10:00 Take a taxi to the YMCA, which is faded, shabby, cracked, etc.
Also full. They direct me to the nearby YWCA, which is not full. I pay
$10 for a double room, which is faded, shabby, cracked, etc., but
reasonably clean. Mind you, there is no power and no running water.
They can't make change—lack of 'small money' is often an *enormous*
hassle in the Third World—so the lady writes *3,000*, the change I am
owed, on the back of my receipt, and tells me to ask for it later.
10:30 Walk a short distance down the street, past gleaming Citigroup,
Subway, and Emirates logos—in a building that has power, from its own
generator—to the Mövenpick four-star hotel, which of course has
power too. Such islands of twenty-first-century civilization are both
common and welcome in downtown African cities. Enjoy AC, eat a jam
doughnut, check expensive Internet, ask them if I can use their gym.
No, I can't: they want to help me, you can see it, but their bureaucracy
doesn't allow it, they don't have a 'procedure' for day memberships.
12:00 Complete long, hot wander through downtown. Through the
area of walled ministries, hotels, and banks, into the thronging,
pounding, intertwining streets near the post office, the nexus of all *dala-
dala* activity in Dar. (*Dala-dala*s are local public transit: minibuses into
which as many as sixteen passengers are crammed, organized by
complex social protocols). It's very hot, maybe 40C, and I'm wearing
jeans, but as long as you keep moving, and stop off in air-conditioned
places (such as the shiny bookstore A Novel Idea which, I'm pleased to
see, sells both of my published novels), it's not so bad. In most places,
despite the power cut, business continues almost as normal. It reminds
me of a Zambian joke: 'What did we use in Zambia before we had
candles?' 'Electricity.'

13:00 Back to YWCA for brief siesta in midday heat. A me-shaped puddle of sweat has appeared on the bed by the time I get up. Still no small money for change. I argue with several taxi drivers before finding one who will take me up to the Masiki district, five kilometres north of the city, for 5,000 shillings (US$4.50).

14:00 It's like a different world up here. Sprawling estates beyond whose high, broken-glass-topped walls can be seen mansions, huge satellite dishes, and manicured lawns and gardens. Security company logos are emblazoned on the gates, which open to allow huge 4WD vehicles. I stop at the Slipway, a wealthy shopping mall with a supermarket full of Western goods, a Japanese restaurant, a smoothie bar, a hookah bar, a coffee house, a pizzeria, another branch of A Novel Idea, a movie theatre, a flashy hotel, and docks used by ocean-going boats, including yachts. This is where the other half lives: expats, embassy staff, Asian merchants, and rich Africans.

Most African cities are set up like this. The bustling, busy, fun but disagreeable downtown; the ministries-and-NGOs district; the green, wealthy, pretty suburb where the rich live lives of Western standards, with pseudo-Western stores and logos; a tiny belt of houses where the vanishingly small African middle class live; and then a long, long stretch of poor exurbs and poorer shantytowns, home to the overwhelming majority of the population.

15:00 Work out at the Dar Fitness Centre, a very nice gym. The hostess speaks English with I've-lived-in-America fluidity. I'm the only one there. I've definitely lost some strength on this trip.

17:00 To yet another wealthy enclave, the Sea Cliff, a luxury hotel at which many presidents have stayed (but they seem proudest of having had Angelina Jolie as a guest) and another nearby luxury mini-mall. I eat an enormous pepper steak at a branch of a South African steak house, and have a beer and read on the cliff over the Indian Ocean, watching the waves dash themselves against the stones as the sun sets. The local paper reports that the power in central Dar es Salaam will be out for *two weeks*—two major transformers have blown. But this district, with better and more recent infrastructure, is unaffected.

19:00 Night has fallen. I argue with taxi drivers outside the Sea Cliff, who tell me that while it may be 5,000 shillings to get from downtown to here, it's 10,000 to get from here to downtown. 'Never mind,' I say, annoyed, 'I'll take a *dala-dala*.' The drivers laugh, calling my bluff.

Then they look at me incredulously as a *dala-dala* appears with Hollywood timing, and I hop on—with, I have to admit, a certain amount of smug self-satisfaction.

But they're probably right most of the time. I suspect only a tiny proportion of the Sea Cliff's clientele would be willing to take public transit, particularly at night. Partly out of inchoate (and totally irrational) fear, and partly, I think, out of a never-articulated belief that it's Just Not Right for a rich white person to get on a minibus packed with poor black commuters.

In reality, said commuters don't give a shit about me; nobody looks twice. And at this hour the minibus isn't even overcrowded. The conductor helpfully gets me to change *dala-dalas* at the right place, and I'm back at the YWCA about as fast as I would have been via taxi, for a total cost of 400 shillings.

20:00 Still no small money at the dark YWCA. They give out candles at reception. I talk to a couple of American girls in a nearby room. They're appalled by the news of the two-week power cut.

21:00 In bed and nearing sleep. I'm a night person in the West, I swear, but in Africa, you adopt a dawn-to-dusk schedule whether you like it or not.

October 2005: Where There Is No Coca-Cola
Bulawayo, Zimbabwe
Gas stations throughout Africa, like everywhere else, display their prices in big bold numbers visible from far away. One in Uganda might say something like:

PETROL 2310

DIESEL 1680

PARAFFIN 970

('Petrol', o North American readers, is the British word for gasoline. 'Paraffin' means kerosene.)

If you walk from Zambia to Zimbabwe, as I did a couple of days ago, you cross over a metal suspension bridge perched 111 metres above the Zambezi River gorge. From your right comes the constant thunder of Victoria Falls. To your left, a bungee-jumping booth stands on the edge of the bridge. If you look over that edge, you may see, far below, amid whitewater wrinkles, yellow Tonka-toy-sized river rafts, full of adrenalinized tourists about to brave twenty-two of the twenty-four rapids of the lower Zambezi gorge. (Of the remaining two, one is grade six, too violent to raft; and you don't raft the last rapid, because then you hit crocodile territory.)

Once past the Zimbabwe border—at which the inspection of yours truly was very cursory compared to the inspection of the US$30 I paid for a three-month tourist visa—almost the first building you reach, after a long, hot, uphill half-kilometre walk, is a Total gas station. Here, in Victoria Falls, once the heart of Zimbabwe's thriving tourist industry, now its last vestigial remnant, the station's price board reads:

PETROL NO

DIESEL NO

PARAFFIN NO

African gas stations also sell sweets, snacks, drinks, and, often, luxury imported goods. Mobil Marts, BP Shops, and La Boutique at Total (they're not being pretentious, it's a French company) are often where you go for European cheese, chocolate, and toiletries, because they're built with gleaming international-standard production values, they feature backup generators that keep fridges running during power cuts, and they are tied into reliable international distribution networks.

If you walk into La Boutique at the Victoria Falls Total, you will see a large Coca-Cola fridge with a crack across one pane. Large and utterly empty. There is Fanta, curiously; there are local Zimbabwean fruit juices; but when I entered Zimbabwe, there was no Coca-Cola available anywhere in Victoria Falls. This was somehow more shocking than the absence of gasoline.

Sometimes the first impression says it all.

There is no fuel here because there is no money. No foreign money, that is; no hard currency. The country is awash in Zim dollars, millions and billions of them, thanks to governmental inability to realize that printing more money is not a valid solution to an economic crisis. When I was here seven years ago, US$1 bought you Z$20. Today's black-market exchange rate is US$1=Z$100,000.

That is, if everyone is honest. They usually aren't. As a sign at my lodge in Victoria Falls said: DO NOT CHANGE MONEY ON THE STREET, YOU *WILL* BE RIPPED OFF. An Aussie couple I was travelling with got cheated twice in Zambia, where they had to change on the streets because the ATMs there accepted Visa but not MasterCard. The first time, the guy made an enormous amount of trouble during the transaction, changing his rate and how much he was willing to change, to cover a con à la *The Sting* in which he switched one of their $100s for a fake. The second time, although they were extra-paranoid and all the money was on a table and in plain sight at all times, the guy somehow, in a performance worthy of the Magic Castle, disappeared 30,000 of their Tanzanian shillings, then cancelled the transaction, claiming he had changed his mind. I know, it's easy to say it wouldn't happen to you, that you'd be more careful. But the thing is, you wouldn't be, not when it's brutally hot, you've been travelling for forty-eight hours straight, you're in a strange country full of worries and distractions, and all you want to do is get to your lodge and into a shower. These two were veteran travellers, but you can't keep your guard up all the time.

I changed $20 at a bank here (it's wise to have an Official Exchange Receipt handy) and the very thorough clerk gave me small change, including a Z$20 note, which has a value of one-fiftieth of one US cent—literally not worth the paper it's printed on. On the other end of the scale, the largest note is Z$20,000, worth less than a quarter. Change a hundred US dollars, and you get a wad of notes—cheap notes, printed only on one side—four inches thick. Every retail transaction is slow here because both sides have to take an appreciable amount of time just to count the money.

Which leads to yet another money-changing danger, the undercount. So how *do* you change money on the black market?

It's actually not an issue that comes up often. In all my travels, I've only found real currency black markets in Nigeria and Zimbabwe. Artificial, unsustainable currency rates are such an obviously bad idea that they only happen in semi-failed states. (Fully failed states like the Congo just use US dollars, eliminating the problem.) In other places, you may get a 5 percent better rate on the street, but the risk isn't worth it.

At land borders, if you need to change money on the street to afford a ride to the nearest town, you just change ten bucks' worth of currency from the previous country—preferably without taking out your money stash—and accept that you're going to get an awful rate. In town, you use a semi-trusted source: ask staff or security where you're staying, or people at a café, somewhere that caters to travellers. They'll know someone or may well be willing to change money themselves. Then the transaction is indoors, in a controlled environment, with plenty of time for everybody to double-check, and you know someone to go to if there's a problem.

If you *must* change a lot of money on the street, agree on a rate first, then take the changer's money and count it, pull the money you previously decided to change—and only that money—from a pocket, give it to him/her/them, and immediately walk away.

In Victoria Falls, at least, the fuel shortage is not that big a deal. The falls are close enough to the border, and there's sufficient local liquidity on the currency black market, that you can often buy fuel smuggled in from rich Botswana for the reasonable price of Z$100,000 per litre. (It's for this reason that the Botswana pula is even more desirable than the US dollar.) Elsewhere in the country, though, if fuel is available at all, it is often only available to those with foreign currency.

I remember, on the drive from Burning Man to San Francisco with A. and M., not two months ago, we stopped in Reno and picked up a newspaper full of Hurricane Katrina news. This was the point at which everyone was still saying things like 'certainly thousands and thousands dead'. Another, similarly histrionic article reported that fuel prices had gone up to $5/gallon in some places and that in some parts of America fuel was not available at all. 'Not *available?*' M. asked, stunned. 'What—what does that *mean?*'

In Zimbabwe, the fuel shortage means that people might go from Harare to their home village to attend their father's funeral, and wind up stranded there for weeks. It means that ambulances have been replaced by oxcarts in certain remote areas. It means that businesses shut down, buses do not run, fields are not tilled, grains are not milled. It means that any drivers who do come into the country make sure they bring enough fuel to get out again. It means that the black market quite literally keeps the country running. If you have some source of hard currency, probably from a relative working in a foreign nation, you're okay. If not, your life is paralyzed.

It's not that there isn't any gasoline available for import. It's that hyperinflation, and the government's subsequent attempts to fix both the price of fuel and the value of its currency, has caused legal importers to throw in the towel and give up. There is no way to bring fuel in, sell it legally, and make a profit—in fact, you'd lose more than half your money. And so the country languishes in stasis: food shortages worsen here in what everyone will tell you was once 'the breadbasket of Africa', a nation that exported food to all its neighbours. Slowly, day by day, the country withers.

The night before last I took the train from Vic Falls to Bulawayo. It's almost the only way to travel cross-country now; the few who *do* manage to get their hands on fuel don't want to expend it all on long-distance travel. The train has decayed greatly from what it was seven years ago: rusted fixtures, doors that don't close, torn seats, worn hinges, cracked glass, screeching brakes. The twin interlinked *Rs* of Rhodesian Railways are still embossed on every window and metal fitting, although Rhodesia ceased to exist twenty-five years ago. We left an hour late, because of a huge line of people buying last-minute tickets, and it took us fourteen hours to travel 450 kilometres, because we stopped anywhere along the line where people waited, to pick them up. It's become a *matatu*—ad-hoc collective transport—on rails. It has to be. For many people there's no other way to travel.

There are a few things you should understand, that may not be obvious if all you know about Zimbabwe is what you read in the media.

The first is that this was once a rich country. It didn't just feed itself; it had thriving tobacco, mining, and tourist industries that brought in stacks of money. Villages that the train passed by were dominated by brick houses with tiled roofs, not the bamboo-and-thatch or concrete-and-tin of east Africa. Bulawayo, 'the City of Kings', Zimbabwe's second-largest city, is a city of wide boulevards lit by elegant street lights, big beautiful parks full of majestic trees, museums, galleries, theatres, department stores, factories, hypermarkets, metered taxis, cinema multiplexes, and golf courses. Once upon a time, not so long ago, these catered not just to white farmers, Asian merchants, and rich government cronies, but to a growing African middle class.

(I remember, when I flew from Cameroon to Harare in 1998, being a little stunned for the first couple of days—bright lights, big city, wealth, bustling civilization. Zimbabwe was an incredible tourist playground back then. I bungee'd and rafted at Vic Falls, rode in the meticulously maintained wood-panelled luxury of the train system, went on game drives in Matopos, canoed in Kariba, explored the ancient ruins of Great Zimbabwe, walked with elephants and wild dogs in Mana Pools conservation area, went hiking in the Eastern Highlands, watched recent-release movies in Harare movie houses, and gorged myself at *braai*s (barbecues) in the late lamented Possum Lodge, and after four rewarding but often difficult months in West Africa, it was all so easy, so affordable, so comfortable, and so much fun. The place was paradise.)

The second thing is that while straits are dire here, it is not in the midst of utter ruin. The government is fascist, but this is not, for the most part, a violent police state. There is no obvious men-with-guns presence. There are roadblocks, but all African countries have these, and I haven't seen anybody trying for a bribe. Local journalists and opposition politicians have been beaten, jailed, tortured, and murdered, yes—but at the same time, there is a very visible political opposition, and while the press carefully watches what it says, it doesn't just parrot government propaganda. Some stores are closed, and others have thinly stocked or half-empty shelves; the streets are half-deserted; there are power cuts, and water cuts, and Bulawayo's water is no longer safe to drink; some people in remote areas are beginning to starve; the papers are full of news of factories that have closed, or agricultural plans that have been abandoned, due to lack of forex; but—from what I've seen so far, mind—somehow, life goes on. People cope. It's an economic crisis, not (yet) a security crisis. Don't get me wrong, these are desperate times for Zimbabwe, but the country is not collapsing. Instead it's slowly rotting away.

The third thing is that there is actually room for a kind of guarded optimism. The country may have finally hit economic bottom. Tourists are returning to Vic Falls: three years ago, the Victoria Falls Hotel had nights with fewer than ten guests, but now, an average of 150 are ensconced in its colonial luxury every night. Two weeks ago, the official dollar exchange rate was US$1=$Z26,000, but the pragmatic new central-bank governor has introduced an 'auction' system (he's not allowed to say 'devaluation' because Mugabe will flip out if he hears the word), which has already raised the rate to a more realistic Z$60,000, and is expected to bring it up to the black-market rate in a few weeks. And the government is now permitting small-scale importers to bring in fuel, which, until a few weeks ago, was exclusively the legal right of the ministry of transport, whose officials siphoned away all forex for themselves. There is a chance that in a month or so the Victoria Falls Total station may once again sell fuel.

It's not much, but maybe it's a start.

(And the Coca-Cola delivery truck arrived in Vic Falls the day after I did.)

So, what went wrong in this country between my first and second visits? That, my friends, is both a simple story, and yet a long and complex one.

November 2005: The Missionary Explorer and the Diamond Tycoon
Bulawayo, Zimbabwe
This is a history lesson. I'll try to make it entertaining.

The history of modern Zimbabwe begins with two dead white men. Extraordinarily famous dead white men: both are more than a century deceased, but you probably know their names. Conveniently, their stories dovetail nicely with where I've been over the last few days.

Almost exactly 150 years ago, on November 16, 1855, David Livingstone (as in, 'Dr. Livingstone, I presume?'), who was in the midst of an expedition across Africa—primarily to carry the word of God to the heathen, but also to survey the continent and open trade routes—was led by his native guides to what still today, from a distance, looks exactly like a bushfire. Then, as you get closer, it sounds like thunder. Hence the African name *Mosi-oa-Tunya*, 'the smoke that thunders'. But Livingstone was a loyal royalist Brit: and so, once he picked up his jaw from where it must have fallen—because this one-and-a-half-kilometre-wide, one-hundred-metre-high curtain of falling water really is a stunning sight—he promptly rechristened it Victoria Falls.

It may not actually have been quite so wide at the time. It would have been, like now, just the end of dry season; and as I type, the entire Zambian side of Victoria Falls is dry. You can walk right along the lip of the basalt gorge that is the falls, if you like, on massive water-worn stones whose bored holes and smooth, fluted edges look uncomfortably like jumbled bones, and then peer over the brink. The Zambezi still tumbles in huge cataracts over the slightly lower Zimbabwe side, though, at a rate of tens of millions of litres per minute, into an opaque white maelstrom beneath, across which arcs a standing rainbow. On a full-moon night, you can see a moonbow.

Even at this minimal flow rate, spray rises high into the sky. When I looked up from the Zambian side at midday, I saw, to my amazement, a perfect rainbow ring around the sun. The colossal gorge over which the river tumbles is narrow enough that you could hurl a baseball across, and it's sheer on both sides. Mist from the falls settles constantly on the patch of land just opposite the permanent Zimbabwe side of the waterfall; this has perpetuated a tiny standing jungle maybe five hundred feet long and one hundred wide, wet and thick with ferns, creepers, and other jungle vegetation not otherwise found for a hundred kilometres in any direction. Between the falls and the micro-jungle, it's an amazing sight.

Other explorers followed Livingstone—one Frederick Courtney Selous, in particular—and discovered that the high plateau to the east of the Zambezi was fertile farmland, relatively malaria-free thanks to its height, and just about dripping with gold. Gold has been mined in Zimbabwe for two thousand years, carried to the Mozambican coast and traded with Arabs; this is the wealth that built the civilization that in circa 1400 built Great Zimbabwe, by far the most impressive ruins of sub-Saharan Africa.

When Livingstone discovered Victoria Falls, in England a little boy named Cecil was two years old. Seven years later, Cecil was diagnosed with tuberculosis. His parents were told he would not live past twenty-one. At age seventeen, in the hopes that the southern air would aid his lungs, his parents sent him to visit his brother, who had recently emigrated to South Africa.

Cecil died before he was fifty. But he had quite an eventful life. During his five decades, two countries were named after him (Northern and Southern Rhodesia); he was named the prime minister of a third country (South Africa); he was also—at the same time!—the managing director of one of the most powerful companies in the world (the British South Africa Company); oh yes, and for the last decade of his life he was widely believed to be the richest man on Earth.

Today, he is best known in North America for the scholarships he endowed in his will. Every Rhodes Scholar attends Oxford on the tab of Cecil John Rhodes's estate. It's not clear what exactly happened with that other section of his will, the one that left money 'To and for the establishment, promotion and development of a Secret Society, the true aim and object whereof shall be for the extension of British rule throughout the world.' His trustees are clearly, to say the least, falling down on the job.

Rhodes made his fortune from the diamond fields at Kimberley, where there was an initial diamond find in 1869, a rush, and then, a few years later, after all the easily accessible diamonds had been mined, a collapse. Rhodes shrewdly bought up all the claims that other miners were selling cheap; then new pumping technology allowed access to a prodigious number of previously inaccessible diamonds, and Rhodes's De Beers Mining Company (named after the farm on which the original discovery was made) owned almost all of them.

A millionaire (in nineteenth-century pounds) by age twenty-seven, Rhodes turned his attention to the colonization of Africa. His creed was summed up with the modest words: 'I contend that we [the British] are the finest race in the world; and that the more of the world we inhabit, the better it is for the human race.' He decided to build a railway from Cape Town to Cairo, to cement British domination of the 'Dark Continent'. He began with the rich areas then known as Mashonaland and Matabeleland, after the Shona and Matabele people who inhabited them, just north of South Africa (known as 'the Cape Colony' at the time). One leg of the railway extended north from Johannesburg; another began at Beira, at the Mozambican coast, and went west; and Rhodes himself designed the city that grew at the place where they met, the city of Bulawayo, in which I sit.

From Bulawayo, the railway went west to Victoria Falls, across a bridge that was built, in 1895, to span the Zambezi, and continued north until it reached the Congo border. En route, Rhodes, the British South Africa Company, and the pioneers it financed and encouraged conquered (or signed extremely unequal and exploitative treaties with) the Shona and Matabele, and created two new countries; Southern Rhodesia (which became simply Rhodesia, and is now Zimbabwe) and Northern Rhodesia (now Zambia).

The railway never made it to Cairo. The Boer War interfered; then Rhodes died of ill health in 1902, and no one shared enough of his vision to force the railroad on. I'm sure he'd be pleased to know that today, though the line to Beira has long since ceased operation, and much of the Zambia line isn't currently running, at least you can connect from the same tracks that he built as far as Dar es Salaam.

Rhodes's grave can be found at a place called Malindzidzi, or 'World's View', in Matopos National Park, where I spent yesterday. During my last visit, my *Lonely Planet* said, in a flight of fancy that has surely since been edited out, 'You don't have to believe in ley lines and crystals to know that the Matopos Hills are one of the power places of the world.' It's an otherworldly place. Incredible crystalline hills and ridges of granite jut out from the African bush, where leopards and rhinos roam. Malindzidzi, a natural ring of colossal boulders atop a huge, solid granite hill, rising above the rest of the park, is one of the most starkly beautiful places I have ever been. I'm grateful I got the chance to see it for a second time.

Rhodes wrote that he chose it for a resting place because of its 'grandeur and loneliness'. I know exactly what he meant.

Let's jump forward to 1948. That's the year that the British Airways Overseas Corporation inaugurated its weekly passenger flying-boat service from England to South Africa. Passengers flew from Southampton to Sicily to Alexandria to Khartoum to Port Bell (now Entebbe) to Victoria Falls to Jo'burg, flying one leg a day, 12,000 feet above the planet, overnighting at each of those destinations. From Vic Falls, you could ride Rhodesian Railways' luxury first-class cars north to the Congo, east to the Mozambican coast, or south to Cape Town.

Does that sound fabulously exotic and romantic? It should. It was. It was the golden age of British colonialism in Africa.

In 1948, my father, born in what was then Umtali and is now Mutare, in eastern Zimbabwe (hence my deep and abiding interest in this country, in case you're curious), was nine years old, and attending a more-British-than-British boarding school in the leopard-infested Vumba rainforest. Note, also, that 1948 was one year *after* India became fully independent. That's an important fact about Rhodesia: it was, in many ways, the absolutely last vestige of true British colonialism on the planet. When my cousin visited here, a decade ago, somebody at an all-white *braai* asked her what she thought of the Rhodesians around her, and she answered, memorably, 'You're like the seaweed flung onto a rock by the highest wave of the highest tide, and left there to dry.'

(Yes, my cousin is a genius.)

Here's something else you should know about colonial life: it was *wonderful.* Whites in Rhodesia lived, for the most part, as well as those in the Raj. No: better. Big houses with spacious verandahs, massive farm properties, vistas of extraordinary natural beauty all around, *braais* and fresh mangos and just-laid eggs, expeditions to Cape Town or Mozambique or to hunt the leopard that was preying on the cattle, days spent on horseback riding across your domain, a tight-knit community of fellow whites, servants to cook your food, make your bed, prepare your saddle, work your fields, build your house. Many if not most Rhodesian whites lived, literally, like medieval kings.

(And many expats in Africa live much the same way today. If you have hard currency, a European pension, say, you too can have that life, those servants, that community, those expeditions. With foreign money, you can live a life here that makes a city or suburban existence in the West seem mean, ugly, cramped, plastic, filthy, and unfriendly.)

There was, however, that inconvenient fact that all this splendour was built on the back of colonized Africans who were little more than serfs.

Why did otherwise intelligent and often kind people fight so hard for the vicious, obscene, evil system in which they lived? Because they knew that if it changed, their lives and the lives of those they loved would never be anywhere near as good. It couldn't last, and it didn't— but note that Rhodesia became Zimbabwe only twenty-five years ago.

Today, Cecil Rhodes lies buried in Matopos National Park, near Bulawayo, a city finally recovering from the horrific mismanagement of the past decade. Zimbabwe remains poorer than it was twenty years ago, but it is no longer racked by hyperinflation and crippling shortages of gasoline and other essentials. Robert Mugabe, enlightened leader turned despot, still clings to power, and no one knows what will happen when he finally dies, but at least there is some hope for the future again. It's a start.

November 2005: Gukurahundi Murambatsvina
Harare (née Salisbury), Zimbabwe

Harare is a very pretty city. Much greener than Bulawayo. There are trees all over, and not just anonymous greenery; many streets are lined with long processions of tall trees, flamboyants and jacarandas aflame with brilliant orange and purple flowers, whose branches arch into one another to form a colourful arboreal shade structure. There is modern architecture in glass and chrome; there are many stores and banks; there is a golf course and a botanical garden, and pleasant suburbs of large houses on large estates. It certainly looks bigger and wealthier than Nairobi, although it's neither.

You'd never know there was a fuel shortage. When it first hit, maybe a year ago, the city shut down. Bulawayo is still semi-paralyzed. But here in Harare, the capital city, between the black market that has swelled to meet the enormous new demand, and the 'fuel coupons' you can buy at banks if you have foreign currency and if you line up for an hour, the streets buzz with activity. People line up everywhere, often at ATMs. Money is so cumbersome that ATMs run out quickly, so everyone takes out their maximum daily amount immediately, which usually means four separate transactions, which means a very slow line indeed. Some things are rare or unavailable—SIM cards for phones, Mach 3 razor blades—but mostly you can get what you need, if you've got the forex, and if you can stand the hassle.

Driving with relatives of mine—which is as thorough a description of them as I'm going to give here—some ten kilometres west of the city proper, we passed a capsule history of the country's last six years.

'You see that field over there?' my relative asked. I looked over. A mostly flat field, studded with the granite boulders and kopjes so common in the Zimbabwe landscape, strewn with trash, rubble, tufts of grass, and occasional one-room tin-roofed shacks. 'That was a big commercial farm, grew maize and potatoes, some tobacco. A white farmer. The "war vets" came five years ago and stole it from him.'

'You know what we mean, when we say "war vets"?' my other relative asked. 'They didn't really fight in the war.'

I nodded. I'd followed the news from far away; I knew. A big, chaotic militia of mostly young toughs who had, over a period of a year, taken over most of the country's white farms, often by violence. A militia too disorganized to earn the name 'paramilitary'; a militia led and supported by the government.

'After they took the land, they started putting up buildings on it. Shacks, like those new ones, but also little houses, vegetable gardens, there was a market, all this land here was covered with them, people everywhere. And then, earlier this year, the government, the same government that put them there, sent in bulldozers and flattened everything, destroyed everything, threw them all off the land. And now there's nothing there at all.'

Operation Murambatsvina, they called it. 'Clean up the trash.' Bulldoze thousands of houses, whole shantytowns, trading stalls, markets—sometimes markets that had been officially constructed by the government, and inaugurated by government officials, within the previous year. Beat up and throw out the flower sellers and artists who have sold their wares outside the hotels and parks of Harare as long as anyone can remember. Render an estimated 700,000 people homeless. Attempt to 'clean up' the entire informal economy. More than half of

Zimbabwe's economy, at a conservative estimate, is informal. Destroy houses built on stolen land by the same war vets you sent five years ago to steal the land.

'The more you think about it,' my relative said, 'the less sense it makes.'

Those war vets weren't war vets; but there was a war here, of course, a long and bloody one, and the country is run by its veterans. Mugabe's North Korean–trained guerrilla army fought Ian Smith's regular forces and Selous Scouts paramilitary for years, until finally, in 1980, in the face of overwhelming numerical superiority and international pressure, Smith handed over the reins of power.

Mugabe, a member of the country's majority (80 percent) Shona tribe, had as his chief lieutenant one Joshua Nkomo, of the minority Ndebele, historically as warlike as the Zulus, with whom they were linked. Two years after independence, Mugabe ousted Nkomo from his cabinet; this sparked civil unrest that resulted in the arrest and massacre of tens of thousands of Ndebele near Bulawayo by the North Korean–trained *Gukurahundi* brigade. (See Peter Godwin's excellent book *Mukiwa* for details.) The newly independent country was already on the verge of cracking and disintegrating—but it didn't. In fact, despite years of terrible drought, it began to thrive. Mugabe turned out to be an intelligent and pragmatic leader. He and his cronies lived the high life, of course, but a lot of money trickled out to the rural poor as well, and with some of the richest agricultural land in all Africa, and a three-legged-stool economy built on mining, tobacco, and tourism, the country prospered. It wasn't quite Botswana or South Africa, but it was miles, leagues better than Zambia or Mozambique, or anywhere in Central or West Africa. It was a success story.

And then, as far as I can tell, about six years ago, Robert Mugabe went crazy.

Samora Machel, the hero of Mozambique, had one piece of advice for Mugabe: 'Don't make our mistake. Don't throw the whites out.' Mugabe didn't—and 50,000 white farmers, twenty years after independence, continued to own and farm most of Zimbabwe's best land. (A brief land-buyback plan, financed by Britain, was cancelled after it was discovered that Mugabe's cronies were getting all the land.) I suppose that stuck in his craw. Rather than wait to buy them out, or wait for the next generation to abandon Zimbabwe for other pastures, which would have happened in many cases, I assure you, he sent the war vets to take all the farms, by force. Some of them were turned into shantytowns; most were given to friends and cronies of the government. Almost none of the farmland went to people who knew anything about farming. The tobacco crop vanished; the food crop vanished; the tourists, spooked by reports of widespread violence, vanished; and the economy went into its current nosedive.

The story is so old it's almost tiresome. Idi Amin and Mobutu did the same thing. Nationalize the economy; blame everything on a local ethnic minority (Asians, i.e., families who hailed originally from the Indian subcontinent, in Amin's case; the Belgians, for Mobutu); steal everything they own, then give all the farms and businesses and other assets to people who know nothing about managing them; watch, sometimes genuinely bewildered, as the resulting businesses are run into the ground, rather than becoming the expected endless supply of golden eggs; then blame 'foreign powers' and the weather, as the government-mouthpiece *Herald* newspaper here never tires of doing.

In the Congo and Uganda, economic disaster was followed by the rule of the gun, simmering violence throughout the country, and eventual civil war. I don't think that will happen here. But you can't rule it out.

Talk to any Zimbabwean about 'the Situation', and eventually they'll mutter something like 'Mugabe is an old man.' Then they'll look at the ground and say, 'You shouldn't really talk about it. People will think you're a spy or something.' They'll half-laugh. Then they'll change the subject.

I'm very aware of being white here, unlike in any other African country; because here, the assumption is that I'm a white Zimbabwean. It's not an assumption I'm comfortable with.

We went to the Bird Park the other day, my relatives and I, an idyllic spot on the shores of Lake Chiveru from which Harare gets its water. Twenty years ago, it was a patch of barren, swampy land. Today, along with the bird sanctuary from which it gets its name, it has a simple hotel, a swimming pool, a pier for yachts, docks for powerboats, horses and Shetland ponies to ride, a café, a football pitch, a waterfront restaurant under construction, a planned game park, and a playground for the underprivileged Zimbabwean schoolchildren who come every day. The owner employs sixty people.

The owner, a white Zimbabwean, middle-aged, bluff and sturdy, intelligent eyes in a weather-beaten face, also, while I was there, sent two of his employees, armed with clubs, to beat and drive off people who had walked for five kilometres to fish from the lake from the edge of his land. When asked why so many wild birds came to roost and feed on his land, he said, squinting with anticipation, 'Because they know they're protected. They know if any coon comes here, I'll whip his ass with a stick until his nose bleeds!'

Mugabe may have gone crazy—that's the only explanation for *Operation Murambatsvina* that comes to mind—but he's crazy like a fox. His latest brilliant political stroke is to reintroduce a Senate, which he abolished in 1985. With this he has thrown the opposition into disarray, and maybe destroyed it.

The leader of the Movement for Democratic Change opposition wants to boycott next month's Senate elections, saying fighting them would be a waste of time and energy, and would simply allow Mugabe to set the agenda. Which is true: between direct appointment (of sixteen positions), violence, and vote-rigging, and Mugabe's continued undoubted popularity in poor rural regions, the government would almost certainly win any contested Senate election. But not fighting means that government Shona officials will represent Matabeleland, scene of the *Gukurahundi* massacres, and that thought incenses the Ndebele, who form a large part of the opposition. So the MDC is riven with arguments and infighting; there is widespread speculation that they might divide or even disappear, victims of their own internecine squabble.

And meanwhile the country continues to rot.

If there's a lesson in Zimbabwe, I think it's this: progress is highly evitable. Places that have bright futures can and do decline and fall.

November 2005: Zimbabwe African National Union—Patriotic Front
Possum Lodge, Harare, Zimbabwe

'If you're willing to play the game,' said D., 'this place can be a fucking gold mine.'

We were in Harare's sole surviving backpacker lodge, which attracts an eclectic mix of travellers, traders, NGO workers, and university-educated, well-employed, been-overseas Zimbabweans—most of them black, like the lodge owner—who you would call yuppies in most places.

Here, though, where everything and everyone is only downwardly mobile, they're just those descending more slowly than the rest.

When D. says 'gold mine', he means it, sometimes, literally. While many if not most of Zimbabwe's 14 million people are down to one meal a day, several hundred people are profiting extremely handsomely from the country's economic ruin. Forex arbitrage, mineral rights in exchange for offshore payments, outright smuggling of gold and fuel: ranking government/ZANU-PF (Zimbabwe is a classic fascist state where the party and the government are one and the same) members and their cronies are doing very well. Rumour has it that one Gideon Gono, head of the Reserve Bank, and in fact one of the country's sources of hope, a man who's acting pragmatically to try to head off hyperinflation, and who has publicly stated that the takeover of the white farms was a disaster, is building an enormous mansion complete with an Olympic-sized swimming pool on the outskirts of Harare, decorated with top-of-the-line luxury goods imported from Europe. Curious how he manages to do this on his on-paper extremely skimpy government salary.

D. has a good, prestigious, professional job, but since January, his salary has only doubled, which means his real income has halved. So he was going to get up at 5:00 a.m. on Saturday morning to drive to and from the Mozambican border, carrying … something … in both directions. I didn't ask what, exactly, and he didn't tell. But whatever is conveyed on this weekly expedition keeps his car in good repair, and D. himself in petrol-and-parties money.

Art, maybe. Seriously. There are thousands of artists in Zimbabwe, still churning out soapstone sculptures and colourful tapestries for tourists—what else are they going to do? In fact most Southern Africa memorabilia comes from Zimbabwe. Traders come here, where supply is enormous and demand almost nonexistent, buy up truckfuls of art, and take it Johannesburg where it's sold for eight times the price, or to London, where the multiplier might be more like eighty. Exploitation? Maybe. Feeds families, too.

Thirty-six hours later, after another late and less-than-comfortable overnight journey on Zimbabwe's once-plush, now rotting and roach-infested trains, I was within sight of that Mozambican border myself. The train left two hours late because the first locomotive didn't work. Wires stick out of holes in the walls, every surface is covered by a patina of filth, you're lucky if the lights and fan work, and even if your fan is operational the compartments are oppressively hot. And that's in first class. But at least the ride is cheap: Z$260,000 from Harare to Mutare, less than US$3 at the unofficial rate.

Mutare itself, where I am now, is a nice little border town just south of tiny Penhalonga, where my father was born, which in turn is just south of the Rezende gold mine my grandfather once managed. It's a pretty town, planted with flamboyants, big trees with widespread limbs bedecked with bright fire-coloured flowers. Once, you could take the train from here to the Mozambican coast. Once, more recently, there were informal open-air markets, carpentry shops, even auto shops. Then they were all razed as part of *Operation Murambatsvina*.

From a certain point of view, destroying the informal economy makes a certain amount of sense. After all, if you're in the government, the informal economy is that sector from which you can't mandate the theft of your 20 or 30 or 50 percent. And if you can't take a slice, why not just bulldoze it, eh?

I didn't go north, towards my roots; instead, having decided it was past time for a splurge, I forked over 10 G B P to a taxi driver to take me thirty-five kilometres in the other direction, to the Leopard Rock Hotel.

Zimbabwe's Eastern Highlands, even today, are a little slice of paradise: rippling ridges of steep, folded hills and valleys covered by green grass and greener rainforest, shot through by burbling, tumbling rivers. The rivers drain east, into Mozambique, and the slopes get rain year-round from the Indian Ocean, keeping the forest green even while the rest of the country is parched and brown.

The Leopard Rock is a four-star hotel that boasts, aside from the usual luxuries, a breathtaking view over the Burma Valley, a game park, one of Southern Africa's premier golf courses (wasted on me; I'm in the good-walk-spoiled camp), horseback-riding trails, elegant dining rooms, a fair-sized casino, and a profound sense that one has entered a bizarre colonial time warp. All that for US$90 a night. My room was between Princess Margaret's Room and the Presidential Suite, and just across from the Queen Mother's Room. They stayed here some decades ago and their rooms have been consecrated to them ever since. Scratch an African, find a royalist.

Seven years ago, I stayed just up the road at the Ndundu Lodge, which, amazingly, is still open, as is Tony's Coffee Shop, next door, which serves extravagant cakes. Once upon a time this was a tourist playground. Those two establishments, and a few other restaurants, have survived because this is a still a deliriously wonderful place to visit. Their market today consists of very occasional tour groups, the local/NGO/expat market, and backpackers coming in from Mozambique (which has seen a backpacker boom over the last few years) to spend a few days in sketchy, exotic, quasi-dangerous Zimbabwe. An exact reversal of roles from seven years ago.

The Ndundu's Dutch owners know both the owner of the Harare lodge and the owner of the place I stayed at in Bulawayo, not surprising considering how tiny Zimbabwe's tourist industry has become. Their sprawling house-turned-lodge is smack between the Bunga Forest Reserve and the Vumba Botanical Gardens, five minutes' walk to either. The gateman at the gardens and I came to the tacit agreement that he would charge me the Zim-resident rate of Z$75,000 (rather than US$10) and I wouldn't ask for a receipt (meaning the money would go straight into his pocket). Normally I'd feel bad about this, but otherwise the money would go to the Zim government, and it's not like I want to contribute to *them*. Another of the many ways in which poor governance leads to corruption, which leads to worse governance, which leads to worse corruption. Feedback-loop death-spiral.

This is one of the few places in the world where, between the height, the climate, the rain, and the soil, you can plant just about *anything* and it will grow: mango and oak side by side, pine and bamboo mixed with jungle ferns and creepers. The Botanical Gardens are just as beautiful as I remember. But they're growing increasingly wild, too. The monkeys have grown aggressive; they jumped around me in the trees, emitting loud nasal snorts, and I swear one of them threw a stick. The little café has long since been closed, and its iron security bars are covered with rust. The main walkway and the lawns around the central pool are still cared for and groomed, but the pathways at the periphery are slowly returning to the wild. There are places you can barely see the trails, others where thick vegetation grows through cracked concrete; what was once a park is returning to jungle. Those seeking a metaphor for the country could do worse.

There are still a few working farms and timber plantations up here, growing tea, coffee, fruits such as mangos and citrus, pine, mahogany. Other farms have been taken over by 'war vets' who live in the rusted, cracked, dilapidated barns and farmhouses, till fields by hand, and just grow enough for themselves. Eagle School, once the boarding school that my father attended, is now a war-vet headquarters; several people independently warned me not to go there. Some estates are open-concept, with colourful signs announcing the name of property and owner. Others are walled, gated, and anonymous, guarded by snarling, howling dogs.

At the Leopard Rock, between lengthy hikes through the glorious landscape, I met a man I'll call K., a South African who works in what I'll call a lucrative and interesting business. *(Ed. note, eight years later: diamonds.)* We drove in his black diplomatic-plates Land Cruiser to have lunch in an upscale restaurant by the road, which was excellent except for the glass in the bread, then kicked back and smoked dope imported from Malawi. K. is (thanks to the government palms he needed to grease as part of his diamond-industry job) by far the best-connected and best-informed person I've met in Zimbabwe. He's also the most pessimistic about its future.

November 2005: The Mutare Club
Mutare, Zimbabwe
The rains have come and the nation breathes a collective sigh of relief. Some years the rains don't come at all. Hopefully they will stay for months. In times not long past, when commercial farms had reliable power and elaborate irrigation systems, the length of the rainy season didn't matter so much: but nowadays, drought means famine.

Mind you, rain doesn't necessarily mean plenty. This is the planting season, but lack of forex and fuel means lack of tractor diesel, spare parts, seed, fertilizer, workforce, everything. On the minibus from Mutare to Harare yesterday, I passed field after field of what were once commercial farms and are now mostly unkempt weeds, with a few small patches being sown with just enough food for the new farmers' families and friends. Zimbabwe will need food relief next year, too, count on it. (Indeed it did.) And yet once upon a time it grew enough to feed itself and half of its neighbours.

On Tuesday I got a ride in the diplomatic-plates Land Cruiser through a hammerblow storm—when I say 'rains', understand that I mean serious tropical downpours, maybe twice a day, for maybe an hour each—to Mutare, where I squelched my way to 99 Fourth Street.

Twenty minutes after I entered Ann Bruce's home/lodge, soaking wet, I was changed, dressed in my most formal clothing (which isn't saying much), and sitting with four Dutch NGO workers and six white-haired Zimbabweans in the faded century-old colonial splendour of the Mutare Club, eating very good Thai food. It was a little surreal.

After dinner I discreetly inquired where I might change money. The answer surprised me. Everywhere else I've been in Zambia and Zimbabwe, unofficial money-changing has been done by burly dreadlocked rasta guys. (This is in part due to my prejudices; I prefer to deal with rastas and/or Muslims, my theory being that they're more trustworthy, albeit for very different reasons.) In Mutare, the transaction was handled in a back room of the club by a portly white-haired grandmother who kept calling me 'dearie'. That was a little surreal too.

I explored Mutare, which didn't take long. It's a nice little city, planted with flamboyants, surrounded by big round hills covered by huge granite boulders like eggs in a nest. Supermarkets, department stores, an interesting history museum, a Nando's restaurant, etc., and its proximity to the Mozambican border (about ten kilometres) means that fuel is relatively easy to come by. By day it's entirely safe.

At night I sat in Ann's comfy living room, watched a very bad British soap named *Doctors* and Samuel L. in a kilt in *The 51st State*, and went out with Jaroon for a beer run. Jaroon and his wife, Karin, are from Haarlem, in the Netherlands, and are working in Mutare on a twin-city volunteer-exchange type of program. They've been here six weeks. The contract is for a year and a half. They don't expect to remain that long. They'd like to, but they think they'll be evacuated before it ends.

Initially they moved into their own house, with an alarm system, an armed guard, and a guard dog. Their home was invaded by gunmen a few weeks ago. Since then they've stayed at Ann's until a more secure place becomes available. Ann has three (very friendly and playful) German shepherds; we took them all on our beer run. 'Ninety-nine times out of a hundred you wouldn't need them at all,' Jaroon explained. 'But a couple weeks ago, a Japanese tourist went out with only one dog and got robbed.'

The word on the street in Mutare—partly rumour, partly based on the type of arms and tactical sophistication used by the home invaders—is that many of them are army soldiers supplementing their hyperinflation-ravaged pay. This is the most worrying thing I've heard since getting here: it'd be far from the first time that an African army started preying on its own citizens, à la Mobutu telling his troops to 'live off the land', and every time it's happened, to the best of my knowledge, it's led to some kind of violent collapse.

November 2005: Human Immunodeficiency Virus
Mutare, Zimbabwe
I haven't really talked about AIDS since coming to Africa, which, to use the world's most tasteless simile, is a bit like going to the Playboy Mansion and writing home only about the food. But what the hell is there to say that hasn't been said already?

'It is encouraging to note that 83 percent of Zambians are HIV negative,' said an editorial in a newspaper I read back in Lusaka, a truly breathtaking attempt at spin-doctoring. And that's only if you accept the government statistics, which of course no one does. (Basically, all statistics emerging from that part of Africa between the Sahara and South Africa are somewhere between 'a good guess' and 'a random number'. And that's without accounting for political massagery.) In Uganda, the continental poster child for AIDS policy, there are already more than *half a million* AIDS orphans. And counting.

In Zimbabwe, estimates of HIV incidence among the adult population range as high as 50 percent. People can't afford antibiotics, never mind antiretrovirals (in the unlikely event they're available at all) and of course hunger and stress speed the disease. A lot of Zimbabweans spend a lot of their time going to funerals. My guide in the Matopos this time around knew my guide in the Matopos last time around, and told me that she'd passed away. Ten years ago, people here didn't tell you that someone had died of AIDS because of the profound social taboo. Today they don't tell you what they died of because it goes without saying.

Get into a minibus in Zimbabwe and you'll notice that you're more comfortable than you would be in that same minibus in Uganda. Because people tend to be skinnier. Hunger feeds AIDS feeds hunger; when it hits, in the space of a few weeks, victims often go from being the breadwinner of their family to being a heavy burden, and poof! their whole family's hope for the future is just *gone*. And then there are the truly grotesque side effects, like the widespread myth that sex with a virgin will cure you of AIDS, which leads to apparently frequent (well, that's pure guesswork on my part, but I've seen several references in local newspapers, and I'm thinking such crimes go massively underreported here) rapes of young women, children, and even infants.

I gather that most people here don't even want to be tested. They don't want to know. And so the epidemic continues. NGOs, not wanting to sound judgmental, delicately refer to 'cultural and social factors' that contribute to the epidemic. What they mean is that a whole lot of HIV-positive Africans are having a whole lot of promiscuous unprotected sex. And years of public education campaigns don't seem to have made much difference.

But, hell, if you live in Zimbabwe, it's not like you're living for tomorrow anyway, right?

November 2005: Last-Day-in-the-Country Blues
Harare, Zimbabwe
Friday I drove with my relatives here out to a game park about a hundred kilometres from Harare. We passed more fields that once were huge commercial farms and are now wastelands decorated with a few wooden shacks and *rondavels* (circular shelters). Can't be an easy row for the 'war vets' to hoe either. The government promised them schools, clinics, and running water, which never materialized, and now those few that remain (many, after moving onto a farm, soon gave up and went back to town) have to scrape an existence out of subsistence farming.

We did pass two still-functional commercial farms; those have had black owners for decades, and are thus exempt from government land seizures. Seizure of white land is still going on; an acquaintance of my relatives lost his farm just a couple weeks ago. Came back to the house after a day in the fields and found a crowd of war vets who wouldn't even let him into his own home. Racial politics aside, it's just insane. Large-scale farming is an advanced science. What they're doing here is like expelling all the mechanical engineers from a country, then grabbing random people from the street, herding them into a newly abandoned factory, telling them, 'Now design and build us some aircraft engines, stat!' and then being surprised when it doesn't work out.

And it's not like they're actually giving the war vets the land, either, you understand—it all becomes state land, they're just allowed to live on it, but since they don't have title to it, they can't borrow against it for little things like seeds or fertilizer or tractor fuel. And so they take over thousand-hectare farms and plant and harvest maybe a hectare of it with hands and hoes, hoping to grow enough food for themselves, if they're lucky. Madness.

The property we went to is half farm, half game park, and white-owned; it's still operational only because it runs the most successful black-rhino breeding program on the planet, and the government (which owns the rhinos) presumably doesn't want to look bad by shutting it down, although apparently they did seriously suggest, last year, that they close down the farm and instruct each of the nearest groups of war-vet farmers to care for one of the rhinos. I am not making this up. Cooler heads have yet prevailed, but I don't expect the place to be around this time two years from now. If the government doesn't get the farm, violence might. The owners' parents, in their eighties, had their home on the property invaded, and their car and valuables stolen by armed thugs, just a couple weeks ago. The farm manager's pickup truck's windscreen is adorned with a large bullet hole, courtesy of a poacher about a month ago.

(Update: I'm pleased to report that I was mostly wrong; the farm is still around today, but, alas, in 2007, poachers shot and killed all of their adult rhinos. Four near-adults still remain.)

The park half of the property is a spellbindingly beautiful place, the bush adorned with the uncanny and seemingly unnatural stacks of huge granite boulders called kopjes, and man-made dams and rivers. It's home to lions and hyenas (caged, and fat and lazy—wild predators ripple with muscle, but these ones are soft); a few elephants, including one who was raised by buffalo and is now the matriarch of a buffalo herd; giraffe, kudu, nyasa, impala, and elegant sable antelopes; and a half-dozen rare, highly endangered black rhinos. The owners' home and guest *rondavels* are in a green oasis of jacaranda and pomegranate trees around a shaded lawn and pool. The farm buildings, by contrast, are large, low, single-room brick warehouses, out in the sun, half-full of feed bags and stacked cattle hides, around which about a dozen black employees work.

On the way back into town, we saw the presidential motorcade: three widely spaced motorcycles (sirens and lights blazing); two police cars (again, sirens and lights blazing); a Jeep full of a dozen helmeted, heavily armed troops; several dark, bulletproof BMWs; another Jeep full of soldiers; an ambulance; and another screeching police car. Mugabe was back from some African summit, where, in you-couldn't-make-it-up irony, he had chaired a session on 'African democracy.'

November 2005: It Don't Mean a Thing if It Ain't Got That Spin
Durban, South Africa
So there[1] I stood, clutching my bared Swiss Army knife[2] in my trembling fist,[3] alone[4] and otherwise unarmed, surrounded by a thousand[5] bloodthirsty[6] Zulus.[7] The witch doctor[8] fixed me with a baleful glare.[9] I knew there was no escape.[10]

---

1. The Warwick Triangle region of Durban, which my *Rough Guide* calls, not without reason, 'an Africanized *Blade Runner* cityscape': a gargantuan agglomeration of mercantile humanity that clogs several massive warehouse-sized market buildings and taxi parks, connected by equally thronging covered walkways, and then spills out into the streets around it for several blocks in every direction, a riot of noise and colour and crowds and goods for sale that makes Las Vegas seem a bit like a sensory-deprivation tank.

2. Bared to initiate the peeling of an orange I had just purchased.

3. I mean, not like but-I-shoot-with-this-hand trembling, but my hands aren't rock-steady, so I imagine I twitched once or twice in mid-peel.

4. 'We live, as we dream—alone.' —Joseph Conrad. Also, I was, in fact, on my own, and also the only white person in sight, which is probably why three white South Africans had independently warned me not to go to the Warwick Triangle. To generalize, white people here who were over twenty-five when apartheid ended seem to treat 'all-black area' and 'high-crime area' as perfect synonyms. Black South Africans, meanwhile, blame the country's crime rate on Nigerians and other immigrants from the rest of Africa, although this is no more convincing than the white prejudice.

5. Well, tens of thousands, really, but only about a thousand of them could reasonably be described as bloodthirsty—

6. —those clustered around the *nyama choma* (grilled meat) stands, in whose vicinity I happened to be standing. Hey, I never said they were thirsting for *my* blood.

7. It's not like I had them fill out ethnicity questionnaires, but, I mean, I am in KwaZulu-Natal, so it does seem likely.

8. Across the street, an old dude was selling wares identified by his cardboard

No word of it a lie!

Durban is a hot, crowded, tropical city, with a busy industrial harbour, a pretty-but-scuzzy beachfront, and a seamy downtown overlooked by hilly, pleasant suburbs. Lines of beach hotels and white-flight suburban shopping malls sprawl down the Indian Ocean coast in either direction. It reminds me a bit of Florida.

The ocean here is warm enough to swim year-round, but the waves are so rough that getting past the breakers is actually something of a physical challenge. And the jagged Drakensberg mountains are just a couple hours to the north. (I meant to stop off there for a few days of hiking, but all the lodges I called were fully booked for the weekend. I've now just accepted that I'm not meant to do any real hiking/trekking this trip, and I'll make up for it next year.)

I'm staying a little way down the coast from the city proper, in a region called the Bluff, at a beachfront backpacker lodge which would be the greatest place in the world if I were a surfer, or a doctor, or better yet, a surfer doctor. As is, it's merely splendid. (I tried surfing once. I might eventually be able to learn the requisite balance, but my high centre of gravity and low flexibility mean it's not for me.)

South Africa is stunningly beautiful, full of all manner of diversions—Big Five (elephant, lion, leopard, rhino, buffalo) wildlife parks! surfing/sailing/swimming/scuba diving! exotic culture! wineries and galleries and posh boutiques! deserts, jungle, mountains, oceans, cities! Charlize Theron lookalikes everywhere! And it's ridiculously easy

---

sign as traditional native medicines, which seemed to consist largely of animal skins, bones, and skulls. In Africa there's a fair amount of overlap between traditional healing and *muti*, black magic, which very many Africans take very seriously indeed, sometimes dying from sheer fear when afflicted by a curse. (And you get occasional newspaper stories about goblins, or *tokoloshi*s.)

9. Okay, I may have taken a little poetic license here, but who am I to measure balefulness? He did give me something of a look. Although the meaning behind it may have been more along the lines of 'I wish you would come here and overpay me for this dried duiker fetus' than 'No one here gets out alive.'

10. The situation being entirely innocent, there was nothing to escape from; hence, logically, there was no escape. Also by this point I'm just kinda makin' shit up.

to travel through. I'm surprised it doesn't get more tourists than Australia. Give it another decade, though, and it probably will. *(Update: These days it does, and rightly so.)*

November 2005: A Home at the End of the World
Cape Town, South Africa
I swear, I could look at the sea all day.

They say most accidents occur within a mile of home. Following that rule, the closest I came to smashing up my rental car was within about a hundred metres of AroundAboutCars, the company that foolishly gave me one. As I very gingerly tried to conduct a wrong-side-of-the-road stick-shift for the second time ever, and the first time in two and a half years, through busy Cape Town traffic, I turned into a side street and found myself on a one-way street, with a minivan barrelling towards me. It screeched to a stop maybe six inches away from my front bumper. I froze a moment, then looked up at the driver with apologetic, pleading eyes, sure that I was the one at fault. Then I looked more closely at the street signs and parked cars. *He* had been going the wrong way. I opened my mouth to shout something—I'm not sure what exactly, but it was going to begin with 'Hey, asshole!'—but my near-collidant was already reversing away at high speed. He nearly crashed into *another* car getting back onto the main road.

The only amazing thing about this is that the minivan wasn't a taxi. South Africa's taxi drivers are legendary for their speed, unpredictability, unroadworthy vehicles, lack of formal training, and apparent belief that they are immortal and invulnerable. Oh, yes—and they're heavily armed. Gunfire breaks out regularly between rival taxi syndicates (at least once in every major city I've visited so far this trip, while I was in said city) and recently, in Johannesburg's notorious Hillbrow suburb, a group of taxi drivers fought a blazing firefight with a police unit that had the temerity to try to arrest them for things like driving with a lengthy list of outstanding warrants but no licence. The police retreated. Several innocent bystanders were wounded.

(I should probably stress at this point that I have yet to feel unsafe here in South Africa.)

Why are there taxi wars here? Because there's a lot of money in the South African taxi business. And why is that? Apartheid. Blacks, i.e., 80 percent of SA's population, were for many years forced to live in vast townships located some distance away from the white cities. Apartheid is gone, but the cities and townships remain. It's a little unnerving to see. It's not just Soweto and co. around Jo'burg, and the Cape Flats in Cape Town; in big cities, this kind of segregation is somehow less surprising. But even little towns, like Knysna and tiny Struisbaai, have their own black townships a few kilometres down the road from the town centre. And they in turn will be divided: orderly areas of small block houses with electricity and running water, in each of which two or three families live; and filthy, squalid, wood-and-tin-roof shantytowns.

The government is trying to improve matters, but progress is slow. And as my friend here pointed out to me the other day, the government's whole approach is suspect. When they build new township housing, they build 'community centre' halls, but there is a complete absence of any space for *commerce*: market squares, shopping stretches. And so the residents have to walk (you're likely to see black people walking, holding their thumb out in forlorn hope of a ride, anywhere within about ten kilometres of a town in South Africa) or take taxis into town, because they can't shop where they live.

Jeez. This is turning into a political-economic rant. It was supposed to be a travelogue. Let me go back to the beginning of this road trip:

Leaving AroundAboutCars, I headed for the N2 from Cape Town. Actually I was going to take the N1 but missed the exit and thought, *What the heck, why not?* East, past the airport, across the vast Cape Flat townships, steeply up the dramatic hills that cup the townships, and then into an endless landscape of rippling hills, green fields filled with new wheat and golden fields littered with hay bales or ostriches, all overseen by the Overberg range of old, folded mountains to the north.

Driving in South Africa rocks. I was instructed to open the lid of the hatchback trunk at night, and also leave the glove compartment open, to show would-be thieves that there was nothing inside. The fuel tank can only be opened with the key. The hard shoulder is a valid other lane, except when it isn't. The speed limit is 120, and is actually reasonably well obeyed. (Mind you, my Fiat Palio—I'm pretty sure *palio* is Italian for 'piece of crap that occasionally makes horrible grinding sounds when you try to put it into reverse'—wasn't going to go much faster anyhow.) Stop in for gas at one of the highway service stops, much like those in Canada, and one attendant will wash your whole car while the other fills your tank. Ah, cheap labour. Outside the gas station, people sell bouquets of wildflowers like nothing I've ever seen before. Which is not surprising, as the Cape has literally thousands of endemic species, including two entire families of vegetation, *protea* and *fynbos*, found nowhere else in the world.

Four hours after leaving Cape Town, I reach, and navigate through the dysfunctional traffic lights of the seaside town of Mossel Bay—first its townships, then its town—which marks the official beginning of the Garden Route. A two-hundred-kilometre stretch of coast so named, allegedly, because the region was called 'the Garden of Eden' by its early (white) inhabitants. Which sounds like tourist hype, and the Garden Route is definitely over-touristed, but honestly? It's easy to believe. Knysna, at the heart of the Garden Route, bills itself as 'Nature's Playground,' and that sounds right too. Miles and miles of glorious coastline, all the beaches and all the rugged rocks you could want; just a bit inland, lakes and rivers surrounded by forest; and beyond them, the ribbed, bat-winged shapes of low, green-clad mountains. You can swim, surf, dive, fish, hike, parasail, bungee jump, ride horses, or go on private-reserve game drives. Yesterday, I spent three hours of the morning hiking through a thickly forested national park (and I didn't meet a soul on the trail), then bodysurfed in the pounding Indian Ocean for an hour, and spent the night in a magical old forest house built in 1874 with a glorious sunrise view of the mountains. And I was taking it easy.

But again I get ahead of myself. From the surfers and fishermen of Mossel Bay to the town of George, which is well-located, has the area airport, and boasts two wonderfully quirky museums featuring huge railway cars and homemade colonial tools, but doesn't have much else going for it: through an area named Wilderness, though it's heavily touristed and really reminds me more of Canada's cottage country; a sojourn among Knysna's little shops and bistros; and then to Wildside Backpackers, with a spectacular location at Buffels Beach, immediately next to a nature reserve that runs for a good twenty-five kilometres, so you can walk along the beach all day if you want. It's a little remote, but hey, I had a car. Did I mention that driving here rocks?

If I had a spare half-a-million dollars, I swear, I'd buy a place here—nothing fancy, just a little hillside cottage with a sea view, a short drive from the beach—come settle in for a few months each year, and write an epic fantasy series.

Today I drove down to the southernmost tip of Africa. Cape Point, south of Cape Town, is an incredibly stark, steep, romantic rocky promontory. It is not, however, the end of the world: that honour belongs to Cape Agulhas, a low-key, non-obvious spot in the midst of windblown bushes and jagged rocks. There is also a rather dramatic lighthouse. I considered overnighting there, but decided to keep going, and am I ever glad I did, because the road between Agulhas and Hermanus, where I sit and type now, is absolutely glorious, winding through rippling fields and ridges of green and gold. I didn't take pictures. I did take a few of the Garden Route and Agulhas, but I don't expect much of them. You can't really capture all this magnificence in pictures.

December 2005: There's Still Crime in the City, but It's Good to Be Free
Cape Town, South Africa
Before dinner last night I built an appetite by climbing Table Mountain, which is both the symbol of Cape Town and its heart: the city encircles the mountain, which rises a thousand steep metres from the sea to an almost perfectly flat top. From the lower cable car station, it's theoretically a two-and-a-half-hour hike: I'm pleased to report that I ascended in just under half that time. There's life in the ol' leg muscles yet, even though they were already battered from cycling fifty hilly, rainy kilometres from Simon's Town to Cape Point and back, a few days ago.

The mountain claims several lives every year, and you're not really supposed to climb alone, but I took a straightforward route up, figuring that if Reinhold Messner could summit Everest solo without oxygen during monsoon season, I could conquer Table Mountain singlehanded. As I reached the tabletop, the clouds that often line it—the mountain's famous tablecloth—were just beginning to arrive, so I only got twenty minutes of the spectacular views.

Just as I attained the top of Platteklip Gorge, I met a South African woman who (like almost everyone else on the mountain) had come up by cable car rather than leg power. 'Did you climb up from the bottom?' she asked. 'I did,' I said. After a moment she asked the inevitable second question: 'And you didn't get mugged?'

Crime, Afrikaans, the Cape Coloured, and the Townships

South Africa is a violent country. It's not near as bad as it once was, and doctors from America no longer go to Soweto to learn how to treat gunshot wounds, but this is still a high-crime nation.

A friend asked me what the feel of the townships was like, compared to American ghettos. I went on a two-man tour through several of them today, courtesy of another friend, and I now feel semi-qualified to answer. But first I want to talk a bit about Afrikaans and the Cape Coloured, which in turn means I have to start with a bit of oversimplified history. Bear with me if I screw it all up.

The Dutch began to seriously settle Cape Town in 1682. It was first intended only as a refuelling station, a place for ships to stock up on fresh produce and water between Holland and the lucrative spice islands of the East Indies. (The reason there's fresh water year-round, incidentally, is Table Mountain: wet air comes from the sea, rises, and forms the 'tablecloth', which condenses and runs down the mountainside.) So they imported serfs from Malaysia to work the company gardens: the Cape Malays. Meanwhile, Dutch sailors, as sailors everywhere are wont to do, got busy impregnating the local Khoikhoi, Xhosa, and Malaysians. The resulting 'coloured' generations, neither black nor white, developed a language that was an odd melange of Dutch sprinkled with Malaysian words: and Afrikaans was born.

Afrikaans wound up being highly associated with the white apartheid government. It was the government's attempt to turn it into the national language of school instruction that sparked the countrywide riots in 1976, one of the turning points in South African history, but the language was in fact created by the coloured community. In the early 1800s, when the British took over the Cape by force (for the second time) and freed the slaves, thousands of Boer settlers, appalled, set out on a fairly incredible migration across the country to settle in a land where they could live free and racist. The famous *Voortrek.* Along with their wagons, they took a dialect of Afrikaans stripped of as many 'coloured' words as possible: but even today, there are more non-whites than whites who speak Afrikaans at home in the Western Cape. The coloureds don't really exist in the rest of South Africa. (Yes, it makes me a little uncomfortable to speak of people purely in terms of racial groupings, but race = ethnicity = culture remains reality here, for the most part.)

The apartheid government classified people as white, Indian, coloured, or black, with decreasing levels of privileges and rights. (Japanese were 'honorary white' because they were rich; black albinos confused the regime no end; and hundreds of people changed classification every year because they passed or failed the 'pencil test', in which their hair was wound around a pencil and its resulting crimping was measured, or other equally bizarre criteria.) Townships, in particular, were divided into black and coloured areas.

To this day, there's a great deal of tension between the black and coloured communities; and to this day, the coloured community, having gone from existing in a white-run country to existing in a black-run country, remain outsiders. This may be why gangs influence and dominate coloured townships far more than the black ones. And this may explain why by far the scariest and most intimidating (though not most appalling) township we went to today was a coloured township called Mannenberg.

The townships are all different from one another, but if I had to generalize, I'd say they feel like postapocalyptic American suburbs. Imagine a very poor stretch of suburban sprawl. Now imagine it *but no one has a car*. The townships are incredibly spread out, in a dizzying and senseless way: a long chain of settlements, connected by (excellent) roads. Everything is low-rise, almost all just one storey and never more than three, and the buildings go on for kilometres. It can easily take an hour to walk from within a township to its taxi park, and another to get into Cape Town in a taxi.

You get the following types of accommodation/street life in a South African township. With the exception of Mannenberg, what a township is like is basically a question of in what combination these elements are found:

Squatter camps. Wooden shacks with corrugated iron roofs thrown up anywhere there's space. Pretty typical in city outskirts anywhere in Africa. The wood is worn and warped; the iron (or tin) roof is rusting, patched with plastic, weighed down against the wind with big rocks and old tires. A makeshift clothesline hangs outside. A lot of them are semi-prefab—other people build and stock pre-made plank walls, doors, and sheets of tin, and when you move into a township from Mpumalunga or the Congo or wherever, you buy all these parts and quickly assemble your single-room shack. Here, unlike anywhere else in Africa, even squatters demarcate their tiny properties with rusting chain-link and barbed-wire fences. Squatter camps are divided by winding, potholed roads—paths, actually, gouged and pitted. Electrical cables dangle by the dozen from every street lamp, illegally tapping electricity. No running water. Some government-provided port-a-potties. Weeds and sand (the Cape Flats are sand dunes). Very lively, people all around, going to and from ... somewhere. Awful and squalid, of course, but not as depressing as you might think, because they're so lively, and maybe because of their temporary feel.

Hostels. Built by the apartheid government to house male labourers. Long, single-storey or three-storey buildings with dozens if not hundreds of tiny cubicle rooms. Awful places that are home, at least in Soweto, to much of the worst township violence. Many have been razed.

Planned settlements. Rows and rows and rows of small houses, with electricity and maybe running water, along roads with scabbed edges. To picture 'small', think of the smallest bedroom you've ever had, and then imagine a family of six living there. (You get more space in coloured areas, or in more recent developments.) Informal businesses beside the road; barefoot children playing soccer on uneven ground littered with debris and broken glass; corrals crowded with sheep; minibus taxis and the occasional private car roving up and down the street; women and men carrying and carting goods of all description to and fro; clothes set out to dry, flapping in the sandy wind. Hustling, bustling, busy, colourful life.

In Khayelitsha, the largest township, these settlements also have huge searchlight street lamps *one hundred feet tall*, built by the apartheid military to turn day into night when conducting operations in the township. To this day there's a military base right next door.

Businesses. These in turn can be subdivided:
• A blanket on the ground: with shoes or produce laid out to sell.
• One notch up: a *braii* grilling meat (word of the day: a severed sheep's head is called a 'smiley', and is barbequed and eaten *in toto*) or an open-

sided lean-to shack, selling dry goods or produce or providing haircuts. Advertised by an uneven hand-painted sign.

• Another notch up: a shipping container in which household goods, bags of rice, phone access, engine oil, and so on are sold. Maybe a bigger, stencilled, painted sign.

• One more: a house that's been turned into a shop, with a big sign decorated with the Coca-Cola logo. (Doesn't mean they sell Coke: across Africa, Coke gives businesses signs in exchange for the ad space.)

•Another: a recognizable commercial shop, with a counter and shelves, maybe even a chip fryer.

• The penultimate notch: a petrol station (owned by a taxi association).

• And, finally: a store in a shopping centre. There are a few shopping centres and their number is growing, although they're weirdly spread out and mostly impossible to get to on foot (see my 'postapocalyptic suburb' comment earlier).

Most businesses are informal, crowded into spaces not intended for them. This is just as true in government-planned townships as in squatter camps. ANC housing officials, many of whom are unreconstructed communists, apparently believe that Commerce Is Wrong and try not to encourage it. Instead they build these massive endless housing projects unleavened by any market spaces, shopping districts, parks, or public squares. Even the soccer fields are improvised. Will this end in disaster, creating a generation of disaffected, ghettoized, angry youth with political freedom but no economic hope? Ya think?

Community buildings. The government does build multi-purpose 'community centres' that as far as I can tell go basically unused except for community meetings. Police stations, walled and guarded like wartime military bases. Primary schools (no high schools), which range from big collections of buildings behind barbed wire to tiny ones the size of portables. Both kinds are shelter behind barbed wire. Taxi parks. (As I've mentioned before, there's a lot of money in taxis, and the taxi industry is incredibly corrupt and crime-ridden, although, oddly, taxi associations are apparently independent of the coloured crime gangs.) Most of these structures are bizarrely designed, full of high production values, and are useless boondoggles (often naïvely tourist-oriented: let's build a walkway atop the highest sand dune in Khayelitsha township, and a wacky-architecture restaurant/pottery centre below! Surely if we build it, tourists will flood here by the thousand!) used only to swell political egos and fatten the wallets of architects and consultants and contractors.

Wasteland. The townships stretch on for miles, and miles, and miles, and many of those miles are empty except for weeds. Space is not at a premium in the Cape Flats, there's plenty of shitty land. So many townships abut empty, uneven fields of weedy sand that go on forever, decorated by all imaginable kinds of trash and maybe a few lonely shacks. You wouldn't want to be in most townships come night: you *really* wouldn't want to be in a wasteland near a township at night. That's where the dead bodies turn up.

Those are the basic components from which townships are formed. But the *feel* of each is totally different.

Mannenberg. Mannenberg is almost all permanent housing. And it felt like bombed-out Mostar in Bosnia. Battered, bullet-scarred, little more than a not-yet-abandoned ruin. Most townships are hives of activity: in Mannenberg, gangs of people stood and sat around on the street, doing nothing but stare, sullen and dead-eyed. My street-smarts alarm pinged off the meter. There's a brand-new shopping centre right across the road. It's built and secured like a fucking fortress.

Delft. The worst place, though, was neither Mannenberg nor the squatter camps, but Delft, a planned settlement that is nothing— *nothing*—but rows of little houses surrounded by emptiness. It didn't feel *post*apocalyptic: it felt like the apocalypse itself. A barren, horrific wasteland, a pit of bare subsistence survival, poverty with no life, no escape, no hope. Hard, flat, empty eyes. Despair made urban flesh. Really. My skin crawled.

Nyanga and Khayelitsha. Nyanga, by contrast, was a bustling district that could almost have been a pleasant little city in Rwanda or Uganda. And the vast Khayelitsha settlement is a city in and of itself; like Soweto, it's getting so close to being just a big, poor suburb that it's actually rather dull. That's a good sign. Dull—trust me on this one, when you're talking about the economic development of poor South Africans—dull is very good.

June 2011: Notes from the Ancient North
Axum, Ethiopia
Let us consider, now, the various modes of transport here in Ethiopa.

First, of course, there is one's feet: very popular, if largely due to necessity. A few people go barefoot, though most wear sandals. Earlier today I followed an elderly man who had one foot sandalled and one bare; we moved at the same pace across gravel-dusted tarmac, though I was booted. Well-dressed women wear heels. And in Addis Ababa (though not here, so far as I can tell) running shoes are also very popular. Running is the national sport. At 6:00 a.m. joggers rove all about Addis. Some are portly office-warrior types. Some are good. Some are *really, really good.* The best of the best—Haile Gebrselassie, the world marathon champion and record-holder—is Ethiopian.

Here in Axum, a ninety-minute flight due north from Addis, the bicycle is also very popular. This surprised me. The Chinese influence again, perhaps? It's not exactly the incredibly dense river of bicycles I encountered in Shanghai in 1997, but I don't think I've been anywhere else in Africa where people regularly bomb down the roads on a knobbled hybrid. I bet the mountain biking would be awesome, once you adjusted to the altitude …

My guidebook claims that horse-drawn carts or *garis* are everywhere, but that was then and this is now; they have been all but replaced by the tuk-tuk, aka the autorickshaw, painted bright blue. The few *garis* I've seen were all scrawny horses dragging overloaded cargo.

Donkeys and mules (embarrassingly, I always have trouble telling them apart: one is smaller and has bigger ears, right?) are popular beasts of burden as well, cushioned with blankets and loaded with bags or bales of firewood. Sheep and goats wander everywhere, but carry nothing.

And there are camels. Camels! Don't get me wrong, I hate the filthy, stinking, malevolent beasts, but they do add a certain wild-frontier air to the place. One hump, in case you're curious, and generally loaded with firewood.

To carry more people requires a minibus, or a bus, or perhaps—I've heard talk of these, but haven't seen them myself—a *luxury* bus, one with a bathroom on board, and free water and snacks. I haven't ridden an inter-city bus yet, to my shame; instead I've been flying. I did frequent Addis's minibuses, which are basically exactly the same as *dala-dala*s or *matatu*s or *tro-tro*s anywhere, albeit maybe in slightly better shape than most. The ones which roll through Axum are in greater disrepair.

And what of the landscape through which one is transported?

Right now it is dry and stony. Watercourses are barren. The trees and grass are thorny, with one notable exception: Australia's backhanded gift to the developing world, the eucalyptus tree. (It grows fast, makes for excellent firewood and construction material, and provides shade and food for animals, but it consumes a *lot* of water.) The rains are coming soon, everyone hopes, and indeed the skies spat a few drops on us today, and their thunderous deluge has already arrived back in Addis.

And the stones—granite, I think, rather than Lalibela's limestone? But I'm no geologist. Regardless, the landscape is hills covered by stones surrounded by rocks resting on pebbles. The new roads they are building everywhere are patterned cobblestones rather than tarmac, not least because the former are available everywhere. Walls and buildings are generally made of stones piled on stones. Doorways and windows are frequently stopped up with stones.

That last seems inexplicable. I would guess it's some sort of cooling thing, but in fact it's not *that* hot here; we are still two kilometres above sea level. The sun is bright and heavy, though, and at midday verges on deadly. I am sunscreened up but have twice worn my hat against the noonday sun nonetheless.

And what else have I discovered about this, my ancient destination?

• It is official: sub-Saharan Africa is *booming.* I mean, I know the numbers have been saying that for some time. Addis Ababa certainly feels like a boomtown, cranes and construction sites everywhere, and even so, the people I talked to there lamented about how Kenya is leaving them behind; but here I am in faraway Axum, an ancient city of some forty thousand near the Eritrean border, and when all the construction projects under way here have been finished, they will have, at a conservative estimate, *quintupled* the number of multi-storey buildings in town. Not to mention all the roadwork under way. Of course, who knows how long some of these projects may have languished half-complete. And yet, even so, their very existence says something, and I heard hammering coming from the couple that I passed …

• The boom definitely has something to do with massive Chinese investment. The blanket in my current hotel is a 'Jin Quo Han' blanket. My Internet connection in Lalibela was established via a China Telecom client. There are Chinese officials, engineers, and tourists everywhere; and instead of complaints about special treatment for whites in the local papers, there are complaints about special treatment for 'whites and Chinese.' Which is progress, I guess, of a sort.

• The most interesting thing about Axum, though, is not its recent boom, but its antiquity. Eighty-foot pre-Christian steles loom over a seventeenth-century church … next to which is the small, inaccessible chapel that is claimed by Ethiopians to hold none other than the Ark of the Covenant. Only one monk is allowed to enter; he lives there all his life. I saw him today, readying a ladder to repair the roof, and he sure had a hell of a beard for an Ethiopian. The deacon claimed he'd been there for fifteen years. The beard made that sound plausible.

• There are also tombs here. Many tombs. The accessible ones have been raided by thieves over the years, but it's estimated that 98 percent of Axum's antiquities still lie buried. The museum, full of ancient illuminated books and dozens of solid-gold crowns and sceptres and the like, hints at the treasures that may lie within some of those tombs. It's all very Lara Croft/Indiana Jones. This is some of the oldest gold country in the world, and there are dozens of goldsmiths on the streets. Don't know if there's a mine nearby.

• Ethiopian Airlines rocks. I flew Addis to Lalibela, then Lalibela to Axum, and in a couple days will fly Axum to Addis, for the combined grand total of US $165, on shiny new-ish Bombardier Q400s.

• It's off season, meaning every tout in Axum and Lalibela has targeted me. They're pretty laid-back as touts go, though, and willing to (eventually) take 'no, I don't want a guide' for an answer.

• Lalibela. Well. It's a major tourist attraction because of its vast and ancient churches carved from single slabs of rock, which are indeed kind of mind-boggling. My favourite part, though, was my trip up to the (also hewn-from-stone) monastery perched on a mountain above the city. Locals and *Lonely Planet* agree that it's only a ninety-minute walk, so when after ninety minutes I seemed nowhere near a monastery, I began to fear that in my haste and confusion I had climbed the wrong mountain. It's true, I had had to stop briefly every hundred or so (vertical) metres to catch my breath, which worried me considering the Himalayas await, but hopefully it was just altitude adjustment. (Lalibela is a more-than-respectable 2,600 metres above sea level.) After two hours, though, I had pretty much given up. And then: blue doors set into a solid stone wall. The monastery. Inside was a bit of a dog-and-pony show with relics and an ancient illuminated manuscript, but the views of Ethiopia's rugged hill country were breathtaking. I glanced at my phone as I left, and again as I arrived at Lalibela's central intersection. It turns out that it took me exactly ninety minutes— moving nonstop at a good clip—to *descend* from the monastery. I retract all my claims that *Lonely Planet* has grown less hard-core.

• Lalibela society seemed to this outsider to be like the limestone on which it is built: rigid and many-layered. When I went to change money, I waited behind a woman with long, carefully braided hair, in a brightly patterned skirt and blouse that looked brand new, tapping her manicured nails on her Nokia as *she* waited for an old man in rags and a poncho-like shawl, in sandals so worn they looked bonded to his feet, carrying a shepherd's crook, who was opening a new bank account with US$5 and two passport photos. (Foreign Exchange and Account Opening were the same window.)

• There were many very poor subsistence farmers in Lalibela, dressed like that old man, walking with both hands on the walking sticks held horizontally across their shoulders, behind their necks; some of the sticks were crooks, some were metal-tipped, some supported jute sacks full of unknown goods, some were just bare sticks. Many were there because Lalibela is also a USAID distribution centre; every afternoon, hundreds of bags of rice and dozens of shining canisters labelled 'Edible Oil', all embossed with the American flag, were given away.

• Next up in the hierarchy, I think, were the poor locals. Did you think shoeshine boys had disappeared with Dickens? They abound in both Axum and Lalibela, and are popular among the members of the upper classes, who would seem middle class elsewhere, I suppose. It's nice to see an emerging middle class anywhere south of the Sahara and north of the Limpopo.

• Table football is very popular; there were a half-dozen public-access tables by the road in various places in Lalibela. Ping-Pong and a variant of pool are easy to find as well.

• Lalibela is very steep. It's probably fifty or maybe even a hundred vertical metres just from the top to the bottom of the town itself. And as a result, the views, oh wow, oh wow, oh wow: expanding out over plains and rippling hills as far as the eye can see. (They're mostly to the not-so-touristy northwest of town, though, so I'm very, very glad I wandered out there.)

• Ethiopia is cheap. I'm following my usual 'sleep cheap, eat expensive', protocol, and travelling on easily less than US$50 a day. I guess when you have a population of 85 million people and not that much in the way of exports, hard currency is highly valued.

June 2011: At the Edge of the World
Djibouti

I'm always amazed by how quickly the alien becomes familiar. On my first day in Mombasa it seemed strange and surreal to be the only guest in a hundred-room Indian Ocean beach resort at the very end of a long, winding road; two days later it seemed perfectly normal. Two weeks ago

I flew into Addis Ababa and made my way through and from the airport dazed and confused, uncertain and nervous lest something go wrong; two days ago I did the same thing and cruised through impatiently without even really bothering to think about the process.

I do not think that will happen if I ever return to Djibouti, though, as the airport process is so comically chaotic. After dancing back and forth and back and forth among three different locations in the arrival hall to get my visa, I emerged into the suffocating heat only to find that the *bureau de change* had closed for the next few hours. Fortunately my enterprising taxi driver took US dollars. Fortunate and unsurprising: we passed a vast US Air Force cargo plane on the tarmac because Djibouti, directly across the Red Sea from troubled Yemen, is home to two thousand US soldiers and eight hundred members of the French Foreign Legion. The latter is the reason I know anything about the place; it's the setting of Claire Denis's brilliant film *Beau Travail*. Otherwise this really is an obscure little nation. To the best of my knowledge, nobody I know has ever been here, which is practically nonpareil. (The only other such countries I can think of are Gabon and various tiny island nations.)

It's easy to see why. To be honest it's a profoundly unattractive city, low-rise and industrial, leached of all colour by the hammering sun, strewn with trash, jumbled with crumbling or half-completed buildings, full of aggressive touts and taxi drivers. On paper it's wealthier than any of its neighbours, thanks to its busy port (and military bases), which also makes it more expensive than any of its neighbours—but it feels like it's been stagnating for years.

It's not the hottest place on Earth. Quite. That's the Danakil Depression, on the Ethiopian side of the border. But it's a contender. My hotel room has only a curtained slit for a window, because the sun is the enemy. There is only one faucet in the bathroom but it provides hot water, not cold. The city essentially shuts down from noon to three every day. Refrigerator-sized air conditioners dominate all the more expensive establishments, and water is sold at roadside stands by the keg. It's actually pretty mild right now, highs around 40c, but it cranks up to 55c in July and August.

At least it has the ocean, and goats, and *chat*, aka *khat*, a mildly narcotic leaf imported from Yemen (which is so close you can practically see it) and chewed all day by pretty much every male inhabitant of the city. Pickup trucks overflowing with the stuff cruise by regularly. Yesterday I wandered past a huge police 4x4; the two officers inside were busily stuffing their faces with *chat*.

I'm mostly here because South Sudan fell through. Originally I was going to spend two weeks there and one in Ethiopia, but the Abyei crisis torpedoed that plan; then Médecins Sans Frontières informed me I wouldn't be able to visit any of their projects after all, which I had hoped to write about; then I was going to get my visa-like South Sudan permit in Kampala, but crazy airline prices torpedoed that plan; then I realized I was looking at US$1500 to spend four days in-country, which just seemed dumb. So here I am in this strange place. Last night I had a beer at a five-star hotel largely populated by Foreign Legionnaires and US military. It was an odd mix. Tomorrow, with luck, I'll visit Lac Assal, and I've booked some diving for Sunday. But I suspect that when Monday rolls around I will have had my fill of Djibouti.

June 2011: The World Is Salt
Djibouti

There were six crew and twenty divers on yesterday's expedition: two Frenchmen who owned the boat; two South African women who were the divemasters; two Djiboutian crew; nineteen members of the US military, ranging from career desk jockeys to some Special Forces dudes, all using their Sunday off to go diving—and one random Canadian tourist. Although at first everyone just assumed I was a new contractor or something, and I wasn't actually outed until just before the second dive.

It was then that the Special Forces dudes started talking to me. It seems the military has implicit but clear social hierarchies. They seemed to approve that I had randomly come to Djibouti, and they seemed pretty plugged-in, too; when I mentioned I had originally planned to visit a friend in South Sudan, they started joking that it was Joseph Kony, a name none of the regular military recognized. Alas, I think they started watching what they talked about, then, too; the best semi-overheard stuff came before that—

'... suddenly every Polish joke I had ever heard made sense to me. Yeah. But the Grom, their special forces, those guys were squared away, and they didn't like their regulars any more than we did ...'
'... dude, I was back in Puerto Rico, man, he was *stupid*. I learned so much here. It's been a great deployment.'

'So you're going career?'

'Yeah, man, totally. I love it. I love being a soldier.'

'That's awesome.'

'… dude ITMed for like an hour, we were watching the whole thing. There were three guys who came in to set an IED, I was watching them from the blimp the whole time, they lit up one guy, shot his arm off, he died, second guy got away on a motorcycle with them shooting all around them, but this guy in a ditch, he'd elbow-crawl, and they'd shoot, and he'd stop moving for five minutes, and we'd start thinking, well, we got him, but then he'd start moving again, and they'd start shooting again … this went on for like an hour 'til he got to the end of the ditch and just booked it into these ruins, and he made it, and they didn't chase him. Low-crawling *works*.'

'… we got three broken treadmills in the gym. Get them from Seychelles, they'll cost like, three thousand—'

'— like *five* thousand—'

'— yeah, maybe, but we gotta get 'em from there, we can't requisition straight from Bahrain, it all has to go through Seychelles.'

'… yeah, we got great video, you can Google it. 'Course the media reports say it was *Afghan* special forces, they don't say nothin' about us …'

About twenty minutes out of the harbour we passed a dead cow floating in the water. Twenty minutes later we passed a pod of *dozens* of frolicking dolphins, leaping out of the water all around us, flashing silver. 'Any day you see dolphins is a good day,' said Kristen, the lead divemaster, happily.

The water was ridiculously warm and clear, visibility out to thirty metres or more. The coral was vibrant and untouched, and we saw massive schools of fish, turtles sleeping on fan coral, and two guys claimed to have seen a moray eel. We encountered a few more dolphins on the way back along the unforgiving shore, a massive jagged wall of solid volcanic rock, as devoid of life as the surface of moon. On the ride back we were more of a big happy family than we had been at the beginning, in the way all dive boats get—though the military lines of social demarcation were still quite apparent.

Back at port a bus picked up the military guys, and I shouldered my bag and walked past them to the gate of the port to look for a taxi. Some of them looked envious. The hotel in which I type this is off limits to them, and there are other strict restrictions on what they can do in town. 'I've been here five months and I've lost twenty-five pounds,' Gareth said, 'nothing to do but work out and dive. Thank God there's diving. Got to spend my money on *something*.'

I got back just in time to make arrangements for today's trip, to Lac Assal, an inland salt sea that marks the lowest point in Africa and the third lowest in the world, after the Dead Sea and the Sea of Galilee: 150 metres below sea level. We (that being me and the driver I hired; I'd say it's low season here except I'm not so sure there's really such a thing as high season) also passed a vast canyon, and endless fields of lava, and a desolate *campement*, and stubborn trees somehow rising out of raw hardened lava, and monkeys and camels, nibbling on acacia trees or simply wandering by.

A long, hot, tiring day, but a great one.

Less than half of the time I've spent travelling has been in Africa, but when I once listed all of the truly great travel days that I can recall, I discovered more than half of them happened south of the Sahara. I don't think this is coincidence. It isn't the easiest place to travel, but it is the best.

II. THE MIDDLE EAST

◈◈◈◈◈◈◈◈◈◈◈◈◈◈◈◈◈◈◈◈◈◈◈◈◈◈◈◈◈◈

My relatively few visits to the Middle East have been sporadic and invariably surreal. My first flight into Egypt was delayed because the pilot ordered the terrified handcuffed man in the seat in front of mine—a prisoner being extradited to Egypt?—removed from the airplane after he shat himself while screaming himself hoarse. My next flight, into the desert city of Dubai, arrived on the heels of a once-a-decade rainstorm. My flight into the American-controlled zones of Iraq was on a US military cargo plane, carrying me because I was theoretically half journalist and half private contractor … but in practice I was still 100 percent tourist.

To me, then, this region of the planet is a zone of hyper-real strangeness. I've been told I'm not alone in this assessment.

June 2003: Moses and Monty Python
Sharm el-Sheikh, Egypt
All credit to Moses. Nowadays Mount Sinai is a straightforward two-hour hike up a well-worn trail, but three millennia ago, when there was presumably no path switchbacking up its steep crags, it must have been absolute murder.

I was expecting a mob of people and was amazed to find myself absolutely alone at the summit for sunset. Amazed and grateful. Standing atop a fantasyland of jagged, pitted, striated crags and canyons, eroded by the wind into twisted coiled dragon shapes, stained by the last crimson rays of the sun, on the very mountain where Moses, so legend has it, received the Ten Commandments—a magical moment. It's not often you get to spend the night in a genuinely mythical place.

I suppose I can't in good conscience leave you with the notion that I have become lone-wolf-in-the-wilderness Intrepid Man. I wasn't *that* alone. Not far below the summit are a half-dozen Bedouin huts/shops providing tea, Coke, chocolate, and mattress/blanket rental; two more overnighters showed up shortly after sunset; and just before dawn an Italian tour-group horde arrived. But still.

In the middle of the night, unless all three of us (wrapped beneath blankets, no tents, a comfortable distance from one another) independently dreamed the very same thing, twenty or thirty monks assembled around the ancient chapel near the summit and sang haunting Latin hymns for half an hour.

I found no burning bush up there. But at the foot of the mountain, in the seventeen-centuries-old Monastery of St. Catherine, grows what is alleged to be an offshoot of the very same bush that spoke to Moses; its remarkably green branches extend over a brick wall that guards its body. They claim that no other bush like it is found in all the Sinai peninsula, and that all the many attempts to cultivate cuttings from this bush in other places have failed. I remain a skeptic, as always, but it's a cool story.

Like other impoverished tourist destinations, Egypt is populated by many, many touts and hangers-on who will attach themselves to you and try to wheedle baksheesh and/or insist on becoming your guide if you either (a) look like a mark or (b) are excessively rude, in which case they may harass you just to piss you off.

Their usual chat-up lines are 'Where you from?' or 'Where you going?' My usual answer to the first is 'What's it to ya?' and to the second 'I seek the Holy Grail.' ('I seek enlightenment' turned out to be too abstract, 'Yo mamma's house' excessively adversarial.) Both usually confuse the tout long enough for a getaway. But today, in a crowded market in Sharm el-Sheikh from where I write, I gave some kid the usual answer, and kept walking, and then I distinctly heard somebody call out to me: 'Hey! My friend! What is the airspeed of a swallow in flight?' And my faith in the universe was newly restored.

July 2003: Aegyptification
Cairo, Egypt

One day in Expatland*

9:00 Wake in luxurious, high-ceilinged expat mansion in expensive Ma'adi suburb. Drink grande cappuccino. Host gives me keys to apartment, introduces me to driver, tells me car and driver are at my disposal.

---

* I would like to stress that this tale is pure fiction, only loosely inspired by actual events, as a thematic exploration of life as lived by certain expats in Egypt.

9:30 Slightly confused by situation; unaccustomed to travelling with own transport. Humbly request of driver that perhaps he could take me to pyramids at Sakkara, if it isn't too much trouble. Apologize profusely for taking up his day.

10:00 Arrive Sakkara. Nobody else here. Visit step pyramid. Hot out.

11:00 Politely ask driver to stop to buy water and then go to Dahshur pyramids, remarkably devoid of any crowds. No water stop. Remind driver of water request. Buy water, visit Dahshur pyramids. Very hot out.

13:00 Ask driver for lunch recommendations. Driver recommends McDonald's. Give driver sidelong look and have him take me to Nile Hilton for lunch; a club sandwich. Hilton pleasantly air-conditioned. Blistering heat makes exterior difficult.

15:00 Have driver take me to Giza Pyramids. Look around briefly. Glimpse Sphinx from behind. Damn, it's hot. Too hot to move or think.

15:15 Argue with driver over whether I have spent enough time viewing the majestic antiquities of Giza. Tersely inform driver that conversation is over and instruct him to take me to Meridien Hotel. Heat nearly unbearable.

15:30 Read *IHT* over a beer in air-conditioned luxury. Occasionally glance up at placid and remarkably blue Nile visible through the window, lined by tourist boats.

17:00 Decide to go to another hotel for dinner. Driver observes that he has a family and would like to see them tonight. Fix cold stare upon driver until he ceases his bleating. Off to Four Seasons for dinner. Driver requests that I leave at 19:00 p.m. Leave car without answering.

19:30 While sitting in bar talking football with American expats, driver approaches and suggests we leave. Tell driver in no uncertain terms (well, possibly slightly uncertain, due to slurring of words) to return to the goddamn car and wait for me if he wants to keep his job.

21:30 Stagger out to car and instruct driver to take me back to Ma'adi. Upon arrival, order driver to go out and fetch me beer. Watch satellite TV. Find self laughing at old rerun of *Married ... with Children*.

22:00 Beer arrives. Driver leaves. Discover beer is insufficiently cold. Make mental note to have driver flogged tomorrow.

23:00 Jean-Claude Van Damme filmfest is on satellite TV. Watch raptly. Decide to stay here in air-conditioned comfort for the rest of my time in Egypt, watching JCVD and colourized Turner Classic Movies, rather than exposing myself to the heat and the dust and the press of the crowds. Catch myself wishing wistfully that I had been born in the days of the Raj. Er, that is, born white, British, and upper-class, of course.

Cairo

'Hell,' Sartre once declared, 'is other people.' He wouldn't have liked Cairo.

It's a monstrous, giddy, dizzying megalopolis, 19 million people crammed into the slender ribbon of the Nile Valley, piloting 2 million cars through perpetual traffic jams despite the terrifyingly efficient use of roads such that two lanes equals four columns of cars. The occasional traffic light performs a useful decorative purpose and serves to lure unsuspecting tourists to their doom. Dust, noise, smoke, soot, blaring horns, bellowed Arabic, screeching brakes, tarnished gray marble. Endless landscapes of concrete blocks sprouting bundles of rebar from the rooftops. Huge hotel and office complexes towering over the wide blue Nile. Rows of pale transplanted palm trees choking in the smog. Curbs a foot high to dissuade Cairenes from parking, or driving, on the sidewalks. Robes, turbans, headscarves, veils, Diesel jeans, Armani suits, bare midriffs, *NSYNC posters. Pale filigreed spires ascending into the sky from enormous, pristine mosques. Fields thick with rotting trash, patrolled by flocks of goats. In the southwest Giza district a block full of papyrus shops ends with a KFC. Walk another hundred metres and you collide with the Sphinx. It's quite a place.

It also boasts the Museum of Egyptian Antiquities, a truly impressive museum which contains (a) the famous King Tut exhibit, in its entirety, solid-gold mask and coffin and all, (b) approximately eighty thousand colossi, steles, columns, statues, busts, and fragments, much of it five or six metres tall, casually distributed, barely categorized, dusty, and occasionally stacked two or three high, the overall effect being the attic of a forgetful pack rat rather than one of the world's great museums, which was fairly charming, and finally (c) the Royal Mummies, nine mummified pharaohs or consorts thereof in various states of deshabille, very cool and creepy as hell.

The Sinai

Previously, when I thought 'Egypt', I did not instinctively associate it with scuba diving, but the Red Sea boasts some of the finest diving in the world. The marine life isn't quite as varied or colourful as in Thailand or Australia, but the coral formations, particularly in Ras Mohammed National Park, are staggering, featuring sheer coral cliffs that drop for hundreds of metres and exquisite fan coral three or four metres in radius. Other people saw manta rays and sharks as well; I, alas, had to content myself with barracuda and a few huge schools of fish.

From the backpacker haven of Dahab I hired a private taxi to drive me to Mount Sinai because there weren't any groups going there. The desert was spellbinding in its utter barrenness. I spent a little more time in it than I intended to because the taxi broke down halfway through. The driver seemed to know only marginally more about engines than I do, which is absolutely nothing, but through trial and error (mostly error), brute force, and ignorance, we managed to reattach the fan belt and suffered only a few seventh-degree burns from the overheated engine en route. Okay, technically first-degree burns, but they felt like seventh.

Luxor and Aswan

Old stuff. Egypt's got a lot of it. Seriously old. When Herodotus visited the pyramids in 500 BC, they were as old to him as he is to us. And seriously big. The ruins of the temple of Karnak, in Luxor, cover more than eighty acres, and the great hall of columns is twice the size of St. Paul's Cathedral. The trouble is that it's all so sprawlingly enormous, and ancient, and elaborately intricately carved with hieroglyphs, and so familiar from countless pictures and documentaries and movie backdrops, that it is actually very difficult to convince yourself that these are in fact real four-thousand-year-old antiquities and not some theme-park reconstruction. Wandering around Karnak I wouldn't have been entirely surprised if Mickey Mouse and Goofy had walked out from behind an obelisk.

The summer heat in upper Egypt—'upper' referring to the Nile, which still defines this land—is blistering, oppressive, average daily highs of 45C. On the other hand it does keep the number of package tourists down. I went to Karnak at 2:00 p.m. and had the entire site pretty much to myself. The Valley of the Kings, which is a little too well-groomed these days to be as haunting as I hoped, was thick with Japanese, but they were far more polite and respectful than the Italians. There were plenty of street hustlers, but even they seemed enervated by the heat, and their cries of 'Felucca!' 'Taxi!' 'See my shop!' 'What country?' 'Where you going?' were half-hearted and rarely repeated.

The Nile Valley really is remarkably beautiful and remarkably slender. For most of the train journey from Aswan to Cairo you can look through the windows on either side and see desert hills in the distance. Egypt's reliance on the Nile's vicissitudes used to be absolute, but in 1967 the Russians built them the Aswan High Dam, one of the Earth's great mute testimonies to man's occasional dominion over nature, and being a hacker tourist ('hacker tourism', as defined by the great Neal Stephenson, is 'travel to exotic locations in search of sights and sensations that only would be of interest to a geek') I went to investigate. It wasn't nearly as big or impressive as I expected—in fact it seemed smaller than, say, Zimbabwe's Kariba Dam—but it's extraordinary to look south from the dam and to think that this basically simple stone structure created an artificial lake that stretches all the way into Sudan and, whatever its environmental downsides, has saved Egypt from both terrible flood and desperate drought since its creation.

From Aswan I also went to Abu Simbel. I went, but I did not arrive. I took a taxi to the airport; I checked in; I went through three equally pathetic levels of security; I boarded the airplane; I buckled my seat belt; I heard the captain announce the magic word 'crosscheck', meaning that takeoff is imminent—and then there was a horrible grinding noise beneath our feet, and the lights flickered on and off. This repeated for some time. After ten minutes the captain announced that there was a very, very minor snag with the engine and we would be en route shortly. Those passengers along the left-hand-side windows were skeptical, as we could see a dozen engineers had already removed the cowling from the port engine and seemed to be doing their best to entirely disassemble it in record time. After half an hour the pilot admitted that, and I quote, 'The airplane is broken,' and we were ferried back to the terminal building. The EgyptAir staff gave us vague cryptic hints of a replacement plane possibly being flown down from Cairo, possibly this week. I decided to save Abu Simbel for the next trip.

November 2004: Too Much Is Not Enough
Dubai, United Arab Emirates
I arrived on the heels of a once-in-seven-years storm. *Desert country, my ass*, I muttered to myself as I sloshed through the inch-deep water flooding Dubai International's arrivals and baggage halls. The water had shorted out the baggage conveyor systems, leaving my planemates temporarily stuck. I, who travel with carry-on only, left them behind and hopped a cab, trying and failing to squelch a sense of soaring moral superiority. The rains had shut down all but one of the highway's outgoing lanes. Two BMWs and one Mercedes were trapped in a gigantic puddle that had swallowed the other two lanes. I found a decent cheap hotel and crashed.

Breakfast on the street, lunch in Oman, dinner in the Burj al-Arab
For breakfast I had an omelette sandwich with tomatoes and cucumbers in greasy Indian bread, with tea, at a sidewalk café. It was tasty and filling. It cost me US$1.

Then I joined my day trip, an intimate little ten-4wD sixty-person convoy into the desert and Oman. We drove down empty, groomed four-lane highways for a while, past scrub that slowly turned into desert, where the fun began. 4wD roller-coaster dune-bashing, the grizzled veteran drivers (including Babylon, the giddy Kenyan at the wheel of our Yukon) carping in an amused way about the amateurs who kept overestimating their own abilities and getting stuck. Thence to a camel farm. I retain my opinion that they're nasty, stinky, loathsome creatures, but I admit they're cuter than I remembered.

And then a really amazing drive that—and I don't say this often—I wish I'd had a camera for. (Was going to pick one up in the morning, but the *souq* wasn't open yet.) We drove for a good fifteen minutes down a kilometre-wide black gravel *wadi* (dry riverbed) flecked with African acacia trees, through a herd of camels coming the other way, with the folded braided furrows of endless red-gold sand dunes to our right, and an impossibly forbidding wall of Mordor-esque jagged black mountains (the Hajar Mountains) to our left, with, the crowning touch, Elvis Presley crooning from the tape deck. It was incredible.

We stopped in Oman for lunch (sandwich, salad, a really bad apple, Coke) in a shockingly green oasis by another *wadi*, this one swept by groaning, howling wind. Then, unexpectedly, back without warning onto another perfect highway, as if it had grown yesterday out of the desert. No customs or immigration; borders are pretty amorphous around these parts, especially when you have a 4WD. In Hatta—which was pretty ghetto for the UAE—we paused to treat ourselves to another gorgeous panorama: red scalloped triangular mountains above a band of pale white marble buildings culminating in the graceful minarets of a mosque, surrounded by the green date palm and mango trees of another oasis, surrounded by more highway-fissured desert.

Back in Dubai, I found a cheap and cheerful gym decorated with heavily rusted but entirely functional weights, picked up a couple necessities for the night, and made my way to the Burj al-Arab—but wait, before I start in on that, I have a shameful admission to make. I only went there because they didn't let me in.

Aside: Five-star hotels are the budget Third World traveller's best friend. They provide oases of comfort, free newspapers, bathrooms well-stocked with toilet paper, swimming pools, and insanely helpful concierges who almost never ask if you're actually a hotel guest until it's too late. In part because of this, in part just to see them, I've made a habit of dropping by the Really Nice Hotels of places I travel to. Despite my often repellently scruffy look, they let me in, thanks to reverse racism, my practised air of confidence, and—in a pinch—a claim that I'm staying in Room 405. Until yesterday, only one hotel had ever turfed me out: the famed Raffles, in Singapore, where the Singapore Sling was invented and a tiger was once (allegedly) shot beneath the billiard table.

(Singapore is kind of like Dubai, come to think of it. Although not as much fun. I'm not saying Dubai is fun—it's actually no fun at all— but Singapore is actively anti-fun.)

The Burj al-Arab proclaims itself 'the world's only seven-star hotel.' Yes, seven. It does have certain advantages; for example, it's as tall as the Eiffel Tower, and it stands on a purpose-built artificial island connected to the rest of Dubai by a dedicated two-hundred-metre causeway. Yesterday, heading nearby(ish) to book my tour, I thought I'd drop by, blag my way in, look around, and have a drink. To their credit, I didn't even make it onto the causeway: hotel guests, invitees, and confirmed restaurant reservations only.

And so I found myself getting into a taxi tonight, wearing just-purchased one-time-use shoes and dinner jacket (fortunately, both are very, very cheap in Dubai), and instructing the cabbie: 'The Burj al-Arab, please.'

The Burj al-Arab: a review
The whole seven-star thing sounds eye-rollingly pretentious, so I decided to arrogantly and arbitrarily give it my own star rating, starting with five stars (pretty much default in Dubai; I mean, not in the kind of US$30 *souq* hotel where I stay, but along the coast or Boulevard Sheikh Zayed) and count from there.

Plus one star for scale. The edifice is immense, and its architecture is undeniably striking. Plus another star for the interior. The Rolls-Royces parked outside are a nice touch. I was expecting Versailles-style incredibly tacky excess, but the two-hundred-metre-tall atrium/foyer manages the trick of being simultaneously cartoonishly over-the-top (apparently everything that looks gold actually is gold, which is kind of mind-boggling) and yet does it in a way that is actually tasteful, and even—dare I say it—elegant. The staff were friendly and inviting. That's seven stars. I was impressed.

Being a half-hour early for my reservation, I took the elevator up to their twenty-seventh-floor restaurant/bar, at which point things began to go seriously downhill. For starters, it's one of the most aesthetically ghastly places I've ever been, with some kind of incredibly wrong-headed tech theme. You walk through tunnels lined with huge circuit-board patterns—I'm not making this up—into a room whose walls are full of LEDs that blink in L-shapes, and whose ceiling consists of garishly coloured *2001*esque, wannabe–Art Deco, but actually really ugly panelled lights. The view is okay but nothing special. Down to six stars.

Then I sat at the bar, ordered a Laphroaig, and they didn't have it.

In fact their Scotch selection consisted of Johnnie Black, Johnnie Red, and Chivas. Yes, yes, Arabic country, but also a massive tourist destination with bars all over the place. Dumbfounding and unforgivable. Docked two stars. Down to four. Had a $15 whiskey sour, which was fine, and headed for their flagship restaurant, Al Mahara.

To get into Al Mahara—remember, this is the flagship restaurant of what bills itself as the world's best hotel—you wait in a room decorated like the inside of a gigantic solid-gold clamshell, and then a faux-airlock door opens, and you get into, I kid you not, one of those incredibly tacky pseudo-motion theatre-on-a-stick things with a dozen seats and video screens on the wall that rocks and rolls a little in a futile attempt to persuade you that you're actually moving. As the video screens try to convince you you're moving fifty metres down and two hundred metres farther into the ocean, the 'captain' of this unbelievably kitschy 'submarine', in this case a guy named Mohammed, wearily recites dialogue about being sorry for the picture of the shipwreck to the left, he'd been drinking last night and crashed. Did I mention his name was Mohammed? Did I mention it's probably not a good sign when your primary emotion as you enter a restaurant is no longer anticipation but a kind of appalled sympathy for its staff? Three stars. If they're lucky. At this point my attitude towards the place is 'nice building, shame about what they put in it,' and I'm beginning to wonder if I should have stuck with the sidewalk cafés for reasons of taste alone.

The restaurant itself is a disc that surrounds a vast (well, forty-foot-diameter, twenty-foot-high) aquarium full of colourful tropical fish. I recognized a leopard shark, blacktip reef sharks, Maori wrasses, Moorish idols, and moray eels, and there were dozens of others swimming in an artificial but convincing coral reef. It's actually quite cool. And, as a bonus, it helps eliminate the occasional social awkwardness of dining alone, as you can always stare at the fish between courses.

The service was excellent, attentive without being in the least intrusive. The staff were impressively well informed. My waiter answered an at least somewhat technical marine biology question. There was a moray eel swimming around (!), which moray eels never do; when I asked why, the waiter explained, in an unrehearsed manner, that of their twelve moray eels, this one was new, and it hadn't worked out its territory yet. The tables and chairs and silverware and so forth were fine, whatever. The wine list was thick and I'm sure impressive; I stuck with sparkling water.

The menu, not surprisingly, focused on seafood, but had plenty of other divertissements. I skipped the 650 dirham (approximately US$180) tasting menu in favour of a bowl of hot-and-sour seafood soup, hold the scallops—I have a recent suspicion that I'm allergic, and I never liked 'em anyhow—and wok-fried lobster with rice (total 445 dirham/US$110).

The meal began with a small *amuse-bouche* of shrimp and tuna in a thick creamy sauce that managed to be simultaneously (a) incredibly bland and (b) so cloying that it leached all the taste out of everything else. Not a good beginning.

The bread was nothing to write home about, though the focaccia blackened with squid ink was at least interesting.

Then the soup arrived. It was in a bowl about ten centimetres in diameter and seven centimetres deep. It was full of the usual hot-and-sour soup stuff, plus a variety of seafood, plus spices. It rested on an elegantly folded napkin. It looked unprepossessing.

Oh. My. God. It. Was. So. Good.

I feel almost embarrassed about the praise I'm about to lavish on a bowl of hot-and-sour soup, but really, it was a religious experience. Every mouthful was an exquisite dance of spices. I want to take up poetry again, for the first time in ten years, just to write an ode to this soup. A world that contains soups like this cannot be all bad. I would vote for this soup for prime minister (or sultan) and I would stand by it no matter what scandals it was accused of. To those who ask if there is a God, I would answer: 'Who else made this soup?'

It wasn't soup. It was divine.

The lobster was okay. There was a lot of it, dressed with pesto sauce, which was interesting but unsuccessful. The rice, though, was *perfect*, big, light, fluffy, tasty, decorated with pine nuts. After finishing the lobster, I ate the whole bowl of white rice with just as much pleasure.

I turned down dessert, but they brought me a trayful of petits fours; they looked good, and the chocolate bits were superb, the rest didn't really work for me, but they never do anywhere else either.

Final note: With two bonus stars for the soup, and one remedial star added because the bathrooms were excellent and didn't have an attendant, and because you can take an elevator back to the lobby instead of going through that cringe-inducing 'submarine' ride again (although it remains an option), we reach a grand total of six stars. I'm so glad you agree.

The Burj al-Arab's clientele, in both hotel and restaurant, was, I'm disappointed to say, mostly incredibly boring: loud, pudgy, and dull, or wrinkly and anxious. There was one redeeming couple—a bona fide sultan/sheikh/emir in full s/s/e garb sitting on a lobby couch with his arm around a drop-dead gorgeous Russian-supermodel type, but mostly, I fear the world's interesting rich (rooms at the Burj start at US$900 a night and go way up in a hurry) stick to boutique hotels. Can't say I blame them. But it's a nice place to visit, as long as you have the soup.

April 2005: Rock the Casbah
Germany to Iraq
Images from the past eighteen hours:

04:00 (German time, GMT+1) Stepping out of a van onto the Frankfurt runway. The looming C-17, its high wings oddly twisted, looks gigantic against the night. The interior is an enormous tubular cave, its ceiling covered by wires, duct tubing, crawl spaces, and access platforms, the metal walls full of racks of odd tools, anchors, buttons, controls, nooks, crannies. The only windows are a few tiny portholes. The floor is all rollers, on which pallets averaging twenty cubic feet are stacked and secured by a mesh of seat-belt-like straps. It's hard to tell exactly what most of the cargo is. Passenger seats line the walls. Most of them are blocked by cargo, but there are enough free for tonight's four passengers.

We listen to the lecture about our oxygen masks, life jackets, and fireproof breathing hood. I strap myself into a seat beneath an axe. The axe is mounted next to a sign that says FOR EMERGENCY EXIT CUT HERE. Tonight, judging from the pallet in front of me, the mighty American war machine needs files. Boxes and boxes of nine-by-seventeen-inch manila files ordered from INDUSTRIES FOR THE BLIND, INC. At the very front of the cave, next to stairs leading up to the flight deck, the loadmaster sits in a cubicle, surrounded by mysterious buttons and controls. We are given lunch-box-sized Air Force meals, which turn out to be not bad.

10:30 (Iraq time, GMT+3) Woken from my sleep on the C-17's steel floor and advised that we will soon begin our 'tactical descent' into Iraq. Better known to the military cognoscenti as the 'death spiral'. I fasten my seat belt. The plane begins to lose altitude, gently at first, like a passenger jet, and then the pilot pushes the nose down and lets it plummet.

The white noise drowns out everything, earplugs are pointless. My stomach first lurches, then feels just weird—not queasy, exactly—and I realize it's because I'm not used to massive sideways deceleration. We start to level off and bank, hard, at the same time, and when the banking ends, the nose goes back down, we're diving again, screaming downwards. From where I'm sitting all I can see is daylight through the portholes. For this I'm a little grateful. The nose eases back up, up, and suddenly we make a perfect three-point landing, we don't even bounce, and then we're braking *hard*, my bag would go flying forward if I didn't corral it with my feet, then slowing to a gentle taxi. Welcome to Iraq.

11:00 The rear gate won't open. The crew chief is fiddling with it. 'Just remember,' the loadmaster says drily, 'we're the superpower.'

11:15 The rear gate opens. Out into the heat and the light, neither quite as intense as I feared. The landscape is as flat as a pounded pancake, baked mud and gravel and pavement, but with more trees than I expected. The first things I see are the surreal hangars; they look like colossal igloos, built out of desert-coloured bricks the size of SUVs, through which huge arching tunnels run. The vehicles nestled within look like Tonka toys. We drive to the arrivals tent, where I sign in, try and fail to connect to my contacts with an ancient field telephone, and am left to my own devices. The arrivals tent is dominated by a massive TV showing *CSI* to dozens of uniformed troops sitting in rows of chairs. At the other end of the room, posters fail to explain the Byzantine procedure of signing up for departures.

12:00 Picked up and taken to the trailer that will be home for the next few days (though I might try a billeting tent, larger and better air-conditioned, tonight). Most of the buildings here are temporary, thanks to a law that requires an Act of Congress to build so much as a single new permanent building on a military base. (Rebuilding old Saddam-era buildings that were smithereen-bombed, however, counts as 'refurbishing' and is okay.) The resulting temporary structures are impressive. Vast segmented tents that look like giant caterpillars. Huge ovoid domes, seamed like circus tents, with gleaming chitinous skins and massive wedge-shaped doors at one end. Countless trailers surrounded by sandbags, walled by intermittent rows of concrete barriers. Massive trapezoidal bunkers from the Saddam era, brutalist and windowless. Everything is pale, low-contrast, all colour drained away by the scorching desert sun.

13:00 Off to DFAC 1 for lunch with my hosts, entrepreneurs who provide Internet access to denizens of US military bases in Iraq. I know them socially from the Internet; previous to this visit I had met only one of them in person, for a grand total of one hour. DFAC = Dining FACility. A huge cafeteria-like structure, where sour-looking Sri Lankans serve surprisingly good food to anyone with a DoD badge. It reminds me of summer camp.

14:00 Exploratory drive around the base in a battered old Mercedes. Pennsylvania Avenue, the main drag, is thick with Humvees, minibuses, Pathfinders, weird armoured military vehicles adorned with .50 calibre machine guns, truck cabs, huge construction vehicles that can carry entire shipping containers with their scorpion-like arms. Troops wait at wooden bus stops or walk up and down, most of them armed with M16s and wearing helmet and armour; that last is unusual, but the threat level has been ratcheted up today for Saddam's birthday. We pass parking lot after parking lot where vehicles of all kinds are arrayed in neat rows. A lot where hundreds of Porta-Johns are arrayed in neat rows. Barriers, fences, razor wire, concertina wire—but that mostly near the airfield proper; it's easy to walk most anywhere in the populated part of the base. Buildings and trailers are often identified by unit names and numbers, sometimes with murals painted outside. The base is littered with weird, unexpected bits of Americana: a US Post Office box, a Subway logo.

We pass the single most extraordinary thing I see all day, the trash dump, massive piles of scrap metal, charred twisted wreckage from the US bombing of this base, and I don't even know what else. It looks like the end of the world, like a jagged rusted hell, and it goes on and on, and at its far corner the 'tire fire'—it's not clear to me whether this is deliberate or not—releases a constant plume of smoke into the air.

Along the fence, which looks flimsy, just chain-link topped by barbed wire, with watchtowers every so often, some low and wooden, some high and metal and camouflage-netted. To the airfield, where a

C-17 is taking off, past where a Marine helicopter bulbous with weaponry is parked next to a long, long line of Blackhawks and a collection of Chinooks. Past the Iraqi National Guard enclave, past the KBR (Kellogg Brown Root) enclave, back 'home'.

15:00 Exploration on foot. The base seems much bigger this way. Twenty minutes in the heat and I start to get a little fatigued. Already the churning cornucopia of traffic, the clutches of Army and Air Force troops, the trailers and sandbags and fences and helicopters above, all seems almost normal. To the movie theatre, showing *The Amityville Horror*. The huge, high-ceilinged recreation centre, where the electronic games room is full and the library empty, alas (and very weirdly stocked; tons of *Left Behind* books and political theory). The main PX (Post Exchange), is a combination grocery, electronics, clothes, and tools store, prices comparable to Back Home, with a Burger King and Pizza Hut out front. Instead of real change you get bright little circular pieces of cardboard with their value written on them; it's suggested this is to prevent pocket-jingling. Back 'home' again, via minibus, which comes promptly and moves quickly. I suppose a base this size needs remarkably good public transit.

17:00 A jarring thump shakes the trailer. Mortar? Controlled explosion? No alarm, so probably the latter. Mortars apparently still hit the base every couple of days; in fact, LSA Anaconda is mordantly nicknamed 'Mortaritaville'.

May 2005: Wasting Away Again in Mortaritaville
LSA Anaconda, Iraq

I'm staying in a billeting tent, which is a tent dormitory with eighteen cots, a few Porta-Johns nearby, and some showers and actual toilets a farther walk away. Don't misinterpret 'tent'. This one has wooden floors, fluorescent lights, two massive air-conditioning units, and a fifteen-foot-high ceiling. 'The only things the army are really good at are erecting tents and lining things up in neat rows,' said one of my hosts. (Presumably they're at least competent at the actual warfighting as well. And their engineers are well respected.) There are twenty-eight such tents in the billeting area, plus a central check-in tent that features another huge TV, a small library, and the Internet/phone centre from which I now type. Backpacking is actually amusingly good training for living at a military base.

There are plenty of bugs, kind of surprising for an alleged desert. (Though there is a nearby canal, and fields of green weeds grow outside the fence.) I showered late, night before last, and there were sand fleas everywhere. The odd mosquito too. At night, driving along Pennsylvania Avenue, you can see surging clouds of bugs and moths flocking to every candy-cane-shaped street light.

It's still easy to get lost, since there are few unique landmarks. Fortunately there are bus stops everywhere, most of which have posted bus maps.

Several times yesterday I asked soldiers how long they'd been here, and they answered with how much time they have left. Most seem to be from the South or the Midwest. One of them said 'It's changed a lot since the first time.' This is his second tour. Last time his unit was living in bombed-out buildings and doing laundry by hand; now they have access to pools, gyms, vast recreation facilities, cooked food every night, and so on.

The food ranges from unremarkable to excellent. Dinner night before last was (good) steak, lobster, and king crab legs. Unfortunately I didn't take my hosts' warning re the spikiness of the crab legs seriously, and impaled my thumb on a thorn-like shell protrusion. Yes, that's right, I went to Iraq and was wounded by shellfish. Do I qualify for a Purple Heart?

Went to the gym yesterday. It's one of the huge (forty-foot-high ceiling, football-field length) circus-type ovoid tents, just past the indoor/outdoor pool complex. Except for the lack of changing rooms, it's one of the nicest gyms I've ever been in. There's a basketball court, an indoor racquetball court, tons of free weights and cardio equipment, a sit-up room, an aerobics/martial arts room, all heavily air-conditioned, of course. The red alert siren sounded partway through my workout. Mortar strike somewhere on base, presumably. No one heard its thin wail, obscured as it was by that Destiny's Child song 'I Need a Soldier', until the music stopped and a sergeant shouted at us all to go to the perimeter of the building and sit with our backs to the wall. This is the new red alert procedure; the old one was to evacuate the building immediately. We sat for about twenty minutes, united by boredom, until the all-clear sounded.

Most of the actual infrastructure—power, water, roads, sewage, DFACs—is contracted out, and most of the contracts go to KBR.

Presumably building a military base isn't all that different from building an oil drilling compound. KBR in turn subcontracts much of the actual work to (judging from their staff) Turkish, Filipino, or Indian/Sri Lankan companies. The last group isn't that surprising—there's a long history of people from the subcontinent coming to the Gulf to make their fortune and support their families.

The nonmilitary Turks, Filipinos, and Indians are known as TCNs (third country nationals) and are treated with some ... not suspicion, exactly, but lack of equality. Iraqis, none of whom I've actually seen yet, are LNs (local nationals) and divided into 'escort required' and 'no escort required'. TCNs also run the local bazaar, where you can buy leather jackets(!), brass lamps, carpets, toiletries, clothes. The bazaar is pretty devoid of shoppers. I feel a certain kinship with the TCNs; after all, technically, I am one myself, though I strongly doubt a Sri Lankan could wander around the base like I do without at least occasionally being challenged. White skin and an American-sounding accent will get you a long way on an American military base.

Most soldiers choose to wear their PT (physical training) gear, black shorts and gray T-shirts, rather than their DCUs (desert camouflage uniforms). Half of them still carry guns, pistols in strapped-on thigh holsters, or various flavours of assault rifles. It's a little bizarre being at the PX and seeing a woman carrying a shopping bag with an M16 slung over her shoulder. There are 'clearing barrels', basically triangular wooden blocks containing barrels lined with sandbags, outside most buildings, into which guns must be pointed while cleared for fear of an accidental discharge. I'm not sure why they're so heavily armed—I've only been here two days, but I can confidently say that a firefight is not going to erupt in LSA Anaconda anytime soon. Maybe they're worried about the Iraqi National Guard unit going rogue.

Freedom Radio plays in the gym and occasionally in cars: a weird mix of rock, country, paeans to the fallen and the decorated, and exhortations to keep up the good fight, call your family, check with your chaplain if you're stressed, and not lose your ID card, along with lectures on how to recognize an IED. (Classic Orwellian milspeak: 'VIED' sounds so much more clinical and innocuous than, say, 'car bomb'.) TV antennas pick up Armed Forces Network channels. There are also Arabic radio stations, mostly devoid of music. The first song played by Armed Forces Radio when Operation Desert Storm began in '91 was, famously, the Clash's 'Rock the Casbah'. There is no longer any sign of that irreverent humour.

Last night, while I was sitting with one of my hosts atop an E-shaped truck-parking bunker (with steep inward-sloping concrete, but exterior slopes gentle enough to walk on) watching the sun set spectacularly over the base, there was a GI perched on the middle branch of the E with a lit candle, a tarot deck, and a knife, performing some kind of pagan ritual. And I thought the place couldn't get any more surreal. Except it isn't; I've been here all of forty-eight hours and living on an Iraqi military base already seems perfectly normal. One thing about us *homo sapiens*, we adapt real good.

May 2005: Black Hawk Up
Baghdad, Iraq

Objectively, a day trip from Balad to the Green Zone involves very little risk. Subjectively is a whole other story. Typically, I was nervous up to the moment when I actually sat down in the outgoing Blackhawk; then I started to grin.

It didn't help that the two passengers I flew out with were Airborne doctors who had chatted breezily during the preflight about their recent patients: a 'star cluster to the face' (don't know what that is, but it sounds nasty) and a piece of shrapnel that lodged on the *inside* of the victim's skull (without any brain damage). They talked wistfully about the 'freedom birds', the airplanes that fly from Balad back to America, and the sad fact that they weren't on one.

To fly a Blackhawk from Balad, you sign up at the space-available tent, and at your appointed hour a minibus takes you out to the flight line, where dozens of helicopters, mostly Blackhawks and two-rotored Chinooks, await. After grisly conversation (see above) you climb in.

There isn't quite enough room to stand. The door gunners sit on padded seats behind the cockpit; a machine gun is mounted on a flexible arm in the open window in front of each them. The space between them is occupied by a rugged military laptop, from which various cables and wires run. Flaps and panels in the ceiling keep storage niches covered. Everything is painted black. Behind the door gunners are three forward-facing seats; behind that are two benches of five seats, facing one another. The seats are canvas and metal pipe, and the belt buckle is circular, with three apertures, for the side and two shoulder straps; to release, you twist its propeller-shaped top. The main doors slide open and shut, and are windowed.

They turn on the laptop first, which I found surprising. Its screen is touch-sensitive and seems to display some kind of map. Then the power, this sounds like an aircraft engine coming alive, and then the rotors start to turn, like fifteen-foot knife blades with the sharp edge away from the rotation direction, the last foot or so of each rotor bent back about thirty degrees, forming a vaguely swastika-like shape. A few slow rotations, then whop, whop, whopwhop *whopwhopwhopwhop* and you better have your earplugs in by now because Blackhawks are *VERY LOUD*.

Taxi out onto the runway; hop up, then down again, standard procedure for some reason, in sync with the other Blackhawk next to you (they almost always travel in buddy-system pairs) and then up you go, like an angled elevator, the ground falls away. But not too far. They fly about fifty to a hundred feet above the ground, at around two hundred and forty miles per hour. It's twenty minutes from Balad to Baghdad.

From the air Balad/LSA Anaconda looks like a child's sandbox full of military toys. The area outside is much greener, a patchwork of farming fields fissured with canals and pocked with clusters of palm trees. Then villages, big L-shaped concrete blocks and crude brick buildings with thatch/mud roofs. Roads, smooth and modern, well-trafficked. Herds of goats flee from the helicopter noise. Lots of people wave; some keep their arms lowered and stare; some just ignore us. We cross wide muddy rivers, vast barren brown patches, more roads, towns, farmland. Not a lot of variety except that the size of the villages increases. On the way back, it was nearing sunset, and I could see street lights in the larger towns, fluorescent tubes mounted on hockey-stick-shaped poles.

A Blackhawk is a remarkably smooth ride. The whole aircraft vibrates, but it's a kind of soothing white-noise vibration rather than anything jarring. Both flights did feature a couple of sudden heart-pumping lurches though. On the way there we repeatedly banked sharply, sometimes by what felt like as much as 45 degrees (but was probably more like 30). I presumed it was standard operating procedure to do this, a kind of evasive action, but the flight back was pretty much a straight and level shot. I guess each flight crew has its quirks.

The ride itself is absolutely exhilarating, landscape zooming past and disappearing under you, like a dream of flying.

On the way out, one door gunner had a bagful of little Tyco stuffed horses, the size of my hand, white with a brown mane, beneath his seat. He placed one stuffed horse in the turret mount in front of him, presumably as a mascot. Midway there, as we flew over a village, he dropped another one out. A gift to Iraq? A sacrifice to propitiate Lady Luck?

On the way there we spent hardly any time over Baghdad, all I saw was a sea of buildings, a busy traffic-jammed highway, then bridges over the wide Tigris, and we were already descending into the Green Zone. The descent takes about five seconds; the landing is gentle, bumpless. On the way back, we spent more time over the city, flying from the palaces of the Green Zone, across commercial streets and built-up areas full of two-and-three-storey buildings on palm-tree-lined streets, drab and sprawling, a bit like a characterless suburb of Cairo except not as built up. Beyond that were the inevitable shantytowns, one-storey shacks, slums smeared across miles—Sadr City, I suppose. Fabulous and exotic it wasn't. I can't imagine there'd be much reason to come to Baghdad if you hadn't convinced yourself you needed to conquer it.

May 2005: The Green Zone Is for Conquering and Unconquering Only
Baghdad, Iraq
Insurgent mortars hit LSA Anaconda on a daily basis. (Don't worry, it's an enormous base, the chance of actually getting hit by one is astronomically small.) The other night a barrage of about half a dozen hit maybe half a mile away from me, waking me up even though they weren't loud—there's something about that *crrrrump* that kicks you into wakefulness. I went back to sleep, was rewoken by the red alert siren, and went back to sleep again, as did almost everyone else in the tent; you're supposed to find a hardened bunker for the duration of the red alert, if you're on active duty, but nobody here takes the siren seriously. It's 'the boy who cried "mortar".' Here it goes again, as I type.

Word is that one shell smacked into a shower trailer in which a soldier was showering. Fortunately for him it (a) missed his stall and (b) failed to explode. No word on whether the hot water was interrupted, or on whether he dried and dressed before leaving.

Last night a strong dusty wind turned into a full-on storm. It rained mud; the wind had kicked the dust up into the air, and the raindrops brought it back down. The storm grew so strong that the main billeting tent (not where you sleep, but where you check in/watch TV/eat/get books/make phone calls/read on the Internet) half-collapsed and had to be rebuilt this morning. The walls of my tent whipped back and forth, the wooden doors slammed open and shut, and outside the wind howled and the mud spattered down.

The Green Zone is a very weird place. It's a vast patch of prime Baghdad real estate, a collection of palaces, embassies, stadia, huge decorated archways, hotels, and government buildings, all tucked into the crook of an arm of the Tigris River. Not that you can see the river much. The huge, continuous wall of twelve-foot-high concrete topped by an endless cylinder of DNA-like concertina wire sees to that. This entire city district called the Green Zone has been sealed off, interrupted only by a dozen or so checkpoints.

Within is the downtown of a poor-but-not-too-poor city—wide streets, uneven cobblestoned sidewalks, and vast tyrant-ego-stroking architecture—turned into a paranoid armed camp. Especially in the district where I arrived. All the roads here are lined by more concrete-barrier walls. Another wall surrounds the helipad. The streets, parking lots, helipad, PX entrance, and compound entrances are watched by heavily armed Gurkha sentries, and believe me, a tougher-looking bunch of hombres you never did see. Smaller concrete barriers, sandbagged, block the traffic. Lines of armoured Humvees with machine-gun turrets are parked on the street. Concertina wire is everywhere; in places you have to watch where you're going just walking down the road, to avoid a dangling strand. And the pièce de paranoid résistance is the US Embassy, once Saddam's presidential palace, now guarded by Gurkhas (Nepalese soldiers), Marines, walls, cameras, and presumably every other form of defence known to mankind. I tried but failed to gain access; you need an active-duty DoD badge or a yellow embassy badge.

Lots of people wear yellow embassy badges. Almost all of them are white, American, thirty-something, trickling in and out of the embassy to the nearby minibus stop (like Balad, the Green Zone is serviced by KBR-operated shuttle buses with Filipino or Iraqi drivers), the PX, or the Chinese restaurant. Yes, there is a Chinese restaurant, reopened after a bombing last year. Past a huge half-bombed-out palace that is now a military base, along a sidewalk demarcated by barriers and concertina wire, past a checkpoint and a shuttle bus stop and Gurkha-guarded compound entrances, then to your left, at the CHINESE RESTAURANT sign that looks like graffiti, through the cloud of Iraqi kids trying to sell you bootleg CDs, along a very narrow path with another huge concrete barrier to your right and property walls to your left—and that's even more surreal, backyards leading to moderate-sized houses in the midst of all this military security —and about a hundred feet in, in the shell of what was once a nice house, a nice Chinese family serves you food on wooden tables, indoor and out. The hot-and-sour soup was surprisingly very good. The vegetable fried rice was, not surprisingly, not.

I mentioned compounds: there are several, each of which has its own walls and wire and security. The embassy is the *ne compound ultra*, then there's a PCO (contracting office) compound, another for the State Department, another for the KDP (Kurdish Democratic Party?), plus the military minibases in the Zone if they count, and the biggest compounds of all, Kellogg Brown and Root, a division of Halliburton, which runs the actual infrastructure of the Zone just as it does at Balad. There are six thousand KBR employees in Balad and probably a comparable number in the Zone. The running joke is 'KBR invaded Iraq; America just came along for the ride.'

There are very few Iraqis in this 'downtown' embassy-compounds-helipad area. The ratio of military to civilian is something like one to one. Some of the civilians look like civil servants anywhere. Some of them carry weapons and wear armour. Mercenary groups such as Blackwater have a significant presence here in Iraq, employed by private companies or sometimes, I think, by the US government directly. I'm not sure if the Gurkhas are mercenaries or part of the 'multi-national force'.

The parking lot outside the PX is like an SUV dealership, an armoured SUV dealership, with a sideline in Humvees. It seems that only Iraqis drive sedans. Past the embassy-compounds-helipad area, the Green Zone opens up a little and starts looking like a city again, one with wide two-lane roads and apartment buildings, although it's still mostly given over to government buildings and hotels. I was denied access to the Al-Rasheem Hotel, to my dismay. Note that in a five-hour visit I only managed to visit the places the local buses take you, which is maybe half the Zone.

Some of the old walls are bullet-scarred. A huge archway covered by a massive golden dome spans the road at one point. Highways lead off into unexplored parts of the Zone. The roads are busy but the sidewalks nearly deserted. A couple of sidewalk stands sell Coke, cigarettes, DVDs, grilled kebab meat. I traded a dollar for a thousand dinars at one, and was offered whiskey in a hushed voice. I rode in a bus empty except for the driver, and, later, in a bus where I was the only non-Iraqi; I'm embarrassed to say that both experiences were slightly nervous-making. The Iraqis were friendly, and laughed and joked with one another. Mostly men, a few women: two middle-aged with dyed hair, one young, very pretty, and heavily made up, dressed all in black with a hijab.

A friendly Scotsman I rode with another time explained that there are still twelve thousand Iraqis who live within the Zone, and as a result only the compounds, whose denizens live and work inside, are truly secure; the Zone itself is only quasi-secure. Being ex–British military, and having fought in the first Gulf War, he also had harsh words about the unprofessional military incompetence of the insurgents. 'I'm from John o'Groats,' he said. 'Isn't that the end of the world?' I asked. (John o'Groats is the northernmost habitation on the British mainland.) 'No, sonny,' he said without missing a beat, 'this is.'

III. EUROPE

❉❉❉❉❉❉❉❉❉❉❉❉❉❉❉❉❉❉❉❉❉❉❉❉❉❉

I've lived in both London (several times) and Paris (twice), but I confess: I actually haven't spent all that much time travelling in Europe. There's a reason for this. I've long figured that Europe will always be there, wealthy and accessible, whereas the trials and tribulations of travel in the developing world will probably grow less appealing as I age. In a sense I'm saving many of Europe's traditional sights for my faraway languid retirement.

But I have managed to wander into a few of its more curious corners: in particular, Albania and the former Yugoslavia, which serve as the setting for the first section of my second novel, *The Blood Price*. I can assure you that they did not disappoint as background for a thriller.

June 2003: An Elaborate Hoax?
Athens, Greece; Albania

Athens. Cradle of civilization, where 2,500 years ago the ancient Greeks invented democracy, philosophy, and the Olympics. Or did they? I ask you: Where's the proof?

Yeah, yeah, I know: 'The proof's all around you! The Acropolis! The Parthenon! The Temple of Zeus! The Olympic Stadium!' Uh-huh. I seen 'em. The Acropolis is a construction site, the Parthenon and the Temple of Zeus are covered in scaffolding, and the Olympic Stadium is flanked by a pair of enormous construction cranes. It really makes you wonder.

Athens itself is a nice place, a bit of a dive, but I like dives. The Greeks very sensibly herd the vast majority of tourists into a warren of shops and cafés just below the Acropolis. The entire rest of the city is under destruction for next year's Olympiad, and the streets are labyrinthine, but fortunately it's a good place to get lost in. I like the way glitzy shopping areas and grimy suburbs alike can suddenly be interrupted by exquisite Orthodox churches that look like wedding cakes, or (allegedly) ancient ruins and pillars. And you can pick up fresh spanakopita on basically any street corner. Mmm.

Also, it's cheap.

'The best-laid schemes … gang aft agley.'
From Athens I took the train north to Thessaloniki, and from there into
Skopje, the capital of the Former Yugoslav Republic of Macedonia. Well,
actually, no. Lesson learned: even if all previously available information
states that Canadian passport holders may purchase a Macedonian visa
at the border rather than in advance, the only opinion that really
matters is that of the Macedonian border police. It might be for the best
that I was bounced, as the way things were going, it looked like
Dragosic, the wild Serbian man who co-inhabited my train
compartment, was going to either challenge me to a duel to the death or
offer me his daughter's hand in marriage before the ride was over.

The Greeks gave me a free ride back to Thessaloniki, where I spent
a pleasant day exploring the café-laden city before hopping a bus to
Albania, which has a truly fearsome reputation in Greece; all passengers
had to go through a metal detector and run their bags through
an X-ray machine, before they were allowed onto the bus. I've passed
through a fair few land borders before, and this was a first. (Ironically
the only other destination for which I can envision it happening is
the USA.)

Then, as always seems to be the way with border crossings, we hit
the border itself at 2 a.m., and I had to do the hurry-up-and-wait
border thing, sleep-deprived and shivering in the night, jostling for
position in the cloud of people to get the Greeks and then the Albanians
to stamp my passport. Amusingly, my sleep-dazed state saved me from
paying a 'personal surcharge' to the Albanian border guard:

ABG: 'Entry tax, twenty euro.'
Me: 'Twenty euro?' *(Not sure if he'd said 'twenty' or 'thirty'.*
A pause. ABG looks at me narrowly. I look back, eyes glazed
with what I guess might have seemed to be skepticism.)
ABG: 'Ten euro.' *(reluctantly)*

Why does a dog wag its tail?
The bus deposited us in Korce, a town an hour from the border. Nicky,
an eccentric British missionary I met on the bus, kindly put me up at
her house in a nearby village. An exceedingly hospitable person, but she
had a disconcerting habit of ranting about the miserable, greedy,
thieving Albanians. If her neighbours (who fed me coffee and chocolate
in the morning) and all the other people I've met here are anything to

go by then she couldn't be more wrong. 'Happy, pleasant, friendly, generous, and welcoming' would be more like it.

In fact all of Albania seems to have been the victim of bad press. It's not near as backward and Third World as its reputation would indicate. The countryside is lovely, featuring red-brick rural villages set amid rippling green hills, olive groves and herds of goats, and Lake Ohrid, a vast, misty lake surrounded by rugged granite hills. Future European cottage country, mark my words. Buy your waterfront property now while it's cheap.

(Weird stranger-than-we-can-imagine aside: Lake Ohrid is home to the European eel, an extremely bizarre species that is born in the Sargasso Sea, swims across the Atlantic, through the Mediterranean, and up the River Drin to live in Lake Ohrid for ten years, then swims back to the Sargasso Sea to mate, reproduce, and die. I couldn't make this stuff up.)

The landscape is admittedly made a little surreal by the 750,000 small, domed concrete pillboxes that the paranoid Hoxha administration placed all over the country, particularly along roads and waterfronts, to protect Albania from the expected hordes of invading armies. Although when you consider events in Yugoslavia in the '90s this sadly seems more sensible than crazy.

Further evidence of Albanians being incredibly welcoming: like most developing nations, transport from town to town is handled by minibuses, here called *furgons*. The driver of the *furgon* that took me to Tirana bought me a coffee at a roadside café en route, drove me to the doorstep of my destination rather than the bus station without being asked … and refused a tip.

(We pause here so that those readers with experience of *furgons*/*tro-tros*/*bemos*/*matatus*/PMVs/whatchamathingummies in other places can recover from the shock, dust themselves off, and sit themselves back on their chairs.)

It's also considerably less isolated than I expected. At said roadside café I wound up trading Cameroonian travel tales, in French (somewhat broken on my side), with a Greek-Albanian kid who had just spent two years living there. This isn't quite as weird as it may sound—most Central African countries have significant Greek communities—but is still pretty weird.

Tirana, the capital, is a pleasant enough city to spend a day in. Poor by European standards, sure, and in that stage of development where urban developers seem to get a bonus for making their cheap new buildings as ugly as possible, but at the same time fairly cosmopolitan, with a thriving café culture and even some interesting architecture in an avant-garde-Stalinist-igloo kind of way. And despite Albania being theoretically an Islamic country the women have adopted the Greek fashion of Skimpy And A Size Too Small. After a brief internal struggle I managed to overcome my natural disapproval.

I'm now in Durres, a nearby city on the Adriatic where cheap tourist hotels have been sprouting like pimples along the waterfront to handle Italian tourists who come here on direct ferries from Bari and Trieste. Unfortunately the waterfront and beach are under ugly reconstruction, but there are remnants—a wall, a big amphitheatre, pillars, and baths—of the city the Romans built here back in the day, and once you get out of the city proper, the coastline is beautiful. It's also a useful setting for my planned refugee-smuggling book. And it was fun watching Real Madrid on TV while sitting atop an ancient Roman guard tower that has been repurposed as a bar.

Next up: another couple of days on the Albanian coast, a refilling of moneybags (the banking system here is kinda primitive, but I should be able to get a credit card advance in *leke*, the local currency, and then convert that to euros on the street) and then off to the UN protectorate of Kosovo. Thence to 'the pearl of the Mediterranean', Dubrovnik, in Croatia.

June 2003: Balkanization

The Discreet Charm of the Kosovarese

Parts of Kosovo are very pretty. It was exhilarating, even after an exhausting eleven-hour bus ride through the Albanian outback, to watch dawn rise above its green, misty, rolling hills. Unfortunately the pretty parts do not include the towns. And definitely not the hotels. I checked into the Stalinist-concrete-block Hotel Iliria, whose terrifyingly pallid receptionist had obviously gone to Gulag charm school, and discovered that my room's 'ensuite bathroom' was a cube of rotting concrete featuring a sink, a shower head, a towel ring, and a hole in the floor (to be fair the rest of the room was reasonable). And then I went down and ate breakfast with two hundred Bangladeshi peacekeepers.

I guess NATO-UN territories tend to have more than their share of Luis Buñuel moments.

Kosovo's cities are squalid arrays of grim concrete cubes, but even the poorest apartment block is forested with satellite dishes, and the countryside is green and beautiful. Its inhabitants love three things: cigarettes, ice cream, and the Internet. In a town of 150,000 there must be at least a hundred establishments vending each of the latter two, and the streets are carpeted with cigarette butts. All three are cheap and high quality. Ah, capitalism.

Not all of life's luxuries are well represented here, but to my surprise there was a reasonably elaborate gym. I went to work out. Not twenty minutes later, an enraged and monstrously huge US Marine emerged from the locker room growling with menacing incoherent fury. It turned out that somebody—he suspected a group of 'Albanian thugs' he had seen earlier—had stolen his wedding ring and mission ring from his locker. He seemed much more concerned about the latter. 'I am *not* the guy to do this to,' he said repeatedly, chuckling with mixed chagrin and malicious glee. As the Brit next to me drily observed: 'I hope those Albanians are as good at running as they are at picking locks.'

On the canonization of John Wesley Hardin
From Kosovo I went to the even uglier town of Peja and then spent a draining day crossing all of Montenegro in a chain of wheezing local buses, although this did include a ride through beautiful Tara Canyon, steep verdant slopes above a roaring river. When I finally arrived at the town of Kotor both spirits and expectations were low. But to my surprise Kotor turned out to be a hidden treasure. At the head of the largest fjord in southern Europe, its old town delimited by thousand-year-old walls that snake steeply up the looming hills, thronging, but in a good way, with Serbian tourists, it was easily the nicest place I'd been since Athens.

For all of one day. Because the next day I bused, taxied, hitched, and boated to the city of Dubrovnik, built around a magnificent walled medieval city, on the shores of the crystal-clear island-laden Adriatic, a truly beautiful spot. The new city could almost be anywhere in Europe, but travel through those walls feels like travelling back in time, architecturally, albeit to a place frequented by hordes of time-travelling tourists. It didn't feel quite as old as Kotor, but then in truth it isn't really; there's a map near the Pile Gate showing which parts of the city were shelled (for no military reason) by the Serbs in 1991 and then rebuilt, resculptured, repaired by the Croatians. Short version of the map: 'all of it'. But these days you'd hardly know; the new repairs look authentically old.

I stayed in the YHA hostel in Dubrovnik, and while it was a breath of fresh air seeing fellow travellers again, I think I may be getting too old and crotchety to stay in hostels. One night I had occasion to stay up late musing on the subject of John Wesley Hardin and how he was a much misunderstood man. Sure, he was a violent, murderous, hair-trigger outlaw; but once, as I understand it, he shot a man dead for snoring too loudly. We could do worse than to follow his example.

From Dubrovnik up to Split, yet another city built around a walled medieval old town, this one boasting Diocletian's Palace, the massive retirement home of that emperor of Rome (and persecutor of Christians). Nowadays the palace is integrated into a thriving, busy city, with offices and restaurants lining its smooth marble streets, instead of being walled off and left to stagnate as a museum: very cool.

One man not in a boat

Two days ago I hopped on a bus to the Plitvice Lakes National Park. Little did I know that this particular bus had assigned seating, and was overcrowded, and—terror of terrors—I had sat in the seat assigned to an elderly German woman. (Who did have a seat; it just wasn't *her* seat, and that *wasn't proper*. The horror, the horror.) After my attempts to play Stupid-Tourist and then Scary-Lookin'-Big-Bald-Guy had wilted in the face of her righteous wrath, the bus conductor intervened, and the problem was righted by having approximately 60 percent of the bus move from the seat they were in to the seat they had been assigned, as none of the Croatians had bothered to match up the two either. To be fair, the musical chairs did manage to eat up a fair chunk of the three-hour bus ride. Didn't do any good for the German reputation in this part of the world though. But in the end I made it to Plitvice Lakes, used my travel radar to sniff out the cheapest accommodations, and crashed.

Plitvice Lakes is a very civilized national park, if you want it to be. There are buses that take tourists up and down the east side of the park, and small ferryboats that ply the largest lake. But I was having none of this. *Such conveyances are for the old! I thought. For the weak! For German tour groups! While I—I am an intrepid explorer!* So I bought a Snickers bar and a bottle of water and set out on shanks' mare, briefly troubled by the nagging notion that perhaps I should arm myself with a better map than the microscopic one on my entrance ticket, but quickly dismissing that as defeatist whining and going boldly forth to the lakes.

Six hours, thirty kilometres, a half-dozen muttered oaths, four paths not on the ticket-map, three trails found only on the ticket-map, two wet blistered feet, one explosive discovery that I had purchased sparkling rather than still water, and approximately three thousand dead mosquitos later, I staggered back into my room and flopped down on the bed like a crash test dummy. But I didn't regret a minute. The lakes at Plitvice are, for my money, the most startling beautiful sight in all of Europe, but almost nobody's ever even heard of them. A chain of shimmering, luminous turquoise lakes, surrounded by verdant forest, connected by two hundred metres of waterfalls ranging from towering hundred-foot cascades to burbling mossy staircases: a peaceful, otherworldly paradise almost like an outpost of some parallel fantasyland dimension.

June 2003: Burn the Bridges
Mostar, Bosnia

Sarajevo is battle-scarred. Mostar is *gutted*.

There has been enough reconstruction that it isn't obvious at first. Stand on one of the hardly used bridges, above the steep and beautiful ravine atop which the city perches, and it looks postcard-pretty. If you look closer you notice it's too pretty. All the buildings are new.

Go a block to the west and you step into a war zone. This is where the front line was. Rows of half-collapsed heaps of grey concrete and brick, torn open by ragged misshapen gaps as if Godzilla took bites out of them, punched full of bullet holes, many of them roofless, covered with dust, full of rubble and trash. Chimneys and random jagged spurs that happened to survive the tanks and shellfire jut out like broken bones.

Don't get me wrong. This is not a dead city. The streets are lined with parked cars, bright billboards are posted right in front of the wrecks, and every second or third lot boasts a brightly painted new EU-funded reconstructed building. The relatively untouched areas, where the buildings are merely pockmarked with small-arms fire, are full of cafés where unemployed men sit listlessly in the heat. But it has been eleven years since the major fighting, eight years since the end of the war, and half the centre of the city is still utter devastation. A twelve-storey-high trapezoidal building stands above the major intersection, blackened by fire, every window blown out.

I passed graveyards, choked with fresh flowers, jammed full of hundreds of graves, every single one of them end-dated 1992.

The west bank of the river is Croatian. The east side is Muslim. (The former Yugoslavia was divided among Serbs, Croats, and Muslims.) Kipling had it right: ne'er the twain shall meet. Not in Mostar. The bridges are not exactly worn thin from overuse.

On the bus back to Sarajevo I sat next to a Bosnian-American girl who told me how the evil Croatians cheat her Muslim relatives there out of all the EU money, how war criminals walk the Croatian streets unmolested, how they sneak over to the Muslim side and steal and vandalize. I'm sure the same tales, with the names reversed, are told on the other side of the river. And then, not five minutes after complaining about anti-Muslim sentiment in Mostar, she's talking about the World Trade Center and how she now fears and mistrusts all 'black people with beards' and they shouldn't let them into America. This from a UCSD law student.

It is to weep, or laugh hysterically.

IV. THE AMERICAS

❖❖❖❖❖❖❖❖❖❖❖❖❖❖❖❖❖❖❖❖❖❖❖❖❖❖❖❖

This is home, of course. I was born and raised in Canada, but even the USA feels like my backyard, now that I've lived and worked there several times. And while I've only scratched the surface of Mexico, I've learned that its capital is one of the greatest conurbations on Earth.

Europeans often pooh-pooh the American attitude to travel, but I think many don't quite realize that you could spend an entire lifetime travelling without ever leaving those three nations—and beyond lies far more: the isthmus, the Caribbean, and the vastnesses of South America, which for some reason often seems an afterthought in travellers' minds. It shouldn't be.

September 2003: Let It Burn, Baby, Burn
Black Rock City, Nevada
Burning Man
Avant-garde apocalypse, beatnik bacchanal, counterculture carnival, discordian Disneyland, Mad Max meets Mardi Gras. Dehydration, dust storms, and decadence, a potluck Las Vegas, a pyromaniacal playland, a true Bazaar of the Bizarre. 'Burning Man is all about finding playmates. It's like recess for kids.' *The Road Warrior* crossed with Fellini's *Satyricon* as co-written by Pynchon and DeLillo. Sex, drugs, and psychedelic trance, sorrow and survivalism, a camping trip in a neon wonderland, a mad scientist's mirage made flesh.

And ashes to ashes, and dust to dust, and only the desert remains.

'Burning Man is a self-service cult. Wash your own brain,' to quote its founder, Larry Harvey. People have written a lot of things about the event, some of it even coherent, but I didn't find any actual description of its mechanics, so I think I'll take a hack at it—partly for others, partly for memory, partly because I think I may be using the playa as a fictional setting sometime soon.

Geography
The Black Rock Desert is not made of black rock. There is nothing black at all. It is grey, the pale grey of cheap computers, a flat featureless monochrome sea of grey forty miles by twelve, decorated only by

windblown clouds of grey dust that occasionally spawn high whirling dust devils. It is one of the most visually barren places on this planet.

Think of it as primer.

It is an ancient lakebed, hence its universal name 'the playa'. The absolutely flat playa, used in the past to set many a land-speed record, consists of talcum-fine dust, layered over an endlessly deep stratum of the same substance baked to nearly the consistency of brick. And nothing else. That's it. That's all you get.

In the week before Labour Day thirty thousand people descend on this wasteland and build a city. Black Rock City. A real city, one of the largest in Nevada, with roads and road signs, a lively city centre, quiet suburbs, a fire department, a hospital, and even public transportation of sorts, though when it comes to food, water, shelter, power, fire, and trash removal, you may rely only on yourself and perhaps your close neighbours.

Black Rock City is a circle maybe two miles in diameter, centred on the Man himself, wooden, seventy feet high, looming (this year) atop a four-storey wooden ziggurat. The southern axis is called the Gate; about midway between the Gate and the Man is Center Camp, an enormous pavilion, canopied, decorated with posters and sculptures and installation art and a teeming overlapping mass of carpets, stuffed full of couches and pillows, through which people wander, sit, pause for an hour of yoga or capoeira or hula hooping or a massage, recruit volunteers, meet, greet, catch art cars, set out for Parts Unknown, or sit and listen to live music or spoken-word pieces.

The geography is radial. People say they'll meet you at '3:00 and the Esplanade' or '8:00 and Dogma'. Think of a clock. No, silly, an *analog* clock. The Man is the centre, Center Camp is at 6:00, the Temple at 12:00. The innermost street is the Esplanade, which circles—horseshoes, really; I'll explain in a second—the Man at a distance of maybe half a mile. Seven other streets, their names varying depending on the year's theme, march concentrically outwards from the Esplanade. They in turn are intersected by streets that radiate from the Man, every half hour, starting at 2:00 and ending at 10:00, resulting in a city that, from the air, looks a bit like a one-third-eaten doughnut. These streets also have names—for example, 6:00 was Paradox this year, 7:00 was Creed, 8:00 was Revered. Every intersection is marked by a road sign, but people generally use the clock coordinates instead. There is too much else jostling for space in your mind to try to remember the names and ordinals of all sixteen radial roads.

Within the Esplanade is a disc of playa about a mile in diameter surrounding the Man. This disc, too, is confusingly often called 'the playa'. As is the dust, the general area, Black Rock City, and one's state of mind. Context is king. This interior disc has no buildings other than art installations. Walkways, lit at night by kerosene lamps hanging from paired rows of fifteen-foot wooden pillars on either side, mark the main 3:00, 6:00, and 9:00 routes from the Man. To the north, in the mostly empty expanse between 10:00 and 2:00, are more art installations, these generally larger and more elaborate, until Black Rock City ends at a three-foot-high 'trash fence' about a half-hour walk due north from Center Camp.

Southwest of Center Camp is an agglomeration of trucks wherein the Burning Man organization keeps various spare parts, services, etc. (Details vague because I never went there.) Southeast is the airport, where thirty or forty small airplanes are parked. The playa as a whole is surrounded by jagged hills which, thanks to the utter featurelessness of the ground, always seem to be no more than a few minutes' walk away.

People set up camp in the blocks delineated by the concentric streets (e.g., the Esplanade) and the radial streets (e.g., 7:00). The Esplanade is occupied by the biggest, flashiest, prettiest, and/or most popular theme camps. (More on those in a second.) The next couple of streets out are occupied by the lower-key theme camps. The remainder of the city is populated by the hoi polloi.

Culture

The general image of Burning Man is of a freaky-hippie-tattoos-piercings-counterculture-naked-drugfest-lovein kind of event. This perception is about 60 percent correct. The 'hippie' thing, in particular, is way off base; there are far more flamethrowers than guitars. It's a mix of various counterculture subcultures—hippies, yes, and New Agers, ravers, goths, technofetishists, avant-garde artistes, hordes of the different-like-everyone-else pierced, tattooed, and purple-haired (I don't mean to sound dismissive; most of them are Very Nice People) mixed with RVers, rubberneckers, and the curiously mundane, plus a very large contingent of people who do not fall easily into any category at all.

One of the most important things to understand is that it's more a genially anarchic bazaar than an organized event. Many—most?—of its thirty thousand participants come as part of more than five hundred 'theme camp' groups, ranging in size anywhere from a few people up to maybe a hundred, and each camp does something to entertain, amuse, aid, delight, feed, bewilder, or annoy the passing crowds. Giving out coffee, or Kool-Aid, or pancakes, or massages, or sunscreen. Erecting a giant geodesic nightclub and hosting raves. Displaying an entire life-sized pirate ship. Showing movies. Constructing a merry-go-round, or a circus trapeze, or a roller-skating rink, or a bowling alley, or a haunted-house ride, or a venue for (padded) mano-a-mano battle. Creating an Irish pub, hosting live music, and giving/bartering drinks to all and sundry. Littering their turf with weird sculptures and croaking menacingly at those who approach. Firedancers and flame guns and naked brunches and yoga and temporary tattoos and DJs and art cars. Especially art cars. More on those later.

All of this is given away, or bartered, depending on who you talk to and your point of view. It's supposed to be a gift economy, but this is more a thin veneer than an actual truth; people bring trinkets and goodies and give them away, or exchange them for other people's tchotchkes. Above this symbolism there is a genuine general sense that Sharing Is Good, and that you take care of your new neighbours and maybe even of complete strangers, though it's worth noting that you get this in all desert cultures, temporary or not.

There are (supposedly) only two things you can actually buy, with US dollars; ice, and coffee. Yes, coffee. Lattes, mochas, and so on. Yes, BM is held in the hostile and unforgiving Black Rock Desert, an absolutely flat moonscape of dusty pale alkaline rock, but I think the coffee shows pretty well that folks aren't really here to rough it. It's actually quite hospitable, as deserts go; the heat rarely if ever broke 40c, the ground is firm and flat and easy to get around on, and I'll take blinding dust storms over skin-grating sandstorms any day of the week.

Most camps—theme or otherwise—go to impressive lengths to construct comfort. Geodesic domes fifteen feet high are covered with parachute fabric (to protect from the blistering sun), bedecked with couches and chairs and art and carpets and pillows, and supplied with coolers full of beer and Coke and Starbucks bottled Frappuccinos and booze and piles, mountainous pyramids, of water—that's all pretty basic. The big elaborate camps have thousand-watt lights, generators, full bars, sound systems, multiple solar showers, all trucked in on rental trucks, erected for a week or two, then deconstructed and packed away for another year.

The people-watching is spectacular. Plenty of us mundanes, plenty of people basically in beachwear, and plenty of retina-scarring outfits. Dreadlocks, tattoos, piercings, body paint, circus outfits, six-foot hats, stilts, veils, theatrical costumes, a hoop dress decorated with a thousand sporks, naked men, bare-breasted women, gold lamé, Saran wrap, parasols, chain mail, far more than I could possibly describe or even imagine, in every colour combination imaginable, all of the above often riding bicycles, a favoured method of getting around.

Me, I'm a natural-born pedestrian, but I understand the appeal. This place is Big.

Art and science

When people talk about Burning Man, they'll often say something to the effect of 'It's an art festival.' This is basically a lie. Not a malevolent one, but one told because the real answer takes up pages and pages (as I am finding even as I write this, to my regret). It is a festival, yes, and there is art, some of it even good, but it's not like people are standing around the art installations in the desert, stroking chins and sipping chilled white wine, murmuring, 'Hmm, yes, very interesting, the influence of Dale Chihuly is clear, isn't it?' Or, if that happens (and it might), they're being sardonic.

It's actually a whole lot simpler than that: lots of different people bring bright colourful cool silly stuff and display it to one another. Kind of a cool-stuff swap meet, and/or the communal construction of playgrounds for passersby. Whether it be costumes, or camps, or cars, or elaborate installations that take days to construct, the idea is to have everything Look Cool, to provoke a raised eyebrow and/or a chuckle and/or a double take, and if it's really big and flashy and neon and colourful, and moving and breathtakingly over-the-top and ridiculous at the same time, that's even better. Is it art? Who knows? Who cares? It's a festival! It's a carnival! Have fun! Look over there, there's a dozen firedancing Santas on stilts chasing the giant lobster car towards that huge house of cards! Let's follow them!

Along with the art there's a lot of science. Wait, no, that's not true.

There is no science. But there's a lot of engineering. Way more than you might expect. Art cars aren't only painted and decorated; they're just as likely to be welded, deconstructed, turbocharged, rebuilt from the ground up, and outfitted with propane and oxygen tanks connected to flamethrowers synced to the onboard electronic keyboard. There was a gigantic gyroscope. There was a man walking around in a suit that looked and acted very much like the top half of one of those giant waldo-robots from *Aliens*. There was an art installation that consisted of a giant ball of flame on the end of a steel pole that robotically whirled and wound itself around another pole, over and over again. (Yes, I'm using the word 'giant' a lot. Get over it.) There was a gigantic metal mushroom cranked up to a voltage high enough that thick, crackling, visible-from-a-great-distance arcs of lightning wove their way around the giggling nervous people who stepped into the nearby (metal, grounded, perfectly safe) cage. And there was fire. Lots of fire. My favourite, up to the Burn itself, was a giant (there we go again) metal hand, maybe fifteen feet tall, each finger of which could spout a hundred-foot torrent of flame. I only saw it once. I'm sure there was plenty of cool stuff I never saw at all. I saw a considerable number of the art cars for the first and last time at the Burn.

Art cars. I should speak to you of art cars. For the most part, you are expected to drive your car from the Gate to your camp, at a non-dust-storm-triggering five miles per hour, and there park it until the Exodus. Except for art cars, Burning Man's public transportation. There are dozens of them, cars so rebuilt and welded-over that the original chassis is no longer visible, or experimental vehicles designed from scratch, or reticulated buses dressed up as whales or neon ships. UFOs, Mad Max machines, crabs, wheeled couches, chariots, moving pyramids, a giant vehicular banana, an enormous solar-powered tricycle that looked as if it had just wheeled its way out of *Alice in Wonderland*, a fire-breathing dragon the length of a tractor trailer.… They wander around at random, picking up and disgorging passengers at stops or while in motion (at one point, as I rode a bus that was dressed up as a Hereford cow, the driver stepped out of the bus while it was in motion, jogged around to the other side of the bus to get a can of beer, chatted with the beer-donator for a little while, and only then returned to the steering wheel) and following no route or schedule, but that's okay; their passengers tend not to be big on routes or schedules either.

Art cars are licensed by the DMV, or Department of Mutant Vehicles, an arm—or rather tentacle—of the vast, impressive, and largely volunteer Burning Man administration, of which I should speak more.

BM.org

Tickets to Burning Man generally go for anywhere between $150 and $250 for the week, depending on how early you buy them. Call it an average of $200, multiplied by the thirty thousand attendees, and you're looking at a $6 million dollar annual income for Black Rock City LLC, the organization that runs the joint. (The story behind the people behind this organization, and the history of Burning Man, can be found at www.burningman.com.) This is spent on a full-time planning office, an eighty-acre ranch near the playa where materials and vehicles and one person are kept year-round, a few paid representatives and administrative folks, and the fearsome DPW, the Department of Public (or Playa) Works.

The DPW are a scary, filthy, attitudinous, bad-tempered set of guys, straight out of *The Road Warrior*, crusty and scarred and foul-mouthed and angry and scary-looking and bearded and completely untroubled by any sense of social norms or courtesy. You would be too if you had spent the last month living and working in the desert, building the bones of the city and the Man himself. As such they have a certain reputation in the city. 'DPW killed a puppy!' I overheard at one point. But even if the various rumours about the gutters from which the various DPW members were press-ganged are true, no one disputes (at least not to their faces) that they're hard workers and skilled carpenters. They stick around for the month after Burning Man, as well, deconstructing the city, collecting MOOP (Matter Out of Place or Manmade Object on Playa, also known as 'trash'), and in general returning the playa to its pristine state. LEAVE NO TRACE it says in bright green neon at the Earth Guardian camp of volunteers who help with cleanup, and they do just that, which is a pretty amazing thought when you stand near the Man during the middle of the week and look around at the madcap neon tent city of tens of thousands around you.

Obviously a few dozen paid employees alone could not organize, construct, maintain, administer, and erase a city. Volunteers pick up the slack. Hundreds of them light the kerosene lamps, work at the café, wield hammers and nails to help finish the Man and the ziggurat, build the Temple, clean up MOOP, don khaki and call themselves Rangers and maintain public order and security, greet incoming cars at the start of the week and/or conduct the great Exodus at the end, work at the medical centre or the fire department or the commissary or the airport or the library (yes, there's a library). Volunteers are Burning Man's lifeblood, and its participants are impressively willing to throw themselves into their new jobs.

The Temple

I have referred, a couple of times, to the Temple, a subject that deserves a section of its own, as it is the emotional heart of Burning Man. For four years now an artist named David Best has constructed, and then burned, a multi-storey temple, which has been adopted by the Burning Man population as a memorial to their lost loved ones.

I did not see last year's Temple of Joy, but I wish I had: the pictures I have seen are of staggering beauty. This year, Best and his volunteer cast of dozens built cardboard and wallpaper into the spires and minarets of the Temple of Honor, looming austerely above the desert. People left offerings, pictures, necklaces or decks of cards or any memory of a loved one, to burn with the temple. They wrote memories, pleas for forgiveness, attempts to understand, and angry bile, on the books chained to the temple and on every available space on the temple walls, much of it so raw and searing that I turned away and left the words unread. It may be the only contemplative place in Black Rock City. It is certainly the only place where tears are more common than laughter.

A brief circumnavigation of the Esplanade, circa Wednesday, 10:00 p.m., Pacific Highly Irregular Time

Standing here facing the Man, it's darkness to our right, light and chaos to our left. Hard to imagine that only a few weeks ago it would have been absolutely dark and empty here, isn't it? With all these hordes of glow stick–laden people streaming past, and the neon lights of the Esplanade covering two-thirds of the horizon, thousand-watt floor lamps and projected video and live bands playing, and the green lasers beaming from the Man flickering in the clouds of dust, art car stereos and rave camps and live music stages booming music that drowns out the din of conversation, it's almost like Times Square here.

Behind us, down 10:00 away from the Man, are a heap of rave camps and nightclubs. At the end is the trapeze. Right here on the Esplanade is Xara, a camp that put down sod and live grass in their tent—it's extraordinary how powerful it is to feel and smell something as simple as grass growing after a few days in the desert. Next door is Paddy Mirage's, the Irish pub, where you can barter for Guinness or get it as a gift; it's insanely crowded and hopping to a live band. And down a little farther are some more of the rave camps, with big projection TVs showing trippy little video loops to the crowds twitching and dancing beneath.

Yeah, I heard this guy too: 'I've never been sober on the playa before. It's okay. It's pretty good. But it's weird.' Probably a common reaction. There is an enormous amount of drug use, licit and il, out here. Plenty of people who stay more or less sober, too, but you do see hundreds upon thousands of people walking around drastically underdressed, wearing glow sticks, drinking water and sucking lollipops. And you smell, and get offered, an awful lot of pot.

Past this arcade of little camps, to a big circus tent with lights spinning around it, and look, there's a firedancing performance, a couple dozen of them taking turns with *poi* (a Maori word for 'ball on the end of a string') and swords and cages and staves and pretty much anything you can set aflame and dance with. Onwards past radio stations, live music, the Turnip Head Cult (acronymize it), artistic videos projected onto a geodesic dome backed by an enormous sound system, and there's the Hookah Camp where they had a topless hula hooping contest earlier today … Oh, hey, there's the whale! A big white whale, might have been a reticulated bus once, unloading and loading passengers before it takes off for wherever. Let's ask. Going to the Temple of Gravity, in maybe fifteen minutes? … Well, that's what the driver said. You can't take anything too seriously around here. There's so much stimulation, everyone's so easily distracted, that minds change in a hurry and promises are quickly forgotten. Hey, look, *La Contessa*! A full-sized, forty-foot-high pirate ship. Just because, you know?

If the lights and noises and people and pirates are getting to be too much for you, we can duck into Sanctuary, where they have quiet tents with pillows for meditation and relaxation. Though they also have a bar. Oh, hi. Nice to meet you. Good, thanks, how about you? No thanks, I don't smoke. A necklace? Um, sure, thanks. Bye. Oh, here's the roller rink, I haven't actually tried it out, but it's big and they've sure put an awful lot of work into it. And here's some enormous rotating metallic-arms-with-spinning-engines thing. I don't think it's finished yet and I haven't the faintest idea what it's for. We're getting close to Center Camp now, there's the Earth Guardian LEAVE NO TRACE neon sign, and there's the giant mock-stone cube with a huge glowing, spinning gyroscope to our right, where the walkway to the Man begins. You can almost always see the Man, his hundred-foot-high neon-blue skeleton. Until he burns.

No, I don't feel like coffee, let's keep going. Now where the heck are we? The monkey cult camp. Lots of weird chanting going on in there. Bollywood, with its prayer wheels that play movies, next to Bunnywood, some kind of bunny-worshipping spinoff. Yeah, haven't spent too much time there. Space Cowboys, not to be confused with the huge Roman columns of Space Virgins farther ahead, and Playa Playland, a chill-out room, literally: they mist it up and keep it cool by day and heap it with pillows by night. Mission to Mars, a kind of theme-park ride, overcrowded and not for claustrophobes. And there's some kind of projection-video art project, and brightly lit pictures from last year's Burning Man, oh and off on your right there's a community burn platform for burning wood, or art, or both, before you leave.

I'm leaving out a whole lot of stuff, and I'm not really describing the feel of being there, of the people walking and cycling and art-carring past, talking or gaping or enjoying their drug or just enjoying the moment or, rarely, in a hurry to get somewhere, and the cool dry desert air and the thin dust it carries which you can always feel at the back of your throat, and the way each camp becomes an instantly recognizable landmark, and the sense you get of Black Rock City as a real city, and this is its Ginza Strip, its Times Square, but you know you're only a couple of minutes from its quiet back streets as well, where people relax in their camps and chat with their neighbours. And the sounds—music and wind and conversation and people barking through megaphones and engines and flamethrowers (flamethrowers are *loud*)—and just the general sensory overload and the way in which nearly everything and everyone you see has been constructed to look memorably cool and fun and over-the-top.

Over there, to the right, those are the glass-blowers, for real, taking semi-liquid gobs of melted glass from their oven and twisting and lathing and cutting and sculpting them into coloured glass flames or bottles or cups. There's Camp Carp's Skychair, two canvas hammock chairs hanging twenty feet high, a great place to watch the sunrise. On a little farther is Thunderdome, as in the movie, hosted by the Deathguild goths, where two people enter, strap themselves into bungee belts that launch them careening around the forty-foot-high geodesic dome, and beat at one another with padded swords. Like in the movie, people cluster around and climb high up the dome to watch the spectacle. Unlike in the movie, both contestants are allowed to leave alive, though one senses that some Deathguild members are unhappy with this concession. Onwards to the conGLOmerate, kind of the town's sordid strip club, and then past more visual art, vertical shimmering lines that stretch themselves into recognizable pictures, this one of the Mona Lisa, when you look at them out of the corner of your eye and twist your head rapidly. Past signs, and another arcade of little camps I never explored much, and now we're beyond 9:00 and going back out to raver territory, the *thumpa-thumpa-thumpa* increasing in volume.

The Burn
One of the most impressive things about the Burn itself was the sheer number of people. It's not often that you see thirty thousand people clustered around a single central figure. The art cars (and trucks and buses and tricycles) were circled around the Man, and two cranes kept an eye on the whole business, and a conclave of drummers started drumming a full hour before the burn began. Those many who had them wore their brightest, flashiest costumes, and covered themselves in glow sticks. The mood was primal, electric, everyone waiting breathlessly for an act of destruction. Good-tempered but impatient.

The crowd was thick, but not so thick that you couldn't easily move around the Man, though getting closer was another matter entirely. As for the edge of the safe area, a circle that began about two hundred feet from the Man and the ziggurat, forget it.

About a half-hour before the burn a couple dozen people held a sign-waving, tongue-in-cheek protest ('Two, four, six, eight! We must not incinerate!'), which was met with good-hearted boos and hisses. Then the firedancing began. I'm not a huge fan of firedancing—with the usual individuals or small troupes, it gets old in a hurry—but several hundred firedancers all spinning and whirling balls and bars and blades of flame at once is a pretty amazing sight.

There was a brief pause after the firedancers finished. The crowd was rumbling with anticipation by now and brief chants of 'Burn him' broke out from time to time in random places. The Man himself, whose arms had been lowered by his sides for the whole week, now had them raised high into the sky for the Burn. Then there was a technical problem, and one arm sagged back down, its neon light switched off.

No matter. The fireworks began. With a *bang*. A dozen huge white plumes rocketed into the air, and the crowd leapt to its collective feet and roared its approval, as clouds and columns and webs of fireworks began to fill the air. They lasted only a few minutes, ending much as they had begun; and then the first tongue of flame began to flicker in the room at the top of the ziggurat and beneath the Man, and people around me literally began to jump up and down in anticipation.

Other flames had been lit (presumably remotely) within the ziggurat itself, and the building was made of dry wood, and it took maybe thirty seconds before the whole thing was aflame and fire had crawled all the way up the Man's skeleton. The light was so bright it hurt to look at it. The heat was like an oven, and I was nowhere near the front, people there must have found it nearly unbearable, but the crowd stood its ground and breathlessly watched and cheered. The roaring sound of the burning nearly drowned them out.

The flames went a hundred feet high at least. Huge flickering vortexes of smoke and burning ash spun off from the centre, thirty feet in diameter, and went spinning off in random directions. Some of them made it deep into the crowd but nobody seemed to be hurt. The cloud of smoke blotted out the stars. It smelled like a campfire, the world's biggest campfire.

When the Man toppled over there was a mighty howl. When the ziggurat collapsed there was another. The Burn lasted maybe twenty minutes, if that. When it was over a few thousand diehards converged on the rectangle of still-ten-foot-high flame that had been the Man, stripped off their shirts, and began to dance counter-clockwise around the flames. I bet a whole bunch of them got first-degree burns. The rest of us slowly streamed outwards, into the Esplanade, for the second-last night on the playa.

The Temple burn the next night was very different. A soprano sang arias for the intro. People sat quietly, holding hands, many of them crying, and when it finally fell, we responded with gasps, not howls.

And ... I'm sorry, our tour is over, and I've only mentioned a handful of things that might be seen and done, those that happened to stick in my memory, and—never mind that, the truth is, I haven't really shown you a damn thing. It's like I'm waving a charred bit of ash at you and trying to make you understand what I mean when I say 'tree'.

It's more an event for high-energy visually expressive people-people than for semi-misanthropic utilitarian minimalists such as yours truly—the HEVEPPs and the SMUMs will never fully mesh, I think— but I enjoyed my time on the playa, and found elements of it truly wonderful, and I admit to feeling a little wistful as I drove away. Not that it could ever work for more than a week.

October 2003: Spelunk, Spelunk, Spelunk
San Miguel, Belize

(Belize, like Burning Man, was a setting in my second novel, *The Blood Price*. I went there purely for research, and found a little-known gem of a nation. Long may it stay that way.)

Today I trekked forty-five minutes upriver through primary jungle into a cave, a cave made of rock forged by the dinosaur killer that hit the Yucatan 65 million years ago, a cave infested by vampire bats and blind chittering spiders, a cave used a thousand years ago for Mayan bloodletting rituals and at least thirteen human sacrifices whose calcified remains still litter the cathedral-like grand chamber.

What I'm trying to say is: You want atmosphere? We got atmosphere.

It was a damp journey. The cave was carved by a cold river which is mostly shallow enough for wading but often chest-deep, sometimes requiring swimming, not to mention a fair amount of (very easy) rock climbing. The river is also responsible for the phantasmagoric rock formations found everywhere inside, formations that look like glittering crystalline curtains, arches draped with rippling 'fabric', frozen waterfalls, enormous columns of melting candle wax, Gigeresque fluted tenebrous ribs, pockmarked by perfectly spherical holes in the ceiling in which the bats live.

Apparently, if you were an ancient Mayan, it was a great honour to be executed there, as it meant a guaranteed shortcut to heaven. And apparently the majesty of your place in heaven was directly proportional to the amount of pain you suffered when you died.

There were four-inch-diameter spiders with eight-inch-long antennae; the antennae are used to navigate since of course the spiders, like all cave dwellers, are completely blind.

On the way to the cave, in response to a challenge from our guide, I snacked on live termites, fresh from the mound—a strange carroty taste, since you ask—and on the way out I was bitten by a spider, hopefully radioactive.

We passed Mennonite corn plantations on the way there and back. The Mennonites came to Belize many years ago, seeking a place to live in peace. It's weird enough seeing communities of blond men in suspenders and straw hats surrounded by the Belizean jungle, and hearing them speak some kind of Old German. It's especially weird if you come from a town with a large Mennonite community and the sight reminds you of what was once your home.

May 2004: Incantatia
Cuzco, Peru

There is nothing quite so head-clearing as four days of hard slogging through tranquil wilderness. The Inca Trail is a busy trail, far from remote, worn smooth by tens of thousands of boots a year, yes; but that doesn't detract even a little from its beauty. Am I glad I walked it. (Though 'I' does not currently include my calf or quadriceps muscles.)

Roughing it

Day One Stride up trail, manfully proud of carrying my own twelve-kilogram pack. Magnanimously make way for our stream of eighteen sandal-clad porters, the largest of whom is six inches and forty pounds smaller than I, each weighed down by roughly twenty kilograms of food, water, tents, fuel, chairs, tools, pots, pans, plates, cups, etc.

A glorious day, surrounded by raw wilderness, as I desired, entirely untrammelled by civilization, making our way on foot down the magical Inca Trail, like the Incas themselves, as it should be! The rest of the world should throw down the shackles of cars and fixed-wall buildings.

Sampled coca leaves, which the porters chew. Results in a strange numbing feeling, not terribly appealing. Does take the edge off the uphills though, and only 1 sole a bag.

Day Two A difficult day. First I scalded my fingers on one of the metal cups of mint tea the porters bring us in our sleeping bags to aid the waking process. Then, at dinner, had no dessert spoon. Ruggedly ate my chocolate pudding with a fork. After all, we're roughing it.

No TV in camp; will make suggestion to tour company. Perhaps two more porters, one with dish, one with television? Also, along with erecting our tents for us, cooking our food, carrying almost of our gear, and bringing us tea in bed, perhaps they could lay out our mattresses and sleeping bags, rather than forcing us to do so ourselves.

Coca leaves very useful in dulling ache in legs. Porter I am buying from has raised price to 9 soles a bag, explaining we are farther from coca growing region. Still reasonably priced.

Day Three Still not there yet. The road goes ever on. Does it bloody ever. Am sick of mint tea and my request for cappuccino was met by unforgivable bemusement. Sole silver lining is my newly acquired taste for coca leaves. In fact, have decided to give up on food and chew coca instead. Pedro now charging 81 soles per bag but better that than the constant suffering of endless up-and-down trudgery.

It is now apparent to me that the Inca Empire fell for good reason. There is nothing here but rocks and trees and an infinity of steep leg-chewing hills. Prospect of another day unbearable. Oh, coca, sweet coca, only you can dull the pain.

I'm kidding, I'm kidding. The trail was magical, it really was. And it was a challenging hike. But it was not exactly a raw wilderness adventure. Nowadays you're required to go in a group with a guide, annoying but convenient. Most of me deplored—deplored!—being waited on hand and foot by the eighteen porters to the extent that pretty much all we had to do was walk. But part of me … um … didn't.

It is fifty horizontal kilometres, probably five vertical, from the trailhead to Macchu Picchu: three days of walking. (Okay, so I have friends who would do the whole thing at a dead run.) In that relatively short span you go from sparse farmland and eucalyptus forest to full-on high jungle, hydrated not by rain but by clouds themselves.

The whole trail, start to finish, is fantabulously gorgeous.

* * *

Day One Six hours of relatively easy walking, parallel to the gorge of the raging Rio Urubamba (which eventually becomes the Amazon) on a trail clogged by mules and porters and local children on their three-hour walk back home from school, between enormous rocky ridges backdropped by snow-capped mountains, past little villages and a rebuilt Inca city, up slopes carved by burbling streams and terraced into cornfields.

Day Two Kicked off with a pair of steep five-hundred-metre climbs (actually, a thousand-metre climb divided into two by lunch in a llama-patrolled field) through cloud forest and past the treeline to Dead Woman's Pass, 4,200 metres high. Fuelled by coca leaves,* Snickers bars, and Audioslave, I soared nonstop up both of those. (My pack really wasn't heavy relative to my weight, and I've done a reasonable amount of higher-altitude trekking before.) The views were astonishing; looking down, the trail we had just taken seemed to disappear into an enormous jagged wall of rock that swallowed half the sky, and the trail yet to come descended into a cloud-draped valley. A thousand feet below, in the saddle between two passes, we camped amid the cloud—romantic but also damply, bone-chillingly cold. Sometimes the cloud retreated, and we could see all the way to the high, snow-smeared peaks of the Andes, and the Inca ruins perched above us. One time a new cloud rushed in, turned most of the world white, then lost momentum and fell back downslope, all within five minutes.

Day Three Past the stony (and largely rebuilt) ruins of Inca communications and religious centres, through rocky tunnels carved six hundred years ago, along the top of a ridge with an astonishing Tolkienesque panoramic view of white peaks above brown rock above furrowed folded green jungly hills to both sides, through cloud forest thickly draped with vines and orchids, nearly every tree covered with diaphanous moss. And then to the downhill. *Ouch.* For me, down is always far more murderous than up, and one thousand metres down in ninety minutes spelled *Aargh.* My bum knee was sending me warning twinges for the first time in months by the time we finally reached the campsite.

---

* If you chew coca leaves by themselves you eventually develop a slight numbness in the mouth; but if you chew them with a little volcanic-ash catalyst, your mouth promptly goes numb like you've been injected with novocaine, your aches and pains fade a little bit, and you get a slight adrenalinesque rush. Non-addictive, I swear, I'm not chewing them as I type this, nosirree.

I think I've mentioned that this wasn't exactly remote wilderness. All the campsites had toilets (well, wooden, thatched-roof, long-drop squat toilets) and up until lunch on the first day you could buy Coke and Snickers and cigarettes (!) from trailside vendors. The third campsite had hot showers and cold beers, and my God, were we happy to see them. It also had fairly amazing Inca terraces right next door, three hundred feet of agricultural terraces with a carved-stone aqueduct irrigation system still trickling happily along six hundred years after construction.

Oh yes. 'We.' Four Americans, four Canadians, two Dutch, two English; average age thirty; half long-term and half short-term travellers: a fairly typical group for South America, and a very good one. The Americans were smart, funny, tough, hardworking, easygoing, and did all they could to dispel the myth of the ugly American traveller. Sadly, a few hours after we reached Macchu Picchu proper, several hundred of that species came up to the ruins by bus, and promptly undid all their good work.

Day Four We woke at 4:00 a.m.* and made our way along a mountainside, looking down at thin tendrils of cloud, past the stupefying Andean landscape that we were all so accustomed to that we no longer bothered gaping, and up one last steep climb to Intipuku, the Sun Gate to Macchu Picchu.

May 2004

Peru: The Dead City of Gold

Macchu Picchu is breathtaking. Not so much the city itself. First, I'm more into wilderness than antiquities, and second, only the bones of the antiquities remain. A lot of bones, but still nothing more than walls and rock, and it takes a lot of imagination to picture it all brightly painted, the temples plated with shining gold sifted from the Urubamba far below, the stone altars darkly stained with blood (some of it human), mummies sitting ominously in temple niches, all of it lit by wall-sconce candles at night.

---

*My waking times for the past six days have been 5:30, 6:00, 5:45, 4:00, 4:30, and 4:45, all times ante meridiem. Oh, the irony. When not travelling I generally refuse to wake before 9:00.

No, if you ask me, it's the setting that makes the place. I cannot imagine a more beautiful location for a city. Though it wasn't a very practical location. There are conflicting theories about why Macchu Picchu was abandoned before construction was complete, but while the Spanish invasion was no doubt a factor, the fact that the area didn't have enough available irrigation water to support even a small city had a lot do with it too. (It's estimated that only five hundred people lived there.) There is a river nearby, but it's about three hundred metres down, which is a long way to carry water. A narrow stone aqueduct brought (and still brings) a trickle from ten kilometres away and a kilometre up, but it's not nearly enough for a city.

You can still see why they chose the place. Symbolic reasons, for one. The city is nestled above a huge bend in the serpentine Urubamba as it flows past far below. At the end of that bend, north of Macchu Picchu, a huge mass of rock rears up a full six hundred metres from the river, in the shape of a colossal resting puma. (Okay, a little imagination is needed to see that, but only a little.) Just south of the puma, Macchu Picchu was built, in the shape of a condor with wings outstretched, across a wide ridge leading south and up. Serpent river, puma mountain, condor city: the Inca totem animals for the underworld, the earth, and the heavens, respectively.

All around are small mountains, gigantic knolls carved by the river, or enormous hill faces carved by little tributaries, all of it densely green with cloud forest, and above these the towering snow-painted Andes. The roar of the silvery Urubamba below on both sides of the city is so loud it can be heard everywhere. As far as the eye can see, in every direction you turn, is the most dramatic jungle mountain landscape imaginable. Pictures don't do it justice, not even close, you'd need a diorama, and even that wouldn't capture the sounds, or the clear, cool mountain winds, or the overwhelming otherworldly feeling.

May 2004: Amazonia
Iquitos, Peru

Iquitos: a strange place. It is the largest city in the world (pop. approximately 400,000) to have no road or rail connections; everything and everyone must come or go by air or riverboat. This lends it a real frontier-town feel, which the DEA helicopters, downtown cafés dominated by a small crew of dissolute British expats, and gutted turtles and caimans (gators) for sale in the local market do nothing to dispel. Still, it's civilization; it has an international airport, banks, pharmacies, a cinema, cheap Internet cafés, a five-star hotel, and a thriving tourist industry, the last focused mostly on expeditions to lodges set in jungle proper.

When you're in the middle of Iquitos it's not at all apparent that you're surrounded by hundreds of thousands of square kilometres of raw primary (never-logged) rainforest, but it's very obvious as you fly in. From a window seat high above, much of the Amazon basin has only two colours: the swirling brown ribbon of the Amazon and its tributaries, and the endless sea of deep blank green that surrounds it. *La selva*, the jungle.

But don't confuse the Amazon River with exotic remote wilderness. Exotic, maybe, but make no mistake, Earth's mightiest river is also a superhighway, dotted with corrugated-roof towns and thatched-roof villages, lined by banana and rubber plantations, plied by countless vessels ranging from handmade one-man wooden canoes through ancient riverboats carrying hundreds of passengers up to modern ocean-sized merchant ships. The river waxes and wanes with the year, right now wide and thick and muddy. The main causeway is thirty-plus metres deep, but sandbanks are frequent and unmarked save for the occasional deadhead log. Vegetal flotsam is everywhere, carried downstream by a current that is surprisingly strong given that the river drops all of two hundred metres during its 6,500-kilometre journey to the Atlantic.

We—myself, a pair of Yanks, and a pair of Brits—travelled upriver from Iquitos to Muyunas Lodge, on a small tributary called the Yanayuca River about two hundred kilometres from Iquitos, surrounded by primary rainforest, next to a tiny village.

It was the atmosphere, more than anything else, that made the place. Oh, sure, we captured a baby caiman, we hacked our way through fire-ant-infested swamp to go piranha fishing* in a remote lake, we trekked through primary rainforest past enormous trees and howler

---

* Quite easy, albeit a little painful: just dip your toe in the water and it inevitably comes out with a dangling piranha attached, ready to be grilled. Surprisingly tasty. It is indeed better to eat than to be eaten.

monkeys and ant nests the size of SUVs, we saw sloths and iguanas and tarantulas and blue-morpho butterflies and an amazing number of vultures and hawks and other birds of prey, we swam in the Amazon with grey (small) and pink (large) freshwater dolphins, and all that was very cool. But it was the feel—the cacophony of jungle noises that echoed all night, the towering trees and ferns, even the bazillions upon bazillions of biting flies and ants and mosquitoes and spiders, the sense of being in a wild place—that I liked the most.

Which is pretty funny because it wasn't in fact all that wild. There exists untouched jungle in the Peruvian Amazon—and not just formally conserved areas, there are still tribes in the roadless Madre de Dios region entirely uncontacted by the rest of the world other than the running blowguns-spears-and-arrows battle they wage against illegal loggers—but getting to real heart-of-darkness wilderness, as with pretty much everywhere else, while possible, is expensive, time-consuming, and difficult, as per my dilemma below.

But the Yanayuca is all the more fascinating because it is inhabited and accessible. The village next door had wooden-stilt houses and thatched roofs, used plastic buckets and metal pots, wore Western clothes, but hunted or fished or gathered pretty much all their food. Mostly a subsistence existence, but its inhabitants—as with the net fisherman we met on Lake Piranha—occasionally catch and salt canoeloads of fish, paddle the three days to Iquitos, sell their fish in the market, and pick up what modern equipment and/or decorations they can buy with the proceeds. There is a church, and a school, and a priest and teacher sent from Iquitos, although some months the teacher fails or refuses to come and the school is empty. And they play football, aka soccer. Everybody plays football, young and old, male and female, the village is literally built around the football field, and every Saturday everyone in the nearest dozen villages gathers in one place for a huge tournament, and the champion village wins a hundred US dollars. It's a thriving community, the little river and all the villages and individual houses on its banks, and there is a constant stream of canoe traffic up- and downstream, and it's fascinating watching ancient and modern all mingled together.

We had a guide. Quite a guide. Octavio, an Indian, 'born in the jungle, like a turtle,' he said (and gave me a dirty look when I pointed out that turtles hatch from eggs). Mid-fifties, small, pot-bellied, nicknamed 'Burro', and totally extraordinary; seven-language linguist, village chief, occasional guide, near-superheroic master of the jungle. Can spear fish from five metres in water so brown it is opaque to anyone else. Also expert with bow and blowgun. Can call nearby birds and monkeys to his side by eerily expert imitation of their calls. Can spot iguanas, sloths, snakes, and anteaters in the thickest of brush. Can use jungle flora and fauna as pharmacy, arsenal, water source, pantry, construction material, and who knows what else. Knows everyone in a hundred-kilometre radius of the Yanayuca. He whips up a mean *chichuwawa* sour (a much-better-than-it-sounds combination of fresh sugar-cane rum, wild honey, egg whites, lime juice, and two types of tree bark). He plays guitar. The man is downright cinematic.

A speedboat took me from Muyunas Lodge back to Iquitos, where for an hour I sat in Ari's Burger (central meeting place for the city), smoked (I've taken it up again, for travel purposes), drank beer (Pilsen, which is, eh, okay, I guess), and pondered a traveller's dilemma.

Traveller's Dilemma

See, the thing is, I'm having lots of fun and all that, but the jungle lodge and the Inca Trail and all the other gringo-trail stuff, enjoyable as it is, seems kind of ... well ... tame. Corny as it sounds, I'd like some sense of adventure, forging new trails, or at least less-travelled-by ones. I was thinking about hopping a local-transit riverboat, slinging up a hammock, and riding it all the way down to Manaus, in Brazil. Now that would be a bit adventurous. It would also mean eight very dull days of sitting on a boat watching the shoreline drift past. (As a German woman I met at Iquitos airport, who had just done that journey in reverse, stressed at some length.)

The same is true wherever I look. I'd like to take the hard road—perverse, maybe, but true—but around here the hard road never seems to lead anywhere worthwhile, and doing it for its own sake just seems pointless. I guess that's part of what I liked about West Africa and Papua New Guinea, that there was no easy road. Granted, I could have hired guides here and gone on a far-more-intense jungle expedition, say carving an overland trail between two tributaries, hacking out campsites with machetes every night ... but it would have been just me and a guide or two, and I'm quite sure that would have gotten old in a real hurry.

... So, in the end, I quailed away, back to the easy road, and while it's the sensible decision, I still kind of regret it. Sure, I'll be taking the occasional overcrowded chicken bus, but fun as that is, for me there's no longer any new-frontier thrill to be found in the well-worn backpacker route.

May 2004: El Camino del Muerte
Coroico, Bolivia

In 1906, Butch Cassidy and the Sundance Kid entered Bolivia with the intention of robbing banks. They were gunned down by the Bolivian military. In 1966, Che Guevara entered Bolivia with the intention of overthrowing the government. He was gunned down by the Bolivian military. About a week ago, I entered Bolivia with the intention of seeing the silver mines of Potosi and the salt flats of Uyuni. While I completely failed at both of these, you will notice I was not gunned down by the Bolivian military, so I think it is still fair to count my visit as a total and unqualified success.

It was the strikers, six thousand angry silver miners marching on La Paz to be exact, who cut off the roads to the south and prevented me from getting to Potosi and Uyuni. Not unusual. Political unrest is as Bolivian as apple pie is American. There have been 190 military coups since the country's genesis in 1920, and blockades, demonstrations, and strikes are the national pastime. It's easy to imagine a typical weekday scene in a typical Bolivian workplace:

> 'Hey, Javier, what's up?'
> 'Not much, Nestor. Kinda bored, you?'
> 'The same. What do you want to do today?'
> 'I dunno ... Hey, wait! I know! Let's bring the whole damn country to a standstill like we did last week!'
> 'That's a great idea!' *(Sound of tools being downed.)* 'I'll notify the rest of the boys, you bring the beer!'

I have to say, I had a good time all the same. Bolivia is poor, but it's a welcoming, beautiful, and fairly-easy-to-travel country, and wow, is it cheap. Like Ghana and Nepal, it's a worthwhile destination where it's quite possible to travel for US $10/day plus whatever you spend on activities.

I spent most of my week there pottering around in Copacabana and La

Paz. Copacabana is on Lake Titicaca, a huge and spectacularly beautiful lake 3,800 metres above sea level, radiant blue water lined by golden shores above which rise the white-capped Andes. The town itself, while it sadly boasted no showgirls named Lola, is quiet and pleasant, and so could not be more different from the capital.

That churning shrieking seething throng called La Paz, comparable to Cairo and Delhi in terms of anarchic developing-world chaos if not in size, is set in what looks like a giant bowl scooped a thousand feet deep out of the mountains. It's a bit surreal; wherever you are in La Paz, you can turn in any direction and see barren rock formations upon the crater rim high above you. The city's shantytowns have spilled out of the bowl and onto the high plateau, warrens of cobblestoned streets crowded by ramshackle mud-brick buildings and patrolled by mangy dogs. The area is dusty and colourless, far too high for any trees or bushes to grow. The downtown, fortunately, is considerably more welcoming, except for the traffic, which between the cars, buses, *colectivos* (sixteen-seat public-transit minivans), motorcycles, riot police, and demonstrators, is more than a little life-threatening.

There are a bunch of cool little places. The Museo de Coca for one—which reports, among other things, that Coca-Cola still uses two hundred tons of coca leaves per year for flavouring, and that Western countries are allowed to legally produce cocaine, but developing nations are not. Also the Witches' Market, about a dozen stalls womanned by fierce old witches (I presume), selling carvings, etchings, unidentifiable herbs, hides, bones, and other animal parts: most disturbingly, large assortments of dried llama fetuses.

I also took a hilarious taxi ride up to La Muela del Diablo, aka the Devil's Molar, a huge tooth of rock jutting out from the lip of the La Paz crater. Feeling very intrepid, I clambered up the loose scree to the top, and promptly discovered that it was the weekend hangout for about three hundred Bolivian teenagers, smoking, drinking, flirting, and looking simultaneously guiltily and suspiciously at the sole adult intruder. I quickly took in the amazing lunar-landscape views and beat a hasty retreat.

My one non-lazy day was spent mountain biking down the road from La Cumbre to Coroico. I SURVIVED THE WORLD'S MOST DANGEROUS ROAD proudly proclaims the T-shirt I did not receive at the end of the day. Because they're out of shirts, not because I write from beyond the grave.

Thirty-six hundred vertical metres in five hours is quite a ride. We began in stark high altitude where nothing grew but lichen and where the sides of the road were limned with ice, and, layered in many clothes, we bombed down steep and exquisitely sinuous asphalt at speeds of around seventy kilometres per hour. Then, suddenly, two lanes shrank to one, asphalt turned to extremely rocky dirt, and the adrenaline began to seriously flow.

To our left, about a metre or two away, sheer drops of up to a thousand feet. To our right, equally sheer cliffs (at one point we rode behind a waterfall for about fifty feet). Before and behind us, enormous trucks oozing their slow way up and down incredibly twisted rocky road. When they stand off, which happens fairly often, the downhill vehicle has to back up to a passing bay, aka one of the little projections of road into emptiness every hundred or so metres.

It's actually less dangerous than it might sound, with the possible exception of the last hour, which is over road so dusty that if you're in the back of a train of bicycles a lot of your navigation becomes guesswork. Mostly it's just a matter of confidence. And it's not lack of confidence but overconfidence that is most dangerous: they've only lost one cyclist on this road (or so they claim), an Israeli girl who went straight over the edge a couple of years ago while trying to pass someone else. Many, many vehicle passengers are lost every year, though, hundreds; but the drops are generally too far and too steep to see the wrecks.

Also lost: the five Martyrs of Democracy. A monument en route reports that in 1944, the Bolivian military took five leaders of the opposition party up onto this road, bound their arms and legs, shot them in the head, and threw them off the edge. A bit redundant if you ask me.

I am now in Coroico, in the Hotel Esmeralda, and there has been a bank error in my favour; I booked a cheap room, but they lost the booking, so I got an expensive one instead. Satellite TV, cushy bed, balcony with amazing mountain view, and a choice of lime or orange soap, all for nine Yankee dollars. And the radio is playing Neil Young, 'After the Gold Rush.' Even the little details of this day have been very good indeed.

March 2007: Rainy Season in the Cité Soleil
Port-au-Prince, Haiti
The first day in the Third World is invariably discombobulating,
especially when the world in question is a mere hundred-minute flight
from Miami. Across the turquoise, cloud-shadowed Caribbean; a quick
descent over silted river mouths and sardine-packed tin-roof slums; and
out into the sun-drenched heat of Toussaint Louverture International,
airport code PAP, for Port-au-Prince, Haiti's sprawling, sweltering, seething
capital, the poorest and most violent city in the entire Western Hemisphere.

Arrival
The streets of a new city are always alien and intimidating, and tenfold
so here. Fortunately my friend L. was there to meet me at the airport
with her on-loan driver, Xavier, a courtly forty-something man who
piloted us in his seriously weathered Toyota Corolla through a city that
at first was all slum. Potholed, mud-puddled streets; packs of feral dogs
prowling waist-high mounds of trash; mangled, skeletal remains of
ancient car crashes, thick with rust; stores set in rotting concrete
buildings, walled with iron bars; high walls topped with barbed wire
and broken glass. It was easy to understand why Xavier checked to see
the doors were locked before departing the airport.

But there were the *taptaps*, too. Haiti's roads are full of these dazzlingly painted pickup trucks and minibuses, filigreed murals on wheels depicting Biblical scenes, soccer stars, American flags, and Nike swooshes, each vehicle emblazoned with its own name: HYPOTHESE, ROMANS 3:51, POURQUOI, DIEU AVANT TOUT, DON'T FOLLOW ME. The predilection for bright art doesn't end with their public transit. Walls are covered with murals, or tiled with paintings for sale, and even the poorest people dress in vibrant colours.

Like most hilly cities, Port-au-Prince maintains a tight correlation between altitude and wealth. Sewage runs downhill, and there's plenty of it, especially now, in the rainy season. We climbed past big schools, private and mission-run, and the city transformed itself into a labyrinth of steeply winding streets lined with high walls and clogged with private, NGO, and UN vehicles. Poorer pedestrians and slack-legged street vendors occupied the narrow and uneven sidewalks. We passed through three sets of gates into the fortress-like compound where L. lives.

Insecurity

L. is a communications specialist for UNICEF. In the two months she has lived in Haiti, half her staff have been victims of attempted kidnappings. Within the past year, a co-worker has huddled in her bathroom and exchanged gunfire with would-be robbers; another ransomed her son at knifepoint. L. is supposed to be driven to and from work, and to verify her safety by radio every night. (But she has never been particularly inclined towards following rules.) She is not allowed to even walk the streets of her neighbourhood lest she establish a pattern kidnappers could exploit. Whole swaths of the city, particularly the dreaded Cité Soleil, are 'red zones', entirely off limits; going there is an on-the-spot firing offence. Other areas, and any out-of-town excursions, are 'yellow zone'; they must be cleared in advance by UN security.

Is it really that dangerous? Well, no. Mostly. These security constraints are dictated more by UNICEF's insurers than by a rational risk-benefit analysis. Private-sector expats live much more relaxed lives. It's generally Haitians, not foreigners, who are kidnapped. Cité Soleil, however, by all accounts, really is that bad, a sea of gangs and anarchy that verges on war-zone status. The one person I spoke to who had actually been there spent the entirety of his visit in an armoured car, wearing a bulletproof vest and helmet. But when I went wandering around L.'s 'hood, I didn't feel the least bit unsafe, except for the traffic.

How much violence is being suppressed by the presence of MINUSTAH, the UN peacekeeping force of eight thousand troops and ten thousand staff, is an open question. It's safe to say that these international troops have not been well received. Haitians derisively call them TURISTAH, and resent their heavy hand; expats sardonically observe that their only notable contribution to Haiti has been full employment for prostitutes.

Mind you, the NGO/diplomatic/expat community are no sexual saints themselves, and that goes for both sexes. 'If I see one more forty-something Frenchwoman with a twenty-something Haitian toyboy,' L. says, 'I'm going to throw up.'

Diplomacy

Constrained by security fears and economic stratification, Haiti's expats live in a tiny bubble, a world of a few dozen cafés, restaurants, supermarkets, hotels, and embassies, plus their own gated residences and workplaces, and the cars and drivers who ferry them back and forth. There's no shortage of activities—the night I arrived, we hopped from a house party bidding farewell to a UNICEF dignitary who was heading off to Mauritania, to a flamenco performance at the Institut Française, and could have gone to a bar afterwards—but the faces are always the same: UN, NGOs, private-sector expats on aid-financed reconstruction projects, diplomats, and the last of Haiti's vanishing upper class of sophisticates and slickster frat-boy types. It's often best not to ask where their money comes from. Sometimes it's old money, sometimes it's from overseas, and sometimes it's from drugs. (Although, curiously, despite Haiti's role as a major smuggling nexus, most of the pot in Port-au-Prince apparently comes from Jamaica.)

A huge proportion of Haiti's (legal) GDP comes from its overseas diaspora. Another massive chunk comes from international aid. Between the two groups you get an interesting crowd armed with interesting passports. L. herself has a sky-blue UN 'laissez-passer', which exempts her from all taxes and visa fees (pretty much worldwide; UN income is tax-free even in NYC) and empowers her to demand immediate personal immigration/customs service whenever she enters a country. But even that pales next to the diplomatic passports wielded by the very nice and very funny Spanish couple we dined with on Monday at Chez Woo, Haiti's one Chinese restaurant. Can you say 'diplomatic pouch'?

In a city full of larger-than-life characters, perhaps the largest is L.'s immediate neighbour, Mme L., who once lived in the high-ceilinged, wood-panelled, colonial-style house where L. now rents a room. Then Mme L.'s hyper-rich husband built a magnificent open-concept mansion across the cobbled road, and the old house where L. now lives was rented to one Rene Préval, who has since become president and moved to Haiti's official presidential residence. Mme L. and the president remain friends … despite the persistent swirling rumours that M. Préval was behind the assassination of Mme L.'s husband some years ago. Today, Mme L. is a formidable figure: grey-haired, rich-voiced, clearly once a great beauty, she radiates presence. She has no formal position, and says she has no time or patience for politics, but diplomats and politicians of all stripes to this day pay court at her Sunday power brunches, where she serves Independence Soup. It's tasty stuff. I probably would have enjoyed it more if she hadn't been so intimidating.

Jacmel

Sunday dawned bright and clear, so we decided to try for the beaches of Jacmel. Conveniently, L. already had her security clearance, and the radio reported the city was safe to traverse. We borrowed another friend's 4wd and driver—an easygoing guy our age named Wilfrid, more friend than employee, unlike Xavier—and embarked on the two-hour drive to the south coast.

Traffic in Port-au-Prince is remarkably bad, but its drivers tend to collaborate rather than compete to navigate through the jams and around the potholes. Once out of the city the road parallels the surreally blue Caribbean, then climbs into misty and verdant mountains, past tiny settlements, green fields, and banana plantations, along a dizzying and seemingly endless series of hairpin switchbacks (fortunately, the road here is excellent, and must have cost a freakin' fortune to build) until finally descending into Jacmel. Even in this laid-back tropical town, the shops and restaurants are caged by iron bars, but we can at least walk the streets and swim in the salty ocean, and play a pickup game of soccer with scarily good Haitian teenagers at one of the town's two beaches not plagued by lethal riptides. It's actually pretty paradisical.

In mid-afternoon, after a meal of barbecued chicken, rice, beans, and bread, dark clouds begin to gather. Mercifully the heavy rain does not begin until after we have descended from the mountains, but the drive back still takes an extra hour. Tropical downpours are disastrous in a poor and steeply hilly city like Port-au-Prince: slopes and streets erode, the city floods with sewage, walls and whole buildings collapse to the subsiding ground, and traffic becomes paralytic. By the time we got back L. had missed her daily security check. But there is a silver lining to this muddy puddle: Luc's concert, which we thought we would miss, has been postponed.

Lucky Luc

Luc (aka Luck) Mervil is a Haitian-born Montrealer and one of the brightest stars in Quebec's galaxy of musical *védettes*, in town to play a few shows in his homeland. Notably, he performed in Cité Soleil (under the watchful eye of scores of heavily armed MINUSTAH) and was doing another show in Champ-de-Mars, a big public square in downtown Port-au-Prince. Of course attending the show is a grievous security violation, but L. decides she's willing to risk it. Wilfrid has gone home to his wife and kids, but fortunately V. is ready to ride to the rescue. A Québécois hydraulic engineer and SNC-Lavalin employee, here to rebuild Haiti's ravaged water networks, V. is a huge Luck Mervil fan, and is armed with his own car and a relatively cavalier attitude towards the mean streets of Port-au-Prince. He once told L., 'If I get kidnapped, I don't want you paying a penny more than $5,000 Canadian for me.'

His Daihatsu 4wD carries us to the field of concrete that is Champ-de-Mars. The stage is professionally set, with mountains of amplifiers and big widescreen projection TVs. Vendors sell bottles of Prestige beer, or plastic cups of unidentified alcohol dispensed from plastic jerry cans. The air is thick with second-hand marijuana, the crowd is sketchy but nonviolent, and the reggae band that opens is fantastic. Then Luc leaps onstage, radiating nova-like charisma that rivals Mme L.'s, and the crowd goes wild singing along with the barrel-chested, gravel-voiced *chanteur*. It's a great show. The rain starts up again midway through his show, but no one really seems to care; everyone goes home exultant.

Graham Greene Was Here

Port-au-Prince's Hotel Oloffson is ramshackle but grand. 'With its towers and balconies and wooden fretwork-decorations it had the air of a Charles Addams house…. You expected a witch to open the door to you or a maniac butler, with a bat dangling from the chandelier behind him.' So said none other than Graham Greene, who lived at the Oloffson while writing his Haiti-set novel *The Comedians* (which to my shame I have not yet read, though it's obviously now at the top of my to-read list), half of which takes place in a thinly disguised Oloffson, and much of the rest in the hill station of Kenzkoff above the city. After the book was published Greene was declared persona non grata and banned from Haiti. A plaque indicates the room where the great man lived and wrote. The door was open, so I went in, discovered the hard way that it remains an active and occupied hotel room, and beat a quick retreat.

With L. at work, I borrowed Xavier from her friend and headed up to Kenzkoff. Communication was difficult. My French is wholly adequate for people who speak it as a second language (though wholly inadequate around mother-tongue French speakers) but Xavier speaks almost no French at all; instead he speaks Haitian *creole*, which descends from French, but is virtually incomprehensible to me. Apparently it's very similar to the Québécois *joual*, equally virtually incomprehensible to me. We made it up into the damp and green and glorious mountains, found that everything was closed on Mondays, and beat a hasty retreat back to P-au-P, and eventually its Museum of Independence.

Context

Haiti was the second American country to declare its independence, and the only country ever forged from a successful slave rebellion. Alas, that victory in 1804 remains the brightest and most hopeful moment in the nation's history. Wealthy Germans soon took over its economy, until 1915, when the Americans invaded. They occupied Haiti for twenty years.

Modern Haitian history begins in 1957 when Dr. Francois Duvalier (aka Papa Doc) came to power in a suspect election. Seven years later he declared himself president for life. His secret police, the Tontons Macoutes—or Uncle Knapsacks, after a local bogeyman—kept his iron fist on the levers of power. When Papa Doc died in 1971, his nineteen-year-old son, Jean-Claude, aka Baby Doc, took over the country, and soon became one of the most infamous, capricious, corrupt, wasteful, and murderous tyrants in modern history, rivalled only by Idi Amin and Jean-Bédel Bokassa (off the top of my head).

A series of coups and corrupt administrations followed the fall of the Duvalier regime. In 1991, Jean-Bertrand Aristide came to power, was deposed in a coup, and was reimposed by a new American invasion. He was succeeded by Préval in 1996, who notably served his term and left office when it was over (the only leader in the history of Haiti to do so). Aristide returned to power in 2001 after contested elections; in 2004, he was overthrown by armed rebels and fled the country, and the USA again sent in troops. (Aristide claims he was deposed and kidnapped by the Americans.) Widespread violence engulfed the country for a couple years. Eventually it simmered down and the peacekeepers came in (with at best mixed results, as noted above).

Power in Haiti has always been wielded in part by unofficial violent forces—gang leaders, private armies, secret police—and influenced by voodoo culture as well. It's a messy, complicated place, and few non-Haitians pretend to really understand it.

Getaway

I rode back to Toussaint Louverture in an official UNICEF vehicle, and American Airlines carried me away. From the sky the country is utterly gorgeous. If it ever stabilizes it will be the adventure-travel capital of the hemisphere: glorious beaches, good diving, mountains, extremely welcoming people, colonial-era ruins, smooth roads (once you leave the cities)—what's not to like? I look forward to the day when there are 'slum experience' hostels in Cité Soleil, as there are in South Africa's townships and Brazil's favelas. But after only four days there I can tell you this much: that ain't gonna be anytime soon.

Lemme finish with a piece of increasingly grey-bearded advice for all you youngsters: if you wish to have an interesting thirties, spend your twenties hanging out with ambitious misfits, 'cause they're where the action's gonna be at.

November 2008: In Search of the Lost City
Santa Marta, Colombia

I blame Steven Spielberg. When I arrived on Colombia's Caribbean coast and learned that the remains of an ancient city lay hidden deep in the nearby jungle, visions of Indiana Jones began to dance in my head. A few days later I found myself trekking for six days along steep, muddy, snake- and insect-infested trails, fording whitewater rivers and crossing

countless stepping-stone bridges, drinking the river water and sleeping in hammocks, all just to reach and return from the thousand-year-old ruins known as Ciudad Perdida.

The lost city languished untouched for centuries, until 1973, when it was rediscovered by treasure hunters. Two years later, after looted artifacts started showing up in the local markets, the Colombian government secured the ruins and brought in archaeologists. A thin trickle of tourists have visited over the last fifteen years, although attendance dropped from low to nonexistent in 2003 when eight were abducted by Marxist guerrillas and held hostage in the jungle for months. Since then the Colombian military has maintained a significant presence at the trailhead and the ruins.

The twenty-five-mile trek there and back is no joke, and travelling with one of the four local tour companies that offer the expedition (for US $240, including all meals and accommodations) is highly advisable. My group included seven tourists, a guide, a cook, and a porter. From the ramshackle coastal town of Santa Marta, once the world's biggest cocaine thoroughfare, we journeyed along trails of red mud and white chalk through the half-cultivated foothills of Colombia's highest mountains, and into jungle populated only by the tribes who have lived there for millennia. There were few other foreigners. Colombia's fearsome reputation keeps out the throngs that have turned the Inca Trail into a superhighway, though the country is safer today than it's ever been.

Countless birds of prey soared high above. We served as a bipedal buffet for armadas of insects, saw frogs the size of small rabbits, hordes of lizards, and encountered two snakes—one dangerous, one deadly. But there were surprising luxuries, too: gorgeous swimming holes, rudimentary gravity-driven plumbing at the huts where we stayed, and beer and Coke for sale en route, their prices rising with the distance from the road.

On the third day we reached the 1,200 ancient stone steps that lead up to Ciudad Perdida proper. What's left of the city are terraced plazas the size of cathedrals on a ridgetop with stunning views on either side. The only artifacts that remain are those too big to move: a local map carved into a fridge-sized stone, and a frog-shaped rock that served as a fertility symbol. The ruins are still mostly overgrown, and in many places its stone trails disappear into dense, implacable walls of jungle. I found no golden skulls, but if I listened carefully as I wandered those ancient streets, I could almost hear Indy's theme song.

November 2008: How to Cross a Border
San Pedro Sula, Honduras, to Livingstone, Guatemala
The efficient way, e.g., my flight from Cartagena, Colombia, to Panama City:
• Embark at Airport A.
• Take off.
• Marvel at the Earth from above.

• Land.

• Disembark at Airport B.

*The simple way, as exemplified by my border crossings
into Nicaragua and Honduras:*

• Go to busy bus terminal in seething city very early in the morning.

• Wait. Check in. Wait. Hand over checked luggage. Wait. Produce ticket. Wait. Board.

• Sit on comfy bus, high above the road, watching the verdant hills that surround the Interamericano highway.

• Hand your passport and US$8 to the bus conductor.

• Disembark at MIGRACION post. Run gauntlet of moneychangers. Change money. Stand around for a while. Get your checked luggage out. Stand around for a while. Queue. Wave luggage past customs guy. Stand around for a while. Return luggage to under-bus compartment. Re-board.

• Listen to your iPod. (Reading is out of the question as the road is unstable and you'll get a headache within minutes.) Watch world go by, or the onboard movie. If you are unlucky, it will be *Vantage Point* three times in a row.

• Disembark at busy bus terminal in seething city at dusk.

The fun way, e.g., my route to Guatemala today:

• Leave San Pedro Sula hotel at 8.30 a.m. Find taxi. Haggle with taxi driver about price to bus terminal.

• Board nice, air-conditioned minibus. Leave with only six people aboard. Be relieved that Central America doesn't follow the insane African model of 'we will leave only when every seat is full, no matter how long that means we have to wait, even though we all know the roads will be full of paying customers wanting to hop on.'

• Stop in town to pick up dozens of other people. Become conduit for money being passed back and forth to conductor. Attempt to pick up still more people, who recoil at sight of the overcrowded bus.

• Drive for an hour. Stop in Puerto Cortes.

• Ask around in broken Spanish for bus to *el frontera*. Get directed to not-quite-broken-down former school bus.

• Leave with only ten people aboard. Pick up more en route, until bus is overflowing.

• Buy snacks and drinks from hawkers who crowd their way onto bus at one stop and get off at the next. (Typical in Central America; in Colombia you can hardly move for them.) Be surprised by the children hawking in Honduras; not seen elsewhere.

• Veer off paved highway into dirt-road small towns. Wait while conductor gets out to get a piece of paper stamped, or driver gets out to chat with a buddy, or driver stops to examine grumbling engine. Collect and disperse dozens of schoolkids, blind men led by their grandsons, old women who argue the fare, entire families laden with bags and boxes. No chickens, though.

• Arrive at sleepy border post. Run gauntlet of moneychangers. Chat to one who speaks good English from having worked in North Carolina for two years. Get slightly ripped off by him. Get waved through by Honduras police.

• Walk across border unaccompanied but for a man on a bicycle and another on a horse. Reach large, all-but-deserted Guatemalan border complex. Run gauntlet of moneychangers. Get passport cursorily inspected by Guatemalan Migracion officer who does not stop chattering into his cell phone. Get waved on.

• Hop onto minibus to Puerto Barrios, piloted and conducted by laughing Guatemalan teenagers. Careen out into the road. Fear for life. Observe teenagers pick up some would-be passengers, and disdain others. Their heuristic is incomprehensible but triggers much mirth. The driver is highly incautious but undeniably skilful. Enjoy self despite self.

• Pass plantations of corn, coconuts, palms, and above all, bananas bananas bananas. (The United Fruit Company, which basically ran Central America in the first half of the twentieth century—hence 'banana republic'—is still active in Guatemala.)

• Survive to Puerto Barrios. Disembark. Dine on really good Portuguese food. Hitch ride with guy who speaks fluent American English to the port. Get escorted by a dozen friendly locals to the next outboard-powered aluminum *lancha* (boat) to Livingstone. Stand around for a while. Wedge self into *lancha* with sixteen others, and as the sunset reddens, set out into the Caribbean.

• Hug shore for half an hour. Observe massive frigate birds circling above. Observe cotton-candy clouds and crimson sun setting behind massive palms. Resist temptation to throw self into water for a quick refreshing swim.

• Arrive Livingstone. Disembark. Be surprised by readiness of touts to accept no for an answer. Note that there are few motorcycles and fewer cars, not surprising, as this town of 17,000 is not connected by road to the rest of the world. Note rich mixed smells of ocean, jungle, diesel, and wood smoke in the air. Note touristy-in-a-good-way cafés and shops. Note amazing lushness. It looks like the jungle is ready to retake the entire city in approximately fifteen minutes once its inhabitants leave.
• Seek out hotel recommended by guy in Puerto Barrios. Find it full. Seek out backup hotel. Find it full. Stumble across lavish luxury room for $11 per night (with fan, no air-con, but that's fine in these sea breezes). Congratulate self.
• Find Internet café and inform world of day's accomplishments.

Option 3 is really not that much harder, and oh so much more enjoyable.

November 2008: An Open Letter to Mexico City
Mexico City, Mexico
Dear Ciudad de Mexico: Don't get me wrong. I think you're wonderful. A bewildering, bewitching, gargantuan kaleidoscope, almost incomprehensibly huge and diverse.

Click! Cathedrals, plazas, and cobblestoned streets worthy of a European capital. *Click!* Grimy and teeming seas of concrete buildings from which bundles of rebar sprout waiting for new storeys that will never be built, full of hard-eyed men and women hustling beneath incredible spaghetti tangles of improvised electrical wiring. *Click!* A magnificent boulevard lined with statues, luxury shops, and gleaming skyscrapers is blocked by hundreds of indigenous protesters, some stark naked, most wearing placards adorned with the face of their oppressor as loincloths. *Click!* A 7-Eleven cheek by jowl with a pre-Aztec ruin. *Click!* A warehouse-sized building full of dozens of food stalls surrounding crowded cafeteria-style benches, redolent with meat and spices and chilis and *cerveza*, resounding with conversation and sizzling-food noises and blaring radio and the mariachis in the corner. *Click!* Vast concrete-block shantytowns rising for miles into the hills on either side of a twelve-lane highway. *Click!* Angular minibuses, rusting white-and-green VW Beetle taxis, pickup trucks, and luxury sedans jostle for position on your perpetually clogged and potholed roads. *Click!* A peaceful, delightful neighbourhood of tree-lined streets, Mediterranean houses built around courtyards, sidewalk cafés and Parisian boutiques, armed security guards, and stone and wrought-iron fences topped by climbing vines that almost hide the barbed wire. *Click!* Swarming rush-hour throngs storm the metro like army ants. *Click!* Retina-searing boats glide peacefully along miles of canals.

And you're stuffed full to bursting with hidden and not-so-hidden treasures—murals and Moorish architecture, converted convents and the Palace of Masks, the Blue House and the Trotsky Museum, the jaw-dropping Art Deco masterwork Palacio de Bellas Artes, twenty-four-hour *churro* stands, markets that seem to sell everything and go on forever, and a pleasing sufficiency of Starbucks. You're like the result of someone taking a major European city, a major American city, and a major Latin American city, kneading all three of them together, rolling them out on this plateau surrounded by five-thousand-metre mountains, and then leaving them to seethe there forever. And with perfectly nice $20/night hotels in the heart of town. Like I said, you're wonderful.

However. I do have a couple of issues. I hope that you will take this constructive criticism in the spirit in which it is intended.

• Those guys who sell CDs in the metro, wandering ceaselessly with backpack boomboxes blaring five-second snippets of their wares? It's not just that they're annoying, though they are. It's their sheer numbers. You're all but guaranteed to encounter one no matter how short your trip. I once saw a good half-dozen file past me in the space of about five minutes. But I have not yet seen any of them make a sale. Do you really need so many of them?

• And the organ grinders. For God's sake. One or two I could see as quaintly amusing. But there are *hundreds* of these guys, all identical, in the same uniform, with 'Harmonipan 1937' boxes decorated like musical instruments and propped up on wooden poles, turning the crank and so introducing a ghastly atonal wheezing-whining into the world, while their assistant tries to collect money in a hat. Again, Mexico City, don't get me wrong, I'm a big fan of yours, I really am. But these organ grinders? Something must be done.

• More a request than a complaint: please don't ever, ever, *ever* make me have to drive in this town.

• It would be nice if you could do something about the smog.

• And the violence. Um, not that I've seen any. *(Note: Shortly after this was written, I was mugged at gunpoint.)* But everyone agrees that crime is rampant, and underreported because the police are terrible (and many moonlight as criminals). '55 muggings a day!' warns my guidebook, though when you consider the population of 24 million, that suddenly doesn't seem so many.

• A bookstore that accepted used English-language books as trade-ins would be a real plus.

• Your metro. Er. This is kind of awkward. But, well, I don't know if you realize this, but it makes other cities feel inadequate. It's not just that it's orderly and efficient. It's that a ride anywhere in its enormous sprawling network costs all of *two pesos*. That's fifteen U.S. cents. I mean, it's nice that you let your millions of very poor travel cheap across town, but could you maybe just double that to four pesos? I bet London and New York and Tokyo and Toronto would feel much better about themselves if you did.

• Finally, and really I feel more passionate about this than any of the above, even the smog: your parks? They're practically inaccessible. I understand that crime being what it is, you want to surround your parks (and your main, colossal, 300,000-student university) with high fences. But most cities, you know, when they build a park, and then a metro station immediately next to the park, they *put an entrance there.*

But don't get me wrong, Mexico City. These are minor gripes. I don't really care if you don't change at all (except the parks bit). You're one of my favourite cities in the whole wide world already, just the way you are.

September 2009: My Saga
Reykjavik, Iceland
Two days ago I travelled through flickers of sunlight to the site of the world's oldest parliament as told in the sagas. (The history/folk tales that all Icelanders know. Their language has changed so little that they can still read the sagas in the original. I haven't read any, myself—though I am eyeing the collected English-language version sold in all the bookstores here—but I get the distinct impression from my *Lonely Planet* that the Iceland of the sagas was an extremely bloody place, and that appearing in a saga pretty much guaranteed a drastically shortened lifespan.)

I went to Kerio Crater and to Geysir and its sulfurous vapours of hell, and to Gullfoss Folls. From there I followed the road, which roughly paralleled the gorge visible to the left, into gravel, pitted and potholed and cratered and gouged. But my trusty Skoda steed was a match for it, and the views were worth the grief. Eventually I made my way to the lonely Atlantic, and rested in a small town there for the night.

Yesterday morning I advanced through Iceland's green-and-gold bowls and meadows, which still seem like deserts thanks to the almost total absence of trees; past the endless vast ridges of dark, upswept volcanic rock, and the frozen rivers of jagged lava stained with green moss; towards the snow-capped mountains of the Snaefellsnes peninsula.

The road beckoned ever onwards, past fjords marked with layer-cake mountains, towards the brooding storms of the Atlantic. Past Iceland's tallest structure, a NATO radar tower, to Snaefellsnes itself, the very mountain where Jules Verne's *Journey to the Center of the Earth* begins. Alas, that shortcut to Stromboli is blocked by ice, so I continued past frozen lava flows and natural amphitheatres.

It's times like this when part of you can't help but wonder about the wisdom of travelling to remote destinations utterly alone. *What if...* part of my mind wondered just after I'd ascended an amphitheatre.

What if I fell and broke my leg here? I've seen all of two cars in the last hour, and that was on the main road half a kilometre away, and there's a storm coming …

Then I checked my phone and saw to my amazement that it boasted a bar of coverage. Ah well. A man can dream.

The wind-whipped storm returned shortly afterwards, and fought a running duel with the sun until Sol emerged victorious, and shone greedily on those lonely stone guardians who watch the uttermost West, vast rocky monoliths jutting from the shore, while the storm retreated to its fastness in the heights. I returned to my trusty steed and then to those very mountains I saw earlier in the day.

Halfway back to Reykjavik I had a bizarre and unsettling experience. A farmhouse stood on the left—I forget its name. (Iceland is so thinly populated that every farm has its own road sign.) Two teenage girls in hunter-orange overalls stood on either side of the road. A few sheep were making their way along the ditch to the left, but if there had been any real herding going on, it was over. A kid of about eight rushed along that ditch. Nothing particularly unusual so far.

Farther along the road, a woman walked casually along its leftmost edge, while a man strode along the ditch on the right, holding some kind of long, thin, walking-stick-like implement—a golf club? a shepherd's crook? As I approached, he stepped up onto the road. Leapt, really, with intent. He didn't so much as turn his head my way, but as I was travelling at the speed limit, ninety kilometres an hour, he would have to have been stone-deaf not to notice my approach.

I made the split-second decision that swerving around him was a better idea than braking to a stop at that rapidly diminishing distance. As I did so, he turned towards me. I caught a momentary glimpse of a dangerously lean man with a scraggly dark beard, his face twisted with fury, with *rage*, as he took a step *towards* the car swerving around him at ninety kilometres an hour and raised his stick-thing high, as if to strike. I can't be sure, but I think he actually did swing at my car as I passed. (And he missed.)

When I glanced in my rear-view mirror I saw the woman walking along the edge hold her hand up towards me, as if to say, *Stop*, or in apology. I'm guessing the latter from her body language. She didn't halt, though, or turn to say anything to him. He stood in the middle of the road, glaring.

V. AUSTRALIA

I love Australia. I have been there three times and can hardly wait to go back. I love its ridiculously gregarious people, its gorgeous coastlines, its endless roads, its gargantuan empty spaces. And I especially love how *different* it is, in flora and fauna and look and feel, from everywhere else; it's like a little parallel dimension, an alternate history, that anyone can visit. All you need is an airline ticket.

I can't say I love New Zealand, but I bet I would if I had spent more than a mere three days there. Its Coromandel Peninsula, which is apparently viewed by Kiwis as a very minor attraction only worth mentioning because it's conveniently close to Auckland, remains one of the prettiest places I have ever been. And I can't say I love Papua New Guinea—Port Moresby is an interesting but disagreeable city, and it can be a challenging place to travel—but I can say it's one of the world's most extraordinary nations, and I'd happily go back.

October 2002: Notes from the Lucky Country
Byron Bay, New South Wales
It is with great reluctance that I leave Byron Bay. This is the chilled-out kind of beach town where people come for a day and stay for a month. I've been here only a week. But verily it is one of life's great truths: you can live in a giant covered wagon for only so long before it's time to move on. And so in an hour's time I'll be on a bus to Queensland and the North.

Understand that I was only staying in the giant wagon because the giant teepee was full. Accommodation at the Arts Factory Lodge is a wee bit idiosyncratic. It's a good place, though, in a good town, with all kinds of things to do. In the last week I've been horseback riding, surfing, mountain biking, scuba diving (twice), and trapezing—yes, trapezing—and I still feel like I've been extremely lazy. In a good way.

It turns out I'm not a natural surfer. After a few hours of patient training I managed to wobble around in front of a few baby waves, but Zonker Harris I'm not. I am pleased to report that the trapezing came easier, and I was doing knee-hang catches and backflip dismounts like I was born to it—maybe it's not too late to run away and join the circus after all.

But enough about me, let's talk about Oz.

The funny thing about Australia's east coast is that if you close one eye and squint with the other it looks a whole lot like California: green mountains, golden beaches, sunshine and surf hippies, and wine regions. It would be easy to believe, riding the bus through New South Wales and looking out the window, that you're in some particularly beautiful part of California. (All the country here is particularly beautiful.) But you would know, somehow, if you looked hard enough, that it's not; maybe because you'd realize that half the plants and trees are species you'd never seen before last week, or maybe because you see a kangaroo by the side of the road.

Roos are just one step up from vermin in Oz. Like baboons are, in Africa. Funny ol' world.

Another example: I went horseback riding a week ago. (My first time on a horse in fifteen years.) The road up to that ranch could have been almost anywhere in Canada or America—until we stopped to investigate the four-foot python on the road ahead of us.

Turns out pythons don't much like having their tail grabbed. And who can blame them, really? I should have known better. Steve Irwin has much to answer for.

October 2002: Notes from the Lucky Country, Part II
Cape Tribulation, Queensland

I have seen the Great Barrier Reef, up close and personal, and—wow! Floating weightless amid breathtakingly gorgeous coral formations, in every colour of the rainbow, teeming with huge shimmering schools of fish of every size, and squid and stingrays and sharks and shrimps and eels and anemones and giant clams and, and, and, and it all went on, and on, and on—and this was just at a few of the smaller dots on the overall reef.

I went on eleven dives in fifty-one hours, living on a boat the whole time; for a while there I thought I was growing gills. I am now officially an Advanced Open Water Scuba Diver, which may impress you, unless you have done the same course, in which case you know it's about as difficult as Basket Weaving 101. Terrific fun though.

The night dives were my favourite. Going headfirst down a towering coral wall, playing my light over the twisting alien formations; I felt like an astronaut. And there were sharks at night, their eyes glowing a poisonous jade green. Little whitetip reef sharks, a mere five feet long, and grey whalers bigger than me. Don't worry, they almost invariably leave divers alone. Almost.

The deep dives were a little disappointing; I waited for the nitrogen narcosis, the famous 'rapture of the deep', to hit; I waited to develop delusions of omnipotence or a sudden hatred for my fellow divers; but no, I just felt a little slower and more thick-headed than normal.

I didn't get at all seasick. Conditions were calm, the ocean nearly flat, the underwater visibility ('viz' to you divers) a good twenty metres—but once I got back on land I kept expecting the ground to slosh back and forth the way the boat had, and my system, particularly the 'balance' subcomponent, was not pleased by this unexpected stability. My attempt to counteract this lack of sway by consuming large amounts of Victoria Bitter, as suggested by my crazy Norwegian dive instructor, was an interesting but total failure.

The next morning, a little worse for wear, I went north, to Cape Tribulation, a point overshadowed by Mounts Misery and Sorrow: quite unfair names, really, for one of the most spectacularly beautiful pieces of real estate on the planet, two peaks towering over a verdant coastline. Apparently Captain Cook ran his ship into an offshore reef nearby, and was obviously still in a foul mood when he went about naming things.

But I guess he was half-right after all. While you can argue about what the deadliest creature on Earth is, there's no doubt that whatever it is, it's Australian, and it probably lives near Cape Tribulation. Here you can find huge crocodiles, poisonous jellyfish, plants laden with neurotoxins, and the usual Aussie contingent of snakes, ranging from thirty-foot pythons to ridiculously lethal vipers.

And then there are the cassowaries. But I'll get to them in a second.

When you think Australia, you think rocks and kangaroos, not jungle; but Cape Tribulation is covered by rainforest, which despite two consecutive failed wet seasons is as dense and diverse as any I've seen in Africa or Indonesia. I stayed a couple nights in a very relaxed jungle hostel called Crocodylus Village. It was just a few klicks up from an absolutely gorgeous warm-water beach, and at the village they assured us that despite the copious warning signs on the beach the jellyfish weren't out yet and the crocs stuck to the rivers. Although come to think of it, they did insist on payment in advance. Hmm. Anyway, I swam and lived to tell the tale.

Cape Tribulation is also infested by cassowaries. Yeah, I never heard of them either before I came here. A cassowary is a black-and-blue-and-orange-and-crimson giant flightless bird, about my height. Allegedly they're extremely rare and highly endangered, but I couldn't get away from the bloody things. After a few sightings yesterday, this morning I woke up and went outside and there was one literally blocking my path to breakfast.

Those of you who know me, know that this is an unwise thing to do, but I hesitated; first, because it was morning and I generally spend all morning in one giant hesitation, and second, because even though cassowaries seem extremely slow, awkward, and ungainly, there is at least one documented instance of a cassowary killing a man—a man sitting on a horse, no less—with a single flying karate kick.

(Who taught the cassowaries karate has not yet been determined, but Pat Morita is apparently wanted for questioning.)

Hunger won out over self-preservation and I gingerly picked my way past the cassowary. I wasn't too concerned about animal attacks anyway, because this was clearly the week for inanimate objects to have a go at me. Thus far I have been bashed by a vengeful scuba tank, blistered by a malicious flipper, bruised by two separate tree roots, and gashed by a bloodthirsty vine. It's a rough country, this, but well worth the visit.

October 2002: Notes from the Last Place on Earth
Port Moresby, Papua New Guinea

But of course you're not *really* an intrepid traveller unless you're crammed into the back of a battered Japanese minibus with a dozen families and their produce and their livestock, picking your way along a stomach-churning Third World road punctuated by roadblocks where menacing, drunken machete-wielding men demand a 'toll' before allowing you to continue on to the rat-infested rooms-by-the-hour flophouse where you're staying. Anything more comfortable than that and you're just a tourist.

Sigh. The sad thing is that I'm only mostly joking.

So I went up to Papua New Guinea for a week, partly just to see what it's like, partly because Australia, while wonderful, seemed a little bit … tame, and partly because having already been through cities and beaches and ocean and jungle, and with deserts next on the agenda, I felt like spending a little time in the one terrain Oz does not offer: mountains.

PNG has an absolutely dire reputation in Australia, but it's actually quite nice. There is a certain culture of violence up in the Highlands—a local museum proudly displays gruesome human-finger necklaces, and traditional tribal 'payback' battles flare up now and again—but nearly all the violence is internecine. The people here are among the friendliest that I have ever met.

(The food is nothing to write home about, but I have been eating a lot of an addictive local delicacy called 'long pig'.)

It is not a good country to be in a hurry. Local transit is slow and irregular, and it can take all day to travel a relatively short distance from A to B, and that's if you're lucky and don't wind up stranded overnight at Z in between. I spent one night in the uninspiring town of Kundiawa because I got up at the unbearably late hour of 7:00 a.m. and missed all the morning transit from the mountain village where I was staying.

Ah yes. Mountains. As I was saying. I'm always climbing something when I travel—Indonesian volcanoes, Mount Cameroon (another volcano, in Cameroon, near the Gulf of Guinea), the Annapurna Circuit in Nepal, the Great Wall, the Chimanimani Range—and I have decided that the main reason I do this is because the mind is a liar. It promptly extinguishes all memory of the hours spent with lungs and legs ablaze, eyes focused on the treacherous muddy trail at your feet, head swimming with altitude sickness; it erases the tedious tricky business of picking your way down steep downhill slopes for hours upon hours; it retains only the triumph and sense of accomplishment that you get at the top.

Mount Wilhelm is the biggest mountain in PNG, and at 4,500 metres a fairly serious mountain anywhere outside of the Himalayas. It wasn't as tough as climbing Mount Cameroon, which remains the most physically gruelling day of my life, but that's only because I'm in considerably better shape these days. It was a tough slog. In retrospect, it would have been a lot easier if I had decided to climb it in the dry season.

I'm tellin' ya, if you haven't climbed a big mountain in the tropics during the height of the wet season, you haven't lived—unless, of course, you have something against being soaked to the skin, chilled to the bone, and gasping for thin air like a fish on land.

I was led up the mountain by a tag team of guides, but as always I foolishly decided to carry my pack myself. I'm always a bit suspicious of guides, but this time having them along, even if I carried my own pack, was a good idea; several trekkers have died on Mount Wilhelm, probably in part because the track was not always easy to follow, presumably thanks to the frequent heavy rains here, especially when oxygen-deprivation stupidity kicks in around four thousand metres.

Guide #1, Francis, led me up to the way-station huts at thirty-five hundred metres. Forty-something, missing half of his teeth, insanely strong, he fussed over me like a mother hen but had an alarming habit of lapsing into violently angry rants about the imminence of World War III between the English-speaking countries and the Middle East (which in Francis's somewhat muddled world view included Germany and Japan), which we oughta nuke right now because they're all commies. Otherwise the nicest guy you'll ever meet. I briefly considered discussing geopolitics with him, but decided that smile-and-nod was the wisest strategy.

Guide #2, Nick, took me up to and from the peak, and he was not so much guide as philosopher-king. I challenge you to find another PNG mountain guide who will quote Kierkegaard to you en route and spend the rest breaks discussing the spiritual and philosophical significance of mountain climbing.

They say that from the top of Mount Wilhelm, on a clear day, you can see both the north and south coasts of Papua New Guinea. I cannot confirm this, but I can tell you that, weather permitting, you may see a lot of clouds.

After a mere ten minutes at the top (it was snowing, windy, and *cold*) I stepped, stumbled, skidded, and swam my way down the mountain and back to the village of Kegsugl, where I received the ultimate accolade from Francis. Speaking of me to the lodge owner there, who expressed surprise that we had made it through the rain, Francis said: 'Oh yes. He plenty strong.' (pause) 'Plenty strong ... for a white man.' Gotta put *that* on my CV.

After a longer-than-necessary journey, thanks to missing a 7:00 a.m. bus and discovering there were no more transport options until the next day, I made it back to civilization in the form of the town of Goroka, which has a cool name, wide tree-lined streets, nice people, and the four-star Bird of Paradise Hotel. Following my usual travel modus operandi I checked into a cheap lodge around the corner and beelined straight to the luxury hotel, where I proceeded to spend an entire day in Colonial Mode: resting my weary legs on the poolside verandah, sipping G&Ts and banana milkshakes, smoking cigarettes, and reading old Agatha Christie novels. If that isn't the life then I just don't know what is.

I am now in Port Moresby, a hot, dusty, and generally disagreeable place, which recently came dead last in a worldwide survey of what expats think of the cities where they live, but not the bullet-drenched anarchy that the Australians think it is. Tonight I fly back to Cairns, and thence to Australia's Red Centre. But I'd love to come back to PNG; the coasts are supposed to be beautiful and the diving the best in world.

Next time. Like the man said (that would be me), you can't go everywhere, and you probably shouldn't try.

April 2004: The Antipodean Times, Vol. 1
Aotearoa (New Zealand)
I spent all of seventy-two hours in New Zealand, which is long enough to realize that the whole country is clearly some kind of elaborate scam. The people are too friendly, the landscapes too beautiful, the atmosphere too agreeable. Actually, I think they're overdoing it. I mean, who hears bus passenger after passenger call out, 'Goodbye, thank you,' to the driver when exiting—during rush hour, no less—without getting a little suspicious? I don't know whether they're trying to lure settlers in, to sacrifice them in some kind of Shirley Jackson–esque unholy blood rite, or if the bodysnatchers have taken over, but there's clearly a catch.

A three-day stopover in NZ is a bit like taking a single sip from a single bottle from one of the world's great wine cellars. All I really had time for was a quick rent-a-car drive to the Coromandel Peninsula, where I took an increasingly narrow and winding road north, ocean to my left, Mirkwood to my right. The road shrank from two wide lanes to two narrow lanes and repeatedly to single-lane bridges and, during one especially exciting bit, to a single lane shared by both directions around several blind turns. Thence up into the hills, where occasional SCENIC VIEW signs were completely unnecessary. New Zealand is so insanely picturesque that my return to the standard-issue urban blight of downtown Auckland was actually something of a relief, like a pimple on Gisele Bündchen.

It's an interesting mix of two worlds. Large portions of what I saw were verdant rolling hills, farms and grazing fields and trees and sheep and cattle that wouldn't have looked out of place in northern England, but every so often—particularly in steep, difficult-to-cultivate places—I encountered pockets of the country's original vegetation, straight-out-of-Gondwanaland giant ferns and palm trees in which a munching brontosaurus would not look out of place. My hike down to majestic Cathedral Cove repeatedly took me in and out of each ecosystem. I felt as if I were flickering between parallel dimensions.

April 2004: The Antipodean Times, Vol. 2
Australia
Sydney
My forty-eight hours in Sydney were spent engaged in extremely alcoholized reunions with old friends; for reasons of brevity, and per the advice of my lawyers, I won't bore you with the details. I escaped while I could still walk. And I do mean escaped. Monday morning, I entered my hosts' bathroom, only to find upon attempting to exit that, while the doorknob rotated just fine, said rotation no longer had any effect on the latch. And my hosts, hereafter referred to as 'my attempted kidnappers', had long since gone to work. Fortunately I foiled their cunning plan by dint of their failure to realize that the bathroom windows were big enough for me to squeeze through. Just. There was one bad teetering moment where I feared I was going to fall and destroy their barbeque, their garden plants, and my entire spinal column, but I managed to land catlike (that is to say, on all four limbs) and limp my way to the airport.

Melbourne
… reminds me a lot of Vancouver. I don't want to praise it too much for fear of offending my Sydneysider friends (there is an intense Melburnian–Sydneysider rivalry) but I liked it a great deal, very laid-back and neighbourhoody. Spent a night and a whole day just about walking my feet off wandering around, and yesterday took a one-day Great Ocean Road tour.

The tour itself was terrific, down one of the world's most gorgeous highways (though personally I still give the overall crown to the stark remoteness of California's Highway 1 near Big Sur) with stopovers to watch koalas, hike down to incredibly dramatic gorges and beaches near the Twelve Apostles, travel a circuit path through temperate rainforest, and wade on the beach and play with local canines.

It also exemplified what I like about travelling in Oz: not only is it cheap and easy, but it's also amazingly social if you want it to be. There's such a critical mass of backpackers that on any given day you have a choice of a half-dozen one-day trips (and dozens of longer ones) you can take, all of which stuff twenty or so people in ones and twos in the back of a van and drive you around to the sights and hikes and events for not much money, and by the end of the day, inevitably, you've got a few—or many—new friends to go for a few beers with when you finally return home. I'm getting a little old for the backpacker scene, but am not, I am pleased to report, quite over that hill yet. (In large part because the scene itself is advancing in age. There's going to be an interesting 'post-backpacker' travel demographic in about five or ten years, for people who don't want lager-soaked party places, but are equally repelled by the Holiday Inn.)

The Blue Mountains

Easter weekend was spent camping in the Blue Mountains, an hour west of Sydney (okay, four hours with Easter traffic), with two old friends of mine, Chong and Andrea. It was an uneventful weekend spent sleeping in tents and walking through peaceful eucalyptus forest. Except for the eventful bits.

The who's-the-driver pointer rotated to me on Saturday, and I was eager to comply, as I'd never driven a left-hand-side stick-shift before— in fact, I had only driven a stick maybe ten times total ever. My travel companions were considerably less eager to let me expand my expertise at their expense. I thought I might get some pointers from them, some benefit from their vast experience, but sadly, and unhelpfully, they spent the whole time thin-lipped and white-knuckled, their only articulations an occasional gasp or devout expression of gratitude for their continued survival, which is very enlightened and all but not particularly useful. I hadn't noticed it the previous day, or, come to think of it, either of the following days, but the car behaved shockingly, stalling and lurching all over the place. I intend to write a sharply worded letter of complaint to the Mitsubishi Corporation.

Saturday night we went rattling down a gravel road into a national park, failed to pay for the park despite repeated attempts, went for a very pleasant waterfall hike and then a plateau hike, and found ourselves with an hour of daylight left. A quick discussion regarding whether two bottles of wine was sufficient for three people for one night quickly came to a unanimous no, and we hopped back in the car and rattled back up the gravel road towards what passes for civilization in remote Australia—a small town whose one bar features a spittoon trough and remarkably good wine—and somewhere along the line, between lurches, punctured a tyre. Eventually we even noticed, changed the tyre, and, muttering about what had become an errand to buy the most expensive six-pack ever, began to seek a new tyre somewhere in the Australian wilderness late on Easter Saturday, as we didn't want to risk a repeat performance without another viable spare tyre.

You might think that this would be challenging. You reckon without the almost pathological friendliness of rural Australians. 'Well, mate, it's my mother's funeral right now ... but, hell, sod the old bag, just wait up a tick while I go tap a rubber tree and make you a new tyre by hand myself! No, wouldn't hear of taking any money.' Phone calls flashed across the country on our behalf, already overworked employees dropped what they were doing to help us, and in the end Nick the Tyre Man whipped us up a brand-new tyre in eight minutes flat. (He did, however, charge us. By this point it was almost a surprise.)

Booze stocks replenished to sufficient levels, we rattled back to our campsite and promptly depleted them again. The next day, Sunday, we went on a five-hour hike down a trail, or rather, an alleged trail. On the map it was a bold dashed line; on the ground, however, it was more a hint or suggestion of a trail, trailesque, a trail that Aragorn himself would have had some trouble following. We lost and regained it a dozen times, doubling back, eyes peeled, knowing each time that if we failed we faced a whole night of being lost in the Blue Mountains, in the dark, surrounded by the usual assortment of lethal Australian creepy-crawlies, with no shelter, minimal food and water, and, most horrifying of all, no alcohol whatsoever. I think it was that last that sharpened our senses to the point where we made it back in one piece. We then rattled yet again to Oberon for beer and wine, rattled back, and proceeded to try very hard to burn down the entire national park. I am half sorry to report that we failed in spite of the fact that eucalyptus bark is amazing stuff, and burns spectacularly, like gunpowder.

Darwin

The next day I flew off to sweltering Darwin, at the northern tip of Oz, a weird amalgam of small town and big city, populated by only 70,000 people but the nearest larger city is at least twenty-four hours' drive away, making Darwin the hub of a vast area and hence the home of lots of stuff you wouldn't normally find in a town of that size. It's also a weird mix of 1970s architecture and tropical overgrowth. The latter is due to its latitude; the former, thanks to the cyclone that smashed the town flat forty years ago, razing nearly every building and resulting in the evacuation of 85 percent of its population before the place was rebuilt from scratch.

I intended to get a day of diving in, but unbeknownst to me, for complicated tidal and climatological reasons dive days are few and far between in Darwin's autumn, and all the dive trips were sold out. Instead I did, er, nothing: sat around, worked on my website, read Keri Hulme's *The Bone People.* I know what you're thinking: 'You travelled all the way to remote Australia to do nothing? You can do nothing at home!' To which I reply: (a) I don't have a home and (b) it's, um, a different kind of nothing. Seriously, long days off every couple of weeks are called for when you travel. Well, when *I* travel, anyhow.

Kakadu

Thence to a very cool three-day/two-night camping tour of Kakadu National Park, a vast and magical place. Endless savannah and tropical forest, pockets of outright jungle, beasts (dingos, wallabies, wild donkeys) and birds and spiders and snakes, twenty-thousand-year-old aboriginal rock art, and just extraordinary views, huge ridges and escarpments of tumbling knobbled limestone surrounding enormous green flood plains surrounding luminously blue pools and rivers, flocks of birds calling and circling as far as the eye can see.

The park's Mary and Alligator River systems have the highest density of crocodiles anywhere on the planet. Signs everywhere warned us:

ESTUARINE CROCODILES
ARE KNOWN TO MOVE INTO THIS AREA UNDETECTED.
FRESHWATER CROCODILES INHABIT THIS AREA.
ENTER THE WATER AT YOUR OWN RISK.

So naturally we spent a plurality of the time swimming.

To interrupt myself: Estuarine or saltwater crocodiles are the dangerous ones, growing to eight metres in length, munching on anything that moves (including, every couple of years, a tourist or two), undoubtedly the most dangerous land-based predator on Earth, so perfectly evolved for slaughter that they haven't changed in about 60 million years. Australians, of course, call them 'salties' in their comically laconic way. Similarly, *chironex fleckeri*, the box jellyfish, with a sting so painful its victims usually lose control of their limbs and promptly drown, and even if they survive there are reports of them still screaming *after* they have been KO'ed with morphine, is a 'stinger'. A plant in the Daintree with tendrils so fine and barbed they lodge in human skin on touch and cannot be removed until they naturally fall out in three to six months, during which they release a constant stream of a neurotoxin so agonizing it has been known to drive victims insane, is the 'stinger plant'. *Pseudonaja textilis*, the most dangerous snake in Australia, with venom twelve times more deadly than a cobra's, of which 'once symptoms emerge they proceed with terrifying rapidity with death being sudden and unexpected', happens to be brown, and so is called the 'brown snake'. It takes a lot to get an Aussie to wax poetic.

VI. ASIA

❂❂❂❂❂❂❂❂❂❂❂❂❂❂❂❂❂❂❂❂❂❂❂❂❂❂❂

The first time I ever really travelled, it was to Asia.

By 'real' travel I mean: travelling solo, and/or with strangers; to a faraway land with genuinely foreign culture(s); avoiding cookie-cutter international-class hotels; and making copious use of local public transit. I apologize for the unfortunate, condescending, and erroneous implication that other kinds of travel are 'fake,' but it would be dishonest to pretend that I haven't used this terminology for many years.

In 1997, when I was twenty-three years old, I visited my eldest sister, who was teaching in Japan at the time; flew to Hong Kong, and spent a few days there; and then took the ferry from Hong Kong to Guangzhou. I did not spend the night there. Instead, I found myself on an overnight bus rattling across southern China, in a sleeper berth demarcated by metal rods rather than solid wall. To this day, I viscerally remember realizing just how far I had gone from anything or anyone I knew. This was pre-Internet China: virtually no one spoke English, and an international phone call was a major undertaking. I was completely alone in an alien world. It was terrifying, but it was also extraordinarily thrilling.

I've experienced echoes of that sensation again and again over the years. Every serious traveller does. But it's never quite as intense as the first time. The two continents where I feel it most, to this day, are Africa and Asia, and that's probably why I keep going back to them both, even though—and/or because—they are the farthest away.

September 2000: The Burning Ghats
Varanasi, India

Less than a week here and the First World already seems like a distant memory. Particularly here in Varanasi, the city of Shiva, which feels about three times older than God—there isn't a building that isn't crumbling, and it's not so much a city as a honeycomb of narrow, twisting cobblestoned streets stuffed full of stalls (mostly selling dry goods), cows, and people. A bit like a Moroccan medina. Except for the cows, which roam these streets free of any ownership, thanks to their sacred status. I already hardly notice them anymore. In a little while I guess they'll be all but invisible to me like they seem to be to everyone else.

The Ganges is in flood, so you can't walk along the riverside *ghats* (flights of steps) to watch the bathing and the cremations. Navigation through the streets is necessary (well, 'navigation' isn't really the right word, since you lose all sense of direction in about thirty seconds. 'Random walk' is probably a better phrase.)

Apparently if you die in Varanasi and if your body is washed in the Ganges and then cremated at one of the burning *ghats*, you automatically achieve *moksha*, more or less the Hindu equivalent of nirvana, which I have to say really feels like cheating to me. You can spend your whole life lying and cheating, building up a mountain of bad karma, then go to Varanasi and step in front of a bus and achieve enlightenment through a loophole? How fair is that?

Then again, no one ever said that Shiva was fair.

There is probably some language in which 'India' translates to 'Land of Many Scams'. Everyone agrees: trust no one. I narrowly avoided a few (ingenious, multi-person, well-organized) scams in Delhi, but fell into one here in Varanasi. Everyone asks for the guidebook-lauded Vishnu Rest House in this town, so the enterprising owner of the Sunrise Hotel took over the building next door, put up a VISHNU REST HOUSE sign, dressed the entryway as a hostel reception area (posters, signs advertising bus tickets, English-language books—quite thorough) and has the man there regretfully inform you that Vishnu is full but he can recommend Sunrise next door ...

The irony is that when I came across the real Vishnu Rest House I found it quite wanting compared to the Sunrise, which was cleaner, better maintained, and friendlier. What are you going to do when *Lonely Planet* doesn't call on you? Hustle your way to success however you can.

November 2000: Tiger Hill
Darjeeling, India
India is growing on me. I'm beginning to realize that if you treat India as a game where the object is to perform activities in the least efficient manner possible, it makes a lot more sense.

For example, changing money or buying a train ticket: go to wicket 1, push your way past the line, spend ten minutes with the man behind the wicket trying to understand each other, get form A, copy details from passport onto form A, get sent to wicket 2, find out that even though wicket 2 is open they're not dealing with your request for another half an hour, wait twenty minutes, discover long line at wicket 2 where requests are now being dealt with, push way into line (my size advantage over the locals is extremely helpful), produce form A and passport, watch man behind wicket 2 copy details from passport and discard form A unread, give money/cheque to man behind wicket 2, receive form B, get sent to wicket 3, find wicket 3, receive ticket/money.

Makes perfect sense if you treat it as a game, but the men treat it very seriously.

I am presently in Darjeeling, which is quite a pleasant place, both pretty and relaxed, in spite of being, clearly, a sad, faded relic of what it was during the Raj. This morning I woke up at 3:30 a.m. (yes, me; no, I haven't been brainwashed by North Korean suicide squads) to drive up to Tiger Hill to watch the sun rise. In the unlikely chance Tiger Hill was deserted, it would have simply been a fairly magnificent sunrise featuring four of the world's five highest mountains. Okay, so Everest/Sagarmatha, Makalu, and Lhotse were so far away that they weren't much more than small white triangular blobs peeking over a ridgetop, but the enormous Kanchenjunga massif more than made up for them.

However, it was not deserted. Oh boy, was it not. Every dawn at this time of year between three and five hundred Jeeps and minivans bring somewhere between five hundred and two thousand Indian tourists, and a handful of foreigners, to Tiger Hill. Depending on your point of view, the experience was either marred, highlighted, or transformed into a wholly surreal experience. After the usual bureaucratic nightmare regarding entry tickets, which I won't go into the details of, but which must have earned someone a lot of points in the above-mentioned game, all one thousand plus of us clustered around an observation tower, on various levels depending on how much we had paid. (General Lounge for me, a step above General Admission but below Deluxe and Superdeluxe.)

Everyone stood around looking very bored as the eastern sky reddened and the vast Bengal plains came into view. Then as the first glitter of sun crossed the horizon, chaos: shouting, bustling, crowds pushing, men screaming at one another and holding shoving matches in a battle for prime camera positions, babies passed back and forth above the jostling maelstrom. Everyone aimed cameras at the sun and clicked madly away, ignoring, for my money, the much more impressive spectacle of a crimson Kanchenjunga. Then the sun was up; the sight was over; and within five minutes the crowd began to disperse for the entertaining game of 'find your Jeep'. Me, I decided to walk.

November 2000: City of God
Calcutta, India
Calcutta was exactly how I had imagined India would be. A huge sea of crumbling concrete blocks dotted by fading mausoleums of the Raj.

Long rows of street stalls selling *chapati*-and-curry in banana-leaf plates, chai in disposable clay cups, pyramids of sweets and fruits, cigarettes and drinks. Lots of beggars but not the feeding-frenzy swarms that I'd feared. Dangerously thin men pulling bored housewives around on India's last fleet of hand-drawn rickshaws—I haven't seen a Westerner on one and don't expect to. Buddhist monks videotaping their visit to the Victoria Monument. Okay, so I never imagined that last one.

Hammer-and-sickle signs spray-painted next to government slogans (to their credit, the Russians did give Calcutta a very impressive metro system, even if it's only one line). Lean, feral dogs prowling the overgrown ruins of cemeteries and abandoned temples. Giggling gaggles of schoolgirls in uniform pouring out of school. Men with bamboo clubs driving back the overzealous crowds clustering to see the latest Bollywood blockbuster. Goats and sheep patrolling the edge of the cricket field on the *maidan* (sort of like Central Park).

The smog is just incredible, a poisonous grey-blue cloud that hangs over the city night and day, visible to the naked eye from dawn to dusk. You can see where it comes from, too, with snot-blackening soot billowing from every vehicle (along with a constant refrain of deafening horn blasts). Cracked concrete, potholed roads, a thick, dark grey patina on every exposed surface, enormous clouds of bugs buzzing around every bright light after dusk falls, filthy children huddling next to their equally filthy parents on the street, a general air of ruin and decay occasionally leavened by a streak of smartly dressed middle-class types in the torrents of humanity.

December 2000: The Backpacker Trail
Bangkok, Thailand
While trekking in Nepal I met a wise South African who said to me: 'Backpackers and package tourists are getting more and more alike— package tourists are becoming more adventurous, and backpackers are following standard trails.' Nowhere is this more apparent than in Thailand and Malaysia, which teem with sunburned Europeans lugging backpacks from one clutch of beachfront guesthouses to another. But the intrepid traveller who goes off the backpacker trail can still find remote, exotic destinations away from banana shakes and beach parties.

Or so I hear. But at present I'm not feeling the least bit intrepid. On the contrary I'm growing very fond of banana shakes, and the beaches remain breathtaking even if they are crowded, and … Okay, so I've had a very lazy few weeks. Is that so wrong?

I finally got around to getting my PADI open-water scuba certification, just finished a couple of days ago. You may be thinking, 'Aha, you haven't been that lazy after all!' But I imagine if you are thinking this, you haven't done much diving yourself. For all the posturing that divers (and particularly dive instructors) do about diving being a tough, macho, man-against-nature adventure, it's hard to think of a lazier, more sedentary activity than recreational diving. A typical scuba day; sit in boat for two hours tanning and reading en route to dive site A, float around underwater looking at stuff for an hour (they repeatedly stress that you should move slowly and never exert yourself), tan and read and eat lunch for two hours en route to site B, float around underwater looking at stuff for an hour, tan and read for two hours en route back to base. Not really up there with the triathlon, is it?

However, the float-around-underwater-looking-at-stuff part is extremely cool. I took the course around Krabi, which has unearthly limestone crags jutting out above the water and big coral reefs seething with life beneath, coral and fish and sponges and starfish and jellyfish and sea turtles and (harmless) leopard and blacktip sharks and unidentifiable aquatic life all over the place, every colour of the rainbow.

From India I flew to Bangkok, which is the cleanest, most modern, friendliest, most efficient city in the world. Granted, that's not the usual reaction, but you try going there after Calcutta and Delhi and see what you think of it. After a couple days of going from wat to wat to Starbucks, I hopped on a bus down to Phuket.

Which is one of the most revolting places I have ever been—horrendously overcommercialized in the worst way possible. Even the once-nice beaches have been ruined by touts, hawkers, and sex workers. I spent about twelve hours there and moved on. I was planning to take the bus down to Malaysia via the city of Hat Yai, but at the last second decided to ask about direct flights to Singapore, found a cheap one, and took it. This turned out to be one of my more inspired travel decisions: the next day a massive monsoon storm hammered Hat Yai and flooded it to around three or four metres, killing dozens of people by the time the water finally drained about five days later.

But instead of treading water I was in Singapore. Which as far as I can tell isn't a country, or even a city; it's just a shopping mall grown so enormous that it has its own currency and airport. People complain about its government being fascist and authoritarian, but now that I've been there it's hard to take them seriously; not a real government, more like mall cops. It's all very clean and organized and gleaming with chrome, and a comfortable place to stay for a couple nights, but you really can see everything worth seeing in one of the two-hour tours they run from the airport. This is travel?

Dubai, United Arab Emirates, to Goa, India
Ah, the time dilation of travel. It's hard to believe I left France only six days ago. Moving at a rate of almost a city a day made Paris, Dubai, Mumbai, and now Goa all feel almost like one contiguous travel experience, difference facets of a single destination. And at the same time those six days feel more like a month. I swear, being on the road actively extends your life, at least in terms of perceived time, and that's probably what it's all about?

Well, 'extends' only if it doesn't 'shorten'. Today I hired a motorbike and bombed down Goa's coastal road for an hour, violating every motorcycle-safety law known to man other than 'no headstands while in motion': no helmet! no protective clothing! first time on a motorbike in eighteen months! unreliable Indian bike with unfamiliar gearing system! narrow Third World rutted, pitted roads, occupied by pedestrians, oxen, dogs, autorickshaws, oversized pickups, and worst of all, other backpackers doing the same damn thing! Gorgeous, way-fun ride though.

(Dear Mom, if you ever read this: uh, just kidding. In fact I've never been on a motorcycle in my life, okay? Great. Thanks.)

Arambol/Arumbol/Harmbol (never trust a place if its name can be spelled only one way) is a classic backpacker paradise: spectacular beach lined by laid-back banana-lassi-and-chocolate-pancake cafés, spartan but livable hostels, fantastic expat-run restaurants, book exchanges, Internet cafés, stores selling knickknacks and saris and sarongs and other tropical wear, yoga ashrams, a paragliding school, and the inexplicably ubiquitous didgeridoo workshop, all yours for as little as US$10 per day—though at that price you'll be living in a rather spartan bucket-shower-and-outhouse place, and will be doing no paragliding.

So far Goa feels a whole lot friendlier than northern India. The locals seem to live in a kind of bemused harmony with their visitors, and while vendors may desultorily hassle you, they're just going through the motions, they don't really mean it. The backpacker crowd is a slightly uneasy mix of twenty-something Israelis, for whom a few months bouncing around India/Nepal is a post-military-service rite of passage, and who, not surprisingly, tend to be exceptionally fit, in a trim-tattooed-dreadlocked way, and exceptionally full of devil-may-care-I-don't, fuck-you attitude; low-key thirty-something Europeans who come back every year (some with children, it's a family-friendly place); the Brits-and-Aussies-on-parade type you see the world over; and Others, like me.

Mind you I'm still on the fringes. The grand techno extravaganzas ended years ago, but the beaches farther south have a package-tour-party reputation. We'll see. Also farther south, this month, is one of India's more macabre and bizarre tourist attractions (which is saying something): the once-every-ten-years display of the desiccated corpse of Saint Francis Xavier. How can I possibly resist? But for now let me look back to far-ago yesterweek and tell you about:

Dubai bai bai
There are a lot of cool things about Dubai. It's probably the only country in the world whose population is 80 percent expat; this gives it a great polyglot feel, as the crossroads of Arabia, India, Africa, and Europe: a dozen languages and cultures all jumbled together and feeding on one another. Women in full *chadors* shop for lingerie in Western department stores, Africans stop work for a cup of tea at a break cued by a muezzin's call, Indian employers hold job interviews at a Second Cup(!). It's a wealthy, First World nation, whose highways and hotels and shopping malls put America's to shame, but the best way to cross Dubai Creek, the waterway that divides the city, is still to jump on an *abra*, an old wooden boat powered by a rattling two-stroke engine that leaves when it's full (my longest wait: two minutes) and on which two dozen people sit cheek by jowl. Other, much larger wooden boats—*dhows*—still prowl the waterways from Dubai to Mombasa and Mumbai and Iran, carrying huge boxes and barrels of wholesale goods for export, and are loaded and unloaded on Dubai Creek, just across from stores selling Armani and Pierre Cardin.

The city is impressively if artificially green. The one public beach is terrific. The sheer quantity of bling-bling in the Gold Souq is jaw-dropping (though the rest of the markets don't even begin to hold a candle to those of, say, Marrakesh or Cairo). The skyscrapers look very cyberpunk twenty-first century. All that said, it does start to feel kind of like a giant shopping mall after a little while. If commerce is not your thing, the rest of Dubai's delights are quickly exhausted. Comfortable, civilized, gleamingly modern, yes. Soul? I didn't see any.

Back to Bom! ... er, for the first time
Mumbai: not so much a city as a raving, screaming, all-guns blazing full-frontal assault on every one of your senses, the physical ones of course but also those of taste, decorum, dignity, proportion, decency, wonder, and awe. Bright lights and tall towers, six million people living in the biggest trash-strewn bamboo-pole-canvas-ceiling or mud-brick-aluminum-roof slums in Asia, mutilated (darker-skinned) beggars weaving past designer-jeans-wearing, cell-phone-toting (generally lighter-skinned) yuppies, heat and noise and dirt and dust and smog, howling car and bus and motorcycle horns, neon-lit Victorian architecture, Ambassador taxis and air-con'd BMWs and cows and feral cats and dogs, street-food stalls and chic valet-parking cafés, and the masses, hordes, throngs, seething churning masses of people, people people people, everywhere everywhere everywhere, a colossal overwhelming fog of noises and smells and sights that threatens to redline every sensory organ—in other words, yep, your basic large city in India. But far more alive than the other two I've seen (Delhi and Calcutta). Also far wealthier. My *Rough Guide* reports the fairly amazing statistic that Bombay's 1.5 percent of India's population produces a good 40 percent of its GDP. And for all its horrific poverty—which is so mind-numbing that you quickly stop noticing it—it's, dare I say it, kind of fun, in its vestigial Raj architecture and signage, in Chowpatty Beach with its brightly lit stalls and mini-rides and children of all ages playing and blowing bubbles and enjoying themselves, in the constant churning of unexpected sights the city flings into your field of vision. It helps that it's on the ocean; the air is better than Delhi's, and the sea, dark and calm as an oil slick at night, helps you mentally shape a city that otherwise might be too immense to navigate.

Bear in mind that I spent all of thirty-six hours there (am flying out, too, though, so there'll be more) and first impressions are often misleading, but it's easy to see why Bombay is the setting for most of the Seven Great Indian Novels *(A Suitable Boy, Such a Long Journey, A Passage to India, The God of Small Things, A Fine Balance, Midnight's Children, The Moor's Last Sigh)*; for all its wrenching downsides, it's a fantastic place, in the literal sense of the word.

The Konkan Railway

I managed to purchase a next-day Mumbai-to-Goa rail ticket despite warnings that tickets usually take a week and despite the usual Kafkaesque Indian bureaucracy, hurrah for me. I wasn't particularly looking forward to an eleven-hour train journey commencing at 7:00 a.m., and I picked up two books (Naipaul's *India: A Million Mutinies Now* and Welsh's *Ecstasy*, both of which seemed appropriate) to go with my half-reread copy of *Midnight's Children*, figuring I'd have plenty of time to read all three.

Boy, was I wrong. The Konkan Railway is an absolute delight. Sure, Indian Railways' hygiene standards seem to have slipped some in the past four years, but it's still the only way to travel. I—we, actually; they tend to cluster people with Western names together, so I rode with two Spaniards and three Brits—sat in '3-tier A/C', one of IR's giddying profusion of classes, where I read, chatted, napped, and ordered from the constant flow of *wallah*s. There was a chai-*wallah*, a coffee-*wallah*, a samosa-*wallah*, a dosa-*wallah*, a cold-drink-*wallah*, a sandwich-*wallah*, an omelette-*wallah* (though he dropped out after noon), and (only once) a ticket-*wallah*, all of them marching up and down the length of the train, bringing food and drink to its needy passengers. Or, and this took up a whole lot more of the journey than I expected, we headed to the doors between cars, opened them, leaned out, and stared at Mother India, for a long, long time.

I'd forgotten how beautiful this country can be. Red earth, golden grass, deep green forest, winding shimmering rivers, all luminous in the tropical sun. Warrens of high rocky ridges, birds soaring above. Madmen's checkerboards of small, ox-tilled fields. The *chemin de fer*, the railway's iron road, carving a neat narrow line through Maharashtra, and the twenty-car train itself hovering at either edge of my vision, and the long rows of other faces, both pale and dark, peering out of the train's other doors, and the hot wind in our faces. Eleven hours passed in a flash. I tossed my just-finished copy of *Midnight's*

Children to a fellow traveller, doubtless earning oodles of much-needed karma, grabbed my pack, and hopped off the train just before it started moving again, into the Goan tropical heat. There are worse places to disembark, believe me.

November 2004: Goa with the Floa
Palolem, Goa
Here it's all about the beach. The single most perfect beach I have ever seen, two headlands anchoring a pale, wide, mile-long, sunset-facing crescent. The thick fringe of coconut palms behind the beach shelters dozens of lodges and café-bar-restos, and the road behind them is full of shops and travel agents and Internet cafés, but it doesn't feel oppressively built up; the locals have kept a close eye on development here, and there are no buildings or hotel complexes taller than one storey, and most people stay in simple, thatched bamboo-stilt huts, rustic but civilized with fans, mosquito nets, electricity, and reliable if communal running water. The beach is big enough to swallow us all up and still leave plenty of space for solitude, if that's your thing.

Or activity. There's a lot of activity. Swimmers and walkers and sunbathers, of course, and mostly placid dogs and cows wandering by, and Frisbee, soccer, volleyball, and cricket. That last is played almost exclusively by intra-Indian tourists, who, as at all Goan beaches, make up a hefty percentage of the population, which I like: de facto whites-only bubble enclaves make me uneasy. There are a few boats, outrigger fishing boats and canoes, but not many. People are reluctant to leave the beach. It's understandable.

I've basically spent the past week hopping from one idyllic beach to another. I understand that your sympathy to anything further I say will now be muted, but really, this has highlighted the fact that chilling-out places like Goan beaches are an exception to my always-travel-solo rule: I'm having fun, and have met some cool people, but places like this would be best as part of a couple or a group. Still, you know, as work goes (yes, I said work; research, remember? a new book, remember?), this ain't been so bad.

The party beach
Long ago, in the vanished mists of yesteryear—about ten years ago— Goa's beaches were host to massive raves featuring thousands of people

every night. This is no longer the case (the scene, I gathered, dwindled for a while, and was all but killed, other than at Christmas and New Year's, by a law that forbade amplified music on beaches between 10:00 p.m. and 7:00 a.m. India being India, this doesn't actually make the music illegal, it just makes the required bribes too expensive except for on big special occasions) but the last vestigial traces of the Goa-trance party scene can be found at Anjuna and Vagator beaches. Nowadays, from what I saw, it's just a couple hundred people dancing barefoot in and around beach cafés to low-end sound systems, but it's a very fun, laid-back vibe. Half the local touts and vendors offer you drugs in hushed voices, and you can't walk down the beach at night without smelling pot. It's like the nineties never ended, man. Although this did make me wonder about the night traffic; like all Goan beach cities, Anjuna/Vagator is so spread out that renting a motorcycle is a near-necessity, and I'm not sure I like the idea of stoned/tripping Israeli bikers at midnight. Okay, points for comedy, but I don't wanna be on those same streets.

Anjuna also hosts a huge Wednesday market, which is both annoying, as the touts and hustlers are out in force, voluble, and persistent—especially the ear-cleaners, who I gather are near the bottom of the tout totem pole—and cool, because it is a great market, with all manner of colourful things and trinkets and cloths and sculptures and carvings and food and Goa-trance CDs and retina-scarring om-decorated clothing for sale, although it does suffer a bit from the usual Third World market problem: sure, there are eight hundred stalls, but that's because there are forty copies each of the same twenty stalls. Oh, and there was a really good ashtanga yoga place, and I'm pleased to report that I went through a moderately tough session and my knee didn't even twinge.

The package beach

In the past decade, as the party scene has dwindled, the package scene has exploded and every weekend nowadays, charter airplanes descend on Vasco da Gama airport and disgorge packs of European tourists who then flood into Calangute and Baga (Goan beaches come in twos; Palolem, similarly, has Patnem just south of it). The Calangute beach is enormous, a good five miles long, and spectacular, and is cambered for great bodysurfing, and still replete with big fishing boats piled high with nets. The town has outstanding food, including a French patisserie and an excellent seafood restaurant, and at least one good place to stay, the Villa Fatima. (Mind you, I have a real soft spot for vast, crumbling, once-luxurious places; a more objective reviewer would be more harsh.)

Uh, that said, I kind of hated the whole area. The hassle—you can't walk down the street without twenty people crudely trying to sell you a taxi ride and/or a souvenir trinket. (The usual annoying sales tactics, too: they try to shake your hand, look appalled if you refuse, and pull you into their store if you don't. Or they cry out, 'Remember me?', taking advantage of they-all-look-alike-ism. Or they just refuse to take no for an answer and follow you for thirty seconds, hoping you'll suddenly change your mind.) The noise—the city has grown too far too fast, and the streets are overcrowded, and Goan driving is more about extremely frequent use of the horn than it is about, say, motion, and you risk deafness or at least a headache walking down the street. And it's *ugly*, all cheap concrete buildings packed too close together, the usual Indian dirty-and-unfinished look times two, and aside from eating, swimming, reading, sitting on the beach, and going to expert but pointless copies of Western bars, there's not actually much to do. So my second day there I hopped on a bus to:

The vanished city
Old Goa would be plenty creepy enough without the centuries-old corpse on display. Once upon a time, this pleasant riverside spot was the capital of the Portuguese colony here, a city of several hundred thousand; but then, struck by the tripartite blow of cholera, malaria, and the end of the colonial empire, it disappeared. Now only the churches remain, distant from one another, connected by new roads lined with market stalls selling cold drinks and coconuts and religious paraphernalia (candles, rosaries, flower garlands, stickers and pictures of Krishna and Jesus and Ganesh), and all around, where hundreds of thousands of people used to live, the jungle has returned, leaving no other sign of human habitation.

It's busy this month because of the once-every-ten-year display of the remains of Saint Francis Xavier. I wasn't actually going to see said remains, but the lineups were much shorter than I (and I think they) expected, so I went. Like much else in India, the festival had a hastily, crudely, slapped-together school-play feel which is either engagingly amateurish or infuriatingly incompetent, depending on one's mood. A covered walkway to the cathedral had been erected to protect pilgrims from the sun, but it was sagging and at one point half-collapsed. You had to pass through several sets of metal detectors, but having erected the detectors, the security guards then proceeded to completely ignore the fact that approximately 50 percent of the pilgrims set them off, and just carelessly waved people through. After about ten minutes in line, serenaded by the constant chirping of metal detectors, I entered the cathedral, where, in a glass coffin, half-covered by an ancient filigreed shroud, Saint Francis Xavier lay.

The story goes that months after he was buried, he was dug up, and despite having been interred in quicklime, his body was as fresh and warm as at the moment of his death. Maybe so. I can report that he has gotten very much the worse for wear since then. I can also report that he was very short. Other pilgrims kissed the glass coffin, or draped (Hindu-style) flower garlands on it, which attendants quickly whisked away. I did neither. I found my way through the jungle-taken vanished city to an unexpected riverboat, which took me back to the coast, from where I continued to:

The perfect beach
... but I told you about this one already, didn't I, right at the start. Palolem. Perfection.

November 2004: And on This Pedestal These Words Remained ...
Hampi, Karnataka, India
Hampi, despite its unprepossessing name, is like another world. Its old name, Kishkinda, a city out of legend from the Ramayana, would be more appropriate. The landscape here is unearthly, dominated by vast jumbled ridges of colossal boulders, balancing and leaning on one another in seemingly unnatural ways, somehow looking crystalline and water-warped at the same time. Roads and villages are built in the shadow of these boulders, like handfuls of fifty-foot-high pebbles dropped by the gods, and it's hard to shake the notion that this place was meant for creatures of far greater scale than us. (It reminds me a lot of Matopos in Zimbabwe, for those of you who have been, though leafier and a little less stark.)

And then there are the ruins. The bones of the once-mighty

Vijayanagar kingdom are visible all around the fields and valleys here, and doubtless hidden beneath as well. Hampi itself is built around an ancient temple to Vishnu dominated by a hundred-foot-high ziggurat carved with figurines and birds and filigree, some of its features worn away by the centuries but still imposing. Other ruins are everywhere: temples carved with figurines of Hanuman and Ganesh and Nigiri and Durga and nagas; elephant stables; sets of kilometre-long pillared colonnades; the crumbling remains of a massive stone bridge that once spanned the palm-tree-lined river. The crude modern(ish) buildings, roads, fields, and banana plantations look wildly out of place. This land clearly belongs to history.

Hampi today has a population of maybe five hundred people, twice that if you include Hindu pilgrims and Western backpackers (mainstream tourism hasn't discovered it yet); Karamapular, four klicks to the north, is only a little larger; and between them, and to the east, where most of the Vijayanagar ruins lie, there's nothing but the river, a few modern temples, and the odd plantation. The whole area has a deserted, postapocalyptic—or maybe 'first colony on a new planet' would be more accurate—feel.

The river is wide, fast, and very pretty, especially when sunrise and sunset light the huge jagged boulders that mark its course. Both the centuries-old stone bridge and an incomplete decades-old concrete one five klicks downstream fail to cross it. Instead, coracles, shallow ten-foot-diameter inverted-dome baskets, covered with plastic and lined with some kind of baked mud, ferry passengers, motorcycles, and goats from one side to the other. Beneath Hampi's Vishnu temple, *ghats* (steps) worthy of Varanasi descend to the river. They are almost deserted.

On the highest ridge, just north of the river, a temple to Hanuman, the monkey deity, has been built. The whitewashed stairs that lead up to it are steep and hard in the midday sun, but the views are spectacular. Somebody forgot to tell the monkeys about the temple built to their god; there are a few, but far more cluster around the Shiva temple across the river. A few entrepreneurs near the temple sell cool drinks and fresh coconuts. Hampi does well with pilgrims and tourism, but the villages north of the river are as poor as any I've seen in India, concrete pillboxes with corrugated-aluminum awnings for the rich, thatched huts for the poor, and the women dress not in the vivid, colourful saris or the other Indian women's outfit (*shalwar kameez*, i.e., pyjama-type pants, long blouse, shawl) you see nearly everywhere else, but in simple, ragged clothes. They were threshing grain in the fields today, a busy communal task. It looked fun at first, and then it looked like a whole lot of hard work.

Sadhus, holy men, in saffron robes with painted ash-smeared faces, chant *namaste* at you as they pass; unlike almost everyone else in India, they don't want money from you. White floral and crystalline patterns are drawn in chalk on the pavement in front of most households every morning. Wandering through the thorny-grassed fields (okay, fine, getting completely lost in an attempt to find a short cut between roads), it's easy to find rocks with straight edges and regular carved patterns jutting from the ground, as-yet-unearthed relics of Vijayanagar.

All in all, an exceedingly cool place. I've met several people who came for a couple of days and stayed for a couple of weeks. Mind you, one reason is that you can plausibly live on US$5 per day here, and you can comfortably live on $10. When your travels are limited by money rather than time, that means a lot. Me, I've got a ticket for the night bus to Bangalore, but I'm very glad of my last-second, on-a-whim decision to come here.

September 2006: Russification
St. Petersburg, Russia
Dump any notion you ever had of Russia as a drab and dowdy place. St. Petersburg is swimming in colour, seething with life. I've only been here a day now, but it's already staking a genuine claim to becoming my favourite European city.

That despite the fact I got pickpocketed in the metro this morning—for the first time ever anywhere—amidst the press of the shoulder-to-shoulder crowd. Fear not, all I lost was a day's spending money (R800/US$30). My ID, credit cards, and US cash are tucked away rather more securely. And a good thing, too.

The theatre part of the hostel/puppet-theatre where I am staying is, alas, closed for renovations. (Had I known this, I would have stayed elsewhere, but it's comfortable enough in a Stalinist-hostel kind of way. I have my own room; I'm kinda too old for dorm beds nowadays.)

Mild culture shock hit before I even got out of the airport: I ordered a Pepsi to change money, and got a Pepsi Cappuccino, coffee-flavour cola, which tastes pretty much like it sounds. Thence a rattling, belching, rusting old bus with a babushka ticket taker, down wide green boulevards into the city proper, into the metro, up at Nevsky Prospket—and up—and up—and up. If there's a deeper subway system anywhere, I've never seen it.

Nevsky Prospekt is the spine of St. Petersburg, a massive boulevard walled by ornate buildings, palaces, cathedrals, department stores, McDonald's, Armani, Citibank, and covered by a tangled spiderweb of streetcar wires. Glittering spires, domes, and pillared colonnades are visible around virtually every corner, and the city is broken up by wide canals, massive public squares, and green patches of public parks. But dig a little behind this glittering exterior and you'll find traces of seventy years of Soviet neglect: interior stairways that appear to have been bombed and then littered with construction materials, scarred and faded walls. When you cross the street you stand an equal chance of being almost run over by a groaning Lada or a sleek BMW.

St. Petersburg women are *exceedingly* stylish, and the attractive ones—who so far as I can tell comprise the great majority—are, let's say, not at all reluctant to show off their looks, and often seem to have been born in three-inch spike heels. The wide sidewalks of Nevsky Prospekt sometimes seem less like a pedestrian thoroughfare and more like a parade of models down the world's longest catwalk. Russian men, to a first approximation, appear to go through three stages after childhood: 'awkward student', 'Cassius', 'Yeltsin'.

In a Strange Land

It's very strange being in a place where I don't even know the alphabet, much less the language. First time in ages. Oh, I can mostly puzzle out Cyrillic already, but it's very odd to read things letter by individual letter rather than six or eight words at a time, the way I read English. Russian is enough of a Latin language that sounding out the letters then helps me understand the word—it's an odd satori, halfway through, the first time you suddenly realize a sign says 'Electronics' or 'Telephone'. I have a new understanding of what it means to be only functionally literate. It's intimidating, not knowing the language. It makes you an idiot. And not in the Prince Myshkin sense.

I suspect travel to alien lands is often only easy, mentally, that is, if you started young; in the same way that people who get their driver's licenses in their late twenties are generally forevermore much more timid behind the wheel than those who learned to drive in their teens. I find myself getting more cautious as I get older, more neurotic about plans and preparations, and I think if I hadn't gone to China when I was twenty-three, and Africa when I was twenty-five, today I'd be an organized-tour kind of tourist. Not that there's anything wrong with that.

Teratology

Today I wanted to see an entire woolly mammoth at the zoology museum, found out that said museum was closed, and went to the Kunstkamera collection next door. The museum was half-closed for renovations. Of the remainder, the Great Gottorp Globe could only be viewed with a pre-booked and expensive guide; there were various collections of cultural artifacts from around the world; and then there was the Kunstkamera collection itself, which was ... well ...

You see, Peter the Great was one morbid SOB of a teratologist, and in this, Russia's first museum, he installed a room full of freak-show curiosities collected and embalmed by the anatomist Frederik Ruysch, who I bet was no fun at all at parties. The Kunstkamera collection is, for the most part, an assortment of horribly deformed fetuses floating in formaldehyde in big glass tubes, with the occasional two-headed beast or lump of coral thrown in for show. Labels include 'Double-faced monster with brain hernia', 'Cyclops with occipital hernia', 'Skeleton of child with two heads and three arms', 'Knife used for amputation'. *Body Worlds* has nothing on this place. It's kind of fascinating—and more than a little disturbing.

September 2006: Kremlinology
Moscow, Russia
So this is Moscow. Eh. You can keep it.

Mostly it's a sprawling labyrinth of concrete towers, shopping complexes, BMWs, and construction cranes. My timing probably has something to do with my reaction. The Kremlin is closed to the public this week, and the Bolshoi is entirely wrapped in scaffolding and canvas, but I'm confident I'd take St. Petersburg over this town any day of any week.

There are some cool bits. The metro is indeed magnificent (but its grandeur is threadbare, and it's full of barricades that herd people into seething bottlenecks). GUM, on Red Square, is surely the world's most architecturally beautiful shopping mall (but it's still a shopping mall). The modern sculpture garden across from Gorky Park is quite cool (but Gorky Park is disappointing; most of it is occupied by a tacky amusement park). The Kremlin, St. Basil's, and the Alexanderovsky Gardens are a bit like having a colossal fantasyland castle in the heart of the city (but they throw the gloomy industrial bustle of most of the rest of the place into sharp relief). The people-watching on Arbat is outstanding (though Arbat itself is half souvenir shops and fast-food joints).

My favourite thing by far, so far, is the Exhibit of the People's Economic Achievements, aka VDNKh, which was once sort of a Soviet Epcot Center. Its kilometres of boulevards and gardens are decorated by huge statues of heroic Communist figures, massive golden fountains, Soviet space shuttles, a titanium spire that has to be seen to be believed, and gargantuan pavilions, one for every republic of the USSR and others with catchy names like 'Pavilion No. 71'. Nowadays said pavilions have mostly been converted to stores selling cheap consumer goods, the airplane hangar has become a farmers' market, and bouncy Russopop booms out of speakers hidden in the columns that dot the grounds. It's the utter apotheosis of kitsch.

The occasional *frissons* of feeling like I'm living in a spy novel are also kind of fun. Stepping off the St. Petersburg train into the Moscow night; walking along the fearsome walls of the Lubyanka, that looming monolith that I think would look menacing even if you didn't know its long and bloody history of dungeons and KGB interrogation chambers; being accosted by a policeman (by the rather unfriendly expedient of coming up behind me and jabbing his finger into my back) who demanded to see my documents—'Passport, visa, Moscow registration!'*—and wasn't satisfied by my attempt to forestall him with a mere photocopy

---

* You're supposed to get your visa paper (not to be confused with your visa) stamped every time you stay at a hotel for three or more days; lack of such stamps will cause great suspicion, apparently, even though it's entirely possible to spend a month in this country without spending three days in one place, particularly if you're taking the Trans-Siberian.

(I'm reluctant to hand out my passport unless it's actually necessary). 'Problem! You come to *polizi stationi*!' When I gave in and surrendered my passport, he scanned my registrations minutely for errors before pronouncing, 'Okay!', passing it back, and waving me on.

It's nice to see that some of the old Soviet traditions like random identity checks haven't died off. Two more cops were doing the same thing outside the VDNKh to anyone who looked Caucasian (i.e., dark-skinned). I wonder why I looked suspicious. I am very obviously a tourist here; I consider myself relatively nondescript, but almost nobody has confused me for a Russian. Perhaps that's for the best.

Aside: There's a lot of money flooding through this city. Luxury brands everywhere, BMWs clogging the street, women in thousand-dollar outfits, enormous numbers of *bahkomat*s (bank machines), and even more enormous numbers of burly security guards, plus a very, very, cool Fabergé retail store. But you still can't drink the tap water. Also, the public toilets are Porta-Potties manned by babushkas who charge you 5 rubles a go.

I'm a little footsore; in this past week I've probably done more sustained walking than at any time since … sheesh, probably since trekking around Annapurna in Nepal six years ago. But my poor feet will get a couple days of rest soon enough: Tomorrow night, we embark on the thirty-eight-hour train journey to Omsk. About halfway there, just west of Yekaterinburg, Europe becomes Asia. I wonder if there's a WELCOME TO ASIA, POPULATION 4,000,000,000 sign at the border.

September 2006: Second Person Siberian
Krasnoyarsk, Siberia, Russia
It's when you fight your way through the crowds and out of Moscow's metro and walk into Yaroslavsky Station that the sheer scale of the journey starts to really hit you, when you look at the time-zone markers under the diagram of the rail network, and the way those numbers mount up as the track sweeps eastwards: +6, +7, +8. Eight time zones. A third of the world.

On the platform, in the night, the #2 Rossiya, running from Moscow to Vladivostok, seems to run on forever, although it's actually a train of only some twenty cars, or 'wagons' in Russian. Your first-class wagon is near the middle of the train, and your two-bed compartment boasts saffron drapes and mirrors, a selection of Cyrillic-language newspapers, a radio, and even a television—although the only channel it gets is CCCCC, the Closed Circuit Corridor Camera Channel, to save you from sticking your neck outside your door.

Mikhail and Natalya, your *provodnitsa*s, or 'car attendants', introduce themselves; they live on this train, will ride it to Vladivostok and back again, and it's their job to care for the car and its passengers, to bring you beer or water or food from the dining car. Without a whistle or warning, and bang on time, you start to move: through Moscow's vast and brimming suburbs, past commuter trains glowing ghostly in the night, tired passengers sitting on wooden benches and staring at nothing. Mikhail comes to take your ticket, gives it a little rip right across the hologram sticker, passes back your copy. One beer later, and it's late, and you wrap yourself in the soft first-class linens and let the train gently rock you to sleep.

You wake to trees. And indeed there will be an arboreal theme to the scenery throughout the rest of the voyage. The forests through which you pass are of birch and pine, almost like the birch and pine you know, but not quite. They are too tall, too straight, nothing but trunk and tiny spoke branches. It is like ten million densely clustered needles sticking straight up, like a sea of spears. Power lines parallel the tracks, sometimes near, sometimes far. Roads run alongside the tracks for a time, then veer away.

Over the next day, when you happen to glance out the window, or when you fold down one of the windows in the corridors that opens and spend a few minutes just gazing at the passing land, you see, mostly, the same unchanging, ever-changing thing: taiga forest. Often there is cultivated land beyond. Sometimes there are clearings of tufted, boggy grassland. Sometimes there are people on or near the tracks, railway workers in orange vests, or random passersby in dark jackets, or old women washing clothes in a nearby pond. Sometimes you pass houses, sagging wood and brick—mostly wood—surrounded by groups of shacks that look like African shantytowns. And sometimes there are only the shacks. Piles of firewood are everywhere. Winter is coming.

There are towns and cities, too. Legoland cities of Stalinist concrete blocks, occasionally leavened by neighbourhoods of wooden houses. Other trains howl past in the other direction, mostly freight trains of shipping containers and tanker cars and logs lashed to flatbeds, more and more as you continue farther east, into the industrial heartland of

Russia, along the world's busiest freight rail line. You pass gargantuan factories, mostly abandoned and rusted and crumbling. In major cities you stop for ten or fifteen minutes, and walk up and down the platform, stretching your legs, wary that the train might leap away at any moment, for there is no warning before it departs, except that of the *provodnitsa*s. It's a little odd to walk on ground that does not move. Wrinkled old women push carts full of chocolate bars and chips and beer bottles, or carry bags full of peanuts and oat-honey bars and bread and dried fish, and try to sell them to the train passengers.

They get few customers. The train is half empty. Summer is high season; autumn is quiet. Half the first-class compartments are empty and locked shut all the way to Omsk. In the dining car, Igor, a huge middle-aged man with a boxer's build and only a few remaining teeth (mostly gold), does all the cooking and cleaning while being henpecked to death by three old women who spend all day sitting at a table drinking tea. No more than two other tables are ever occupied by passengers while you are there. You spend the second night drinking beer, swapping tales of Russian bureaucrats, and not playing cards with the friendly Swedish couple next door. In the morning a knock comes on the door, and Natalya slides it open. 'Omsk,' she says.

Siberia begins some 2,300 kilometres from Moscow, or one-quarter of the way to Vladivostok. Omsk is its first major city. It has a history. Dostoevsky was exiled there for four years, almost flogged to death, and dragged out to face the firing squad for an execution that turned out to be mock. For a couple of years, during the civil war, it was the capital of White Russia, until the Bolsheviks came. Today it has a city core of public parks and nineteenth-century stonework, not unlike those in St. Petersburg, surrounded by rings of squat Stalinist architecture.

But the twenty-first century has caught up, and how. Omsk's buildings may be shabby, peeling, faded concrete, but the ground floors of all those along the major streets are brightly painted, brightly lit, brightly branded boutiques and bars and salons and restaurants and supermarkets that wouldn't be out of place in London or Frankfurt. You stay at a sparkling new hotel at the junction of two rivers, go for a quick run on a pedestrian trail that runs along one of them, eat cheap pizza and drink overpriced Czech beer, and watch *Gladiator* on cable TV.

In Omsk you observe, not for the first time, that Russians look very Russian. Especially the men. Even more than you had expected. The whole country is straight out of Central Casting, from the burly middle-aged men and women to the lean soldiers on the streets, the fine-boned kids who run the Internet cafés, the beshawled babushkas on the Moscow metro, and the heavily dolled-up women on the boulevards (spike heels and tight jeans or miniskirts seem to be the twenty-something woman's uniform here, from sea to shining sea).

The next morning, armed with the scantiest of Russian, a phrasebook, patience, and a sense of humour, you buy tickets to Krasnoyarsk from a woman who speaks no English. This time you ride *kupe*, second-class, in four-bed compartments. The train is two-thirds full, and all your fellow passengers are Russian—this is no international train, Krasnoyarsk is the end of its line. The compartment is uncomfortably heated, but the bedding is comfortable enough, there are cups and saucers, tea bags free in the dining car, and of course the samovar at the end of every car, next to the *provodnitsas'* cabin, providing endless boiled water. Next to the samovar is a thirty-seven-point four-colour diagram detailing its design and operation. The *provodnitsas* here are brusque but friendly; so far, their reputation as battleaxes does not seem deserved.

Here the taiga forest appears only in fits and spurts; the trees are smaller, branched more elaborately against the wind, often lonely in a landscape of colossal, marshy grassland on which the courses of flood-plain rivers are marked in brown. Feathergrass and cattails sprout waist high, swept into ephemeral patterns by the ever-gusting wind. In the night, just west of Novosibirsk, you cross the kilometre-wide River Ob, dark water full of barges and the multicoloured streaks of reflected city lights, the fifth longest river in the world.

Today you arrived in Krasnoyarsk (on the shores of the Yenisey River, seventh longest in the world). You were driven through a bustling downtown with some amazing, lace-like wooden architecture, then through long suburbs of scarred apartment blocks, past swastika graffiti, to your homestay in one of the endless anonymous Legoland buildings. The stairwell, like those in St. Petersburg, is dank and grim and crumbling, ominous and inhuman, decorated only by a huge heating duct, but the apartment into which you are invited is cozy and comfortable, all lacy curtains and flowerpots. Your hostess is a formidable old woman named Galina. It's a bit like living with your grandmother; that is, if your grandmother spoke no English.

Tomorrow, you will venture out into the taiga for the first time, into the jagged outcrops of the Stolby Nature Reserve, and soon thereafter, to Lake Baikal. After fifty-nine hours of train travel, at an average speed of sixty to seventy kilometres per hour, you are slightly more than halfway to Beijing. You are not yet halfway to Vladivostok.

October 2006: Places You Only Know from Risk
Irkutsk, Siberia

Yes, it's more than just a territory on the Risk game board. (Though incidentally it's considerably farther south than in the game. The Trans-Siberian, like the Trans-Canadian, stays fairly close to the country's southern border all along its route.) It's famous for … er … not a whole lot, other than being the place of exile for many of the Decembrist aristocrat-revolutionaries, back in the day.

Krasnoyarsk is quite an interesting and cosmopolitan city, and one conveniently located a mere seven kilometres north of the Stolby Nature Reserve, a trip to which answered in part: Why is the life expectancy of Russian men so low? (It's sixty years—*extremely* low for a country so wealthy—compared to seventy-four years for Russian women.) It's not just the rampant alcoholism, the vodka-drinking for breakfast, the continuing classification of beer as a soft drink. It has a lot to do with the fact that, so far as I can tell, Russian men disproportionately tend to be psychotic adrenalin junkies.

'Someone fall off and die here,' Kostya, our guide at Stolby, said, and he paused to think a moment. 'Every week? No, no. Every two week.' He waved a negligent hand at Pillar No. 1, the first colossal pile of karst granite thrusting its way eighty metres into the sky from the taiga forest below. Around us, schoolchildren on day trips shouted excitedly, climbing all over the smaller rocks, and a few beginning expeditions up the pillar. 'You see those marks?' Kostya pointed at two parallel sets of vertical striations. 'Last year, a boy fall off, he grab with his fingernails.' He shook his head sadly.

There are about ten such huge heaps of granite protruding from Stolby—Pillars 1, 2, 3, Grandmother, Grandfather, Crocodile, Monkey, Wild Rocks, and so on—many of them used by the Krasnoyarsk alpine club, among Russia's finest thanks to a rather ruthless process of elimination. A sizable memorial near the entrance to the reserve pays tribute to the many local alpinists who have fallen to their deaths and in doing so presumably improved the club's average skill level. A few years ago, to celebrate their sixtieth anniversary, a few of them climbed Pillar No. 2, the highest and hardest, to celebrate. No big deal, right? Except this group *brought a cow along.*

The cow successfully summitted. No word on whether it went back down the hard way or the easy way, and if the latter, whether it has its own space in the memorial.

A hundred years ago, the local Bolsheviks huddled and conspired in Stolby's caves, plotting and waiting for their revolution, still a decade away. And today, loners and outcasts live in the nature reserves, even through the vicious Siberian winter, in hidden houses and caves, hunting to survive. Kostya—friendly, well educated, thirty-something—spent three weeks in Stolby himself, some fifteen years ago, surviving on cat soup and pine-needle tea. He seemed reluctant to elucidate exactly why.

It's easy to see how you could live here undetected if you wanted to. At ground level, the colossal pillars of the taiga's birch and pine trees seem to stretch all the way up to heaven; this forest that carpets the land all the way up to the circumpolar treeline near the Arctic Sea is vast, cool, mysterious. The air is damp and cold—we were snowed on as we scrambled to the top of one of the rock formations. The undergrowth is sparse enough to permit walking in any direction, but thick enough to obscure vision after only a hundred feet.

For a moment I thought I saw, from the corner of my eye, a strange, ornately carved little wooden house standing on four tall bone-like stilts. When I turned to look, it was gone. Just my mind playing tricks on me.

Olkhon

Every so often, when travelling, you run into a genuine oasis: remote and laid-back, cheap and comfortable, set amid stunning natural beauty, a haven for fellow travellers from around the world, a genuinely magical spot somehow not yet overrun by tour buses, gap-year teenagers, crowds of hawkers or rows of souvenir stalls.

Oases I have found over the years:

    Yangshuo, China
    Tetebatu, Indonesia
    Kokrobite, Ghana

The Vumba, Zimbabwe
Nepal, all of it
The Daintree, Australia
Dahab, Egypt
Caye Caulker, Belize
Hampi, India
Nungwi, Zanzibar

I wasn't expecting to add to that hallowed list while in Russia, but I am pleased today to append the name *Olkhon Island.*

It's a four-hour drive from Irkutsk to the ferry, along a wide black highway divided by a dotted line largely ignored by the swarming Russian traffic. Past smokestacks belching filth into the sky (Irkutsk, like most Russian cities, is smelled before it's seen), airfields above which light aircraft perform unlikely acrobatics, roadside produce markets, farmland, Siberian cowboys herding cattle through the rolling hills, and then back into wilderness: rippling hills of treeless, grass-covered steppe alternating with dense carpets of taiga forest, a kaleidoscopic palette of soft yellow and green. We stop at a Yukos gas station, then at a busy café. Half of its customers are Slavic, tall and fine featured, descendants of settlers and exiles; half are the local Buryat, short and stocky, their Asiatic features a reminder that we're a long, long way from Europe.

Eventually there are no more trees, just sand-coloured grass that looks from a distance like raw desert. Lake Baikal's appearance is so sudden it seems like a mirage. Banana-shaped, sixty kilometres across, Baikal is smaller than any of North America's Great Lakes, but so deep—an incredible 1,637 metres—that it contains more water than all of them put together, a full fifth of the planet's unfrozen fresh water. (By comparison, Superior bottoms out at 405 metres.) Baikal's water is deep blue, crystal pure, sharply cold even in summer. It is surrounded on all sides by high, folded mountains. A single promontory of these mountains extends into the lake, and is cut off from the mainland by a narrow channel. A ferry takes us efficiently across this channel, to the stark, barren, wildly beautiful steppe hills of Olkhon Island.

It isn't all steppe; half the island's soil is too salty to support anything but grass, and the rest is occupied by a great forest of green and golden pine. Colossal jagged rocks and headlands jut into the lake. On both sides, but particularly the east, huge cliffs fall almost vertically

into the water; the island's highest point, 1,230 metres above lake level, is almost immediately next to the deepest trench in the lake, almost three vertical kilometres below. The island's shape mimics that of the lake that surrounds it, a banana seventy-two kilometres by fourteen.

With its shining mountains, the glittering lake, the windswept grassy hills, and the green and golden forests, all on an epic scale, Olkhon is shockingly gorgeous. Well into this century it was inhabited only by Buryats, nomadic and Buddhist, who herded their cattle north and south depending on the season. Their offering places and prayer poles wrapped with colourful fabrics still dot the landscape; they believe Olkhon to be one of the world's central power places. Particularly its northern tip, a jagged rock called Khoboy, or 'the Tooth,' which incidentally is exactly where my watch stopped the day before yesterday.

The Slavs were sent here by Stalin, who established a gulag on the northwestern edge of the island, and exiled trainloads of Estonians, Latvians, and Lithuanians here. Those who survived the nightmarish journey then had to face Olkhon's brutal winters (though at least their summers were presumably beautiful). Nothing is left of that gulag but ruins; the island's one real village, Khuzhir, occupied by some twelve hundred of its fifteen hundred inhabitants, is farther south, halfway up the coast from the ferry, inland from a harbour guarded by colossal rocks.

Khuzhir is a town of wooden fences, wooden houses, rutted, uneven dirt streets covered with dung. Cows outnumber motorized vehicles by about three to one. Its tiny industrial port area is half-collapsed, all but defunct. At first, it looks like one of the most uninviting towns imaginable. But look a little closer, and you'll see that some of these houses are shops; some are hostels; one even provides satellite Internet access (though it wasn't available when I tried it); and a surprising number of Western tourists are wandering around. Wander around a bit, and eventually—very soon, actually, given the size of Khuzhir—you'll find the main reason for this: Nikita's Homestead.

I don't want to portray Olkhon as an undiscovered paradise. Both Western and Russian tourists come here by the boatload, particularly in high summer, when you sometimes have to wait in line overnight on the mainland side to catch the ferry. There are guesthouses and B&Bs not just in Khuzhir but also in tiny (fifteen-building) hamlets that dot the coast. In summer, up to twenty Jeeps a day drive tourists around to see the island's sights. But it's fair to say that much of this is down to one man, a former Russian table-tennis champion named Nikita,

who fell in love with Olkhon, built his house here, and has expanded it into a cozy, comfortable, welcoming guesthouse complex with room for maybe twenty. For room and full board at Nikita's Homestead you pay 600 rubles a day, or some US$25.

Of course it's not ultra-luxury. There's power, but no running water; you have to make do with a *banya* sauna-bath and bucket toilets. If you want a beer, it's delivered in a litre jar from a local brewmeister; if you want to rent a mountain bike, you may be sent down the street to another local entrepreneur; and if you want something not found in the small local mini-markets, well, there's a minibus to Irkutsk every morning. But such desires are rare to unheard of, when you can chill, wander, tramp along the pebbly beaches and through pine forests, hop on the daily Russian Jeep tours to the wilds of the island's north, take a boat out into the lake, watch the incredible sunsets, or explore the lakes and highlands of the rugged interior. Maybe in summer the crowds will find you, but I doubt it. It's very easy to find peace on Olkhon Island. I hope it never changes.

October 2006: In the Footsteps of Chinggis Khan
Ulaan Baatar, Mongolia

Ulaan Baatar: a godforsaken outpost that time forgot in the middle of Mongolia's squalid, all-but-abandoned wasteland, right?

Guess again. This is a thriving, humming hub of commerce— German breweries, Korean restaurants, French bakeries, Irish pubs, Hollywood movie theatres, American missionaries, billboards advertising mining equipment and Western cosmetics, horn-honking traffic jams of Hyundais and Mercedes and Land Cruisers, plentiful cheap Internet cafés (600 tögrög/US60 cents/hour), new construction everywhere you look, and the Mongols themselves slouching about in laid-back Western-cool brand-name black and denim, tattoos and coloured hair. There's even a goth scene. There's money sloshing all over the place in today's UB. Looks a bit like an overheated bubble economy to me, but what do I know?

The lost boys of Ulaan Baatar

It's not a pretty city. In fact it's an impressively ugly one. Most of the buildings are still Stalinist blocks. The streets and sidewalks are battered and cracked. The smokestacks of two massive power plants vomit smoke into the air around the clock, and the city is set in a bowl of mountains; the air is thick with smog. Street urchins and beggars are few but remarkably aggressive. They'll grab you, or follow you for blocks, and one (twenty-something) one followed right behind me one night, trying to match my pace while opening the zippers of my daypack. (He failed, and hence did not score the one-dollar sunglasses I keep in its outer pocket.)

Their aggression is understandable. You see, an amazing network of hot-water pipes bigger than most tree trunks extends from those power plants all through the city, running aboveground at first, along overpasses where they meet roads or rail tracks, and plunging underground when they reach downtown. There are many uncovered manholes, beneath which you can see these water pipes not ten feet below. It's in these passages, in this Dickensian underground labyrinth, that UB's street people live when winter comes and the outside temperatures plunge to -40c. Some are adult alcoholics. Most are orphan children and teenagers, loosely organized into street gangs that emerge by day to scavenge and thieve. Once there were hundreds, but now, apparently, their number is diminishing, as the newfound wealth above trickles slowly into the underworld. But I doubt these lost boys will disappear for a good few years yet, if ever.

The middle of nowhere, the centre of the world
Driving out of UB feels like time travel. Ten minutes west of the city's edge, deep in the Mongolian steppe, it's hard to believe that such a thing as a city ever existed. A single road parts an endless sea of rolling hills of golden, treeless grass. Rippled layers of hills and highlands jut from the horizon on all sides, some barren, some snow-capped. Occasional jagged granite spines protrude from the earth like the half-buried remains of some long-vanished race of monsters.

The road continues past, and sometimes through, herds of horses, camels, yaks, sheep, goats, and cows. Sometimes the livestock is watched by men or children on horseback. Birds fly low over the road: magpies, crows, kites, buzzards, sometimes vultures. Tiny white discs are visible out on the distant steppe or on the slopes of some hills: *gers*, aka (in Central Asia) yurts—crosshatched panels of wood lashed into a circle, then topped by a shallow conical roof, all covered by a thick felt covering. These are home to nomad families who move with their herds

from pasture to pasture over summer, and later to hillsides to shelter from the bitter winter winds. Less than an hour's drive from the capital, Mongolia's main east–west highway is heavily potholed. For one lengthy stretch it's so bad that all drivers take parallel dirt tracks instead, leaving the tarmac to the animals. There is hardly any traffic. A few vans carrying passengers; articulated trucks, many laden with hay; motorcycles with three or four passengers; and a very few private cars.

The occasional 'towns' are single strips of battered, shabby buildings on either side of the road: shops, cafés, gas stations, tire repair places. They feel a lot like the Old West, especially since horses are still the primary means of transport for many. But look closely and you'll see that many of these *gers* have solar panels, wind turbines, and satellite dishes. Mongol's nomads move increasingly by pickup and motorcycle rather than on horseback. They make a pretty good living if they're good at raising and selling their livestock; after all, they pay no rent.

We overnighted at a tourist camp (a bunch of *gers*, a bar/restaurant, an ablution block) beside 'the little Gobi', an eighty-kilometre-long strip of sand dunes beside the ominously named Strangling Mountains, and went for a long hike. (We won't be going to the Gobi proper except when we take the train through, due to time/cost/end-of-season constraints. Next time.) The subsequent day we went to the Zanabazar Monastery next to the town of Karakorum.

Mongolia is primarily Tibetan Buddhist (of the Yellow Hat sect, same as the Dalai Lama). The Soviets, as part of their brutal repression of all Mongolian religion and nationalism during their de facto Cold War occupation of the country, razed all but three monasteries and killed some 30,000 monks. The Zanabazar Monastery has since been rebuilt, but its famous 108 stupas surround a mostly empty plain; still, the rebuilt buildings and the surviving paintings and sculptures within are striking. Most were hidden for decades by devout families who in doing so risked their livelihoods if not their lives. After the monastery, en route to our second tourist camp, we passed through the small, windswept, desolate near-slums of a town named Karakorum. Its population is maybe 10,000. Locals lead goats down its main streets, and they cart wood to the city on foot, in rickety wheelbarrows. Alone in the middle of the vast steppe, a six-hour drive west of Ulaan Baatar, with nothing to signify it but the rebuilt monastery, Karakorum feels very much like the middle of a postapocalyptic nowhere.

But once upon a time, believe it or not, this was the very centre of the world.

You've heard of Genghis Khan, of course. (Actually, 'Chinggis' Khan, mistranslated by a Persian way back when.) Leader of the savage Mongol hordes that raged across the world, their vast numbers overwhelming every army that they faced, looting and pillaging, destroying and despoiling civilization wherever they found it, right?

You might not have heard of Genghis Khan as the Great (albeit often brutal) Civilizer—the man who began as an illiterate slave but went on to forge the world's largest empire and make it a shining bastion of meritocracy, religious freedom, sexual near-equality, free trade, and high technology; the man whose dynasty lasted for generations; the man who always offered peace before he made war, whose forces besieged countless fortified cities occupied by professional armies who generally outnumbered the Mongols two or three to one, and generally conquered the cities in a matter of days, not with numbers but with overwhelming superiority in strategy, tactics, and technology. It's a heck of a tale.

Karakorum was for thirty years, seven centuries ago, the capital of that empire, a city that dripped with silk and caviar and Damascus steel, where a huge tree made of gold and silver poured wine and fermented mare's milk from its branches for the guests of the Khan. But even then, the city was still a long way from other cities—so long that the Khan rewarded merchants who brought trading caravans there by giving them asking price plus a bonus for all their wares. Despite its remoteness Karakorum was the capital of the greatest empire the world has ever seen, one that stretched from the Mediterranean to the Pacific, and from the Indian Ocean to the Arctic.

Nowadays, almost nothing remains. The lone and unlevel steppe stretches far away.

Home, home on the range, where the yak and the camel herds play
On the way back from Karakorum we saw some wild horses, reintroduced from European zoos after they went extinct in Mongolia. The national park they were in was a spectacular landscape of rippling golden hills. The horses weren't that exciting, but it's an interesting project, and seems to be going well. (The local wolf population is doing quite well off it too; apparently every year they eat half the new foals.) We didn't see any of the plentiful marmots in the area, which is perhaps just as well, as many/most carry bubonic plague.

We also stopped by a nomadic *ger* to say hi to its denizens. They were chosen at random by our guide and driver and didn't know any of us from Adam, but apparently nomads welcome visitors at any hour. After a quick snack of fried Cheeto-like dough and fermented mare's milk (like yoghurt mixed with millet beer) we exchanged pleasantries and wandered off again, after agreeing to drive one of the local men to the nearest town.

I don't usually like forced meet-the-locals encounters, but at least this one wasn't preplanned, and while there wasn't much to do but sit around awkwardly, the *ger* was interesting. None of the herds were visible; the only animals around were the people's riding horses (not to be confused with their meat/milk horses), hitched to a temporary wooden fence. The first *ger* had electricity powered by a car battery recharged by a solar panel; the second had a satellite dish, too.

Saddles, tack, plastic jerry cans, and general debris were scattered around the *gers*, but the inside of the one we visited was extremely clean and very cozy. The walls were lined by lacquered orange furniture—beds, sofas, cabinets—all painted with Tibetan-mandala patterns. To the right there was an iron stove in the middle, from which a pipe periscoped up through the roof. Next to the stove there sat a sheep stomach filled with intestines, and other hunks of meat were hung drying from the ceiling above the stove. Posters hung on the walls, and on the cabinets there were family pictures, a picture of the Dalai Lama and a Buddha sculpture. There were a couple of toddlers, too. (Most nomads have relatives in permanent cities, and send their school-age children to live with them during the school year.) All in all, very comfortable. The lack of running water's a bit of a drag, but if they could solve that problem, I could totally set up shop in a *ger*.

October 2006: 'An Especially Tricky People'
Beijing, China

What a difference a decade makes.

On the train from Ulaan Baatar, after we finally escaped the huge, blasted gravel-and-sand plain of the Gobi Desert, after bogies were changed so the train's wheels would fit the rails across the border, and passports were stamped, and we finally entered the Middle Kingdom—in my case, for the first time since March 1997—we rolled to a ten-minute halt at some nameless station in inner Mongolia, and I laced my boots up and wandered out onto the platform to stretch my legs—

— and I stopped dead. Because I knew that smell, I remembered it in my bones, in my deep cortex; smell is the sense most strongly linked to memory. The platform smelled like China.

I suppose I shouldn't have been surprised. And maybe it was just jasmine and cheap cigarettes. But for a second I froze in my steps, remembering.

You'll forgive me if I wax nostalgic a moment. The very first time I went seriously travelling, ten years ago, I backpacked solo across China for a month. In 1997 that was a pretty major feat. There was no Internet. Nobody, but nobody, spoke English; I spent a week without speaking a word of my mother tongue. Instead I had to get by with the exceedingly broken Mandarin Chinese I'd picked up from a single book language tape I read/listened to in the couple of months before I left San Francisco.

In retrospect I don't really know why I decided to go solo through China in '97. I wanted to see the Three Gorges before the dam went up, and I did, but I could have waited a few years. God knows it wasn't the easiest of destinations; quite the opposite—it was diving in at the deep end. I guess that was part of its appeal. Maybe most of its appeal.

I remember very well my first night there, lying in a bumpy sleeper bus travelling between Guangzhou and Yangshuo in the company of two Europeans I'd met just hours before, stopping at an inn halfway and looking around at the dark landscape and having a piercing revelation of just how far I'd come, just how far away I was from anyone or anything I knew, just how *alien* a place I had brought myself to without hardly knowing why.

I got by, even after I left Yangshuo and went way off the backpacker trail. I communicated, navigated, coped, bought tickets, took trains, found hotels. During that week when I spoke no English I was the only white guy on a boat that took three days to coast down the Yangtze from Chongqing to Wuhan, through the Three Gorges. To this day I can count to ten and order beer in Chinese.

Not that I've needed either skill this time. The language wars are over, and we won: English is now more widely spoken in Beijing than in Moscow. The city's once-shambling main streets have become wide boulevards lined by trees, fountains, flower gardens, massive government edifices, colossal shopping malls, five-star hotels. Wangfujing Dajie is like Fifth Avenue as a pedestrian walkway. McDonald's, Starbucks, Sizzler, Pizza Hut, Häagen-Dazs are everywhere. One thing about a totalitarian state, it sure makes for speedy urban renewal.

It is kind of fascinating to watch development in action. Ten years ago China was First World only in very isolated pockets and islands; now it's whole strips and zones, and not just downtown. Gargantuan fields of brand-new apartment buildings (and, to the government's credit, stands of newly planted pine trees) were visible as the train rolled into Beijing. Poke a little farther, one block behind, and you'll still find narrow alleys, ancient courtyards, jerry-rigged wires hanging low over the roads, crowds of bicycle rickshaws and street vendors, heaving throbbing masses haggling for cheaper dumplings; but these *hutongs* are being destroyed as I speak—literally. Just around the corner from where I type, the demolition crews work twenty-four hours a day.

Sometimes Beijing smells like China. Mostly it smells like a smokestack. The pollution, construction/destruction dust, and windblown Gobi sand add up to an incredible, constant, clinging, oozing smog. Today I went for a run around Tiananmen Square and barely managed twenty-five minutes before my breath got ragged. Maybe I'm out of shape. Maybe not. Tonight we walked back along the square, and could barely see through the dust and smog to the other side, and while it's big enough that it's served by three separate subway stations, it's not *that* big. My friend in the British Embassy says he's heard claims that breathing in Beijing is like smoking seventy cigarettes a day.

Modern Beijing is very pleasant, very easy, very nice to visit, still very colourful, lots of stuff to do, I recommend it. The smog won't affect (most of) you if you're only here a week or two. China has gotten rich and is getting richer, and that's good for China, and it's not like it's being culturally colonized by the West, its own culture is much too strong and vibrant for that, soon it'll start throwing its own snowballs back into the global cultural mix like Japan does. But it's no longer even remotely alien, and that's what China was for me ten years ago when for whatever reason I needed alien, and I miss that.

There are other alien places still. But one day, maybe one day not too far from now, there won't be any left at all, and that will be a shame.

October 2006: Top of the World, Ma
Beijing to Lhasa
Bureaucratic preparations for travel to Tibet these days are surprisingly straightforward. I arrived in Beijing and headed straight to BTG Travel in the I-thought-forlorn hope of scoring both Tibet permit and ticket inside of a few days. Couldn't have been easier. The permit required seventy-two hours to arrange (and cost a whopping 900 yuan, more than US$100). The train ticket was 1,216 yuan for an upper-berth soft sleeper. The flight back from Lhasa to Shanghai was 2,580 yuan, and BTG Travel themselves charged me a mere 100 yuan for booking it.

Three days later, I turned up at BTG and got my tickets and two A4 sheets of paper covered with official stamps certifying that I was an Official Tour Group that was Officially Permitted to enter the Tibet

Autonomous Region. (Or so they told me. I don't read Chinese.) The letter of the law still states that only tour groups can go to Tibet, but in the past few years said law's interpretation has been relaxed to include tour groups such as mine (one member, zero guides) and in fact if you fly into Tibet you will probably never actually see the permit.

I understand this permit process would have been much, much trickier if I had applied for a Tibet permit at the same time as I applied for a China visa, rather than after I was in-country, or if I was in-country as a journalist or diplomat rather than a tourist.

A train to Lhasa leaves Beijing every night at 9:30 p.m. I arrived early at the gargantuan *Blade Runner*ish hive that is Beijing West Railway station, stocked up on supplies (AA batteries were surprisingly difficult to dig up), and, at the appointed hour, filed with hundreds of other people through the Ticket Inspection checkpoint.

The ticket-takers barely glanced at my permit, then directed me to someone else, who directed me to someone else, who gave me a Chinese form and managed to translate its necessary fields into English. Then down to a clean, spacious, modern platform and onto a clean, spacious, modern train.

What the Chinese call a 'soft sleeper' is their equivalent of first class. Each soft-sleeper car has eight four-berth compartments, plush and comfortable, although the upper bunks are a bit tricky to get into if you're typical Chinese size. These bunks had a TV at the foot of every bed, with four Chinese channels, though you had to plug your own headphones in. (They showed *House of Flying Daggers* at the very end of the journey, which was a welcome diversion.) First class even includes complimentary slippers. Oh, yes: and a nasal oxygen cannula, i.e., a thin tube that goes into your nose.

Contrary to wild rumour, the trains to Lhasa are not pressurized. (I heard loose talk of a 'tourist train' next year that will be, but I'm skeptical.) The journey tops out at 5,070 metres above sea level. There are nozzles labelled 'Oxygen' in Tibetan, Chinese, and English next to every berth in soft and hard sleeper, and beneath every seat in soft seat (which are comfy enough but no comparison to the full-length sleeper beds) and the dining room. Some hissed apparently without provocation once we hit the Tibetan Plateau, upping the O_2 content of their compartments; most had to have a cannula plugged into them before they fired up. Or so I surmise; I'm pretty good with altitude and, like most of the passengers, never used mine.

We rolled out of Beijing at exactly 9:30, right on time, moving so smoothly at first that I didn't realize we were under way for at least a minute, and soon accelerating to speeds of over 150 kilometres per hour. Each compartment has scrolling LCD displays at either end that inform you (in Chinese and English) of the train number, departure station, terminal station, next station, speed, outside temperature, date and time, along with a couple of phone numbers (only in Chinese), and the frequent exhortation 'Have a good trip!' We didn't stay at 150 kilometres per hour the whole trip, though; across the Tibetan Plateau, we averaged more like 90 (still pretty impressive).

There are two toilets at the end of every car except the dining car: one Chinese (squat) and one Western for soft sleepers; two Chinese for all others. The soft sleeper has three sinks with soap outside the toilets, along with an automated samovar dispensing boiled water.

The dining car served food that ranged from edible to pretty good, for very reasonable prices: around 20 yuan for a greasy but tasty meal of meat, fried vegetables, and rice, 5 for a Coke, 10 for a Budweiser, which alas was the only beer they served even though China's Qingdao is far better. (The exchange rate was about 8 yuan to the US dollar.) The menu was only in Chinese, but pointing-at-random served me reasonably well, and pointing-at-what-looks-good even better. The staff were typically brusque, and kicked passengers out for a few hours each day so they could have the car to themselves. There were also a couple of food carts that rolled up and down the length of the train every so often.

From Beijing, the train was about half full. There were three Westerners: me and an Austrian-Slovakian couple who had been working in China for several months. When we reached Xining, some twenty-four hours after departing Beijing, more people flooded on, including a large Japanese tour group that took over almost my entire car, and another eight Westerners. The soft-seat cars were, mercifully, empty enough that many people were able to sprawl out over three chairs, and a whole hard-seat car was deserted. Strangely, no one took advantage of this.

The train was well-windowed, and though the windows grew streaked over the course of the journey, the (usually eye-catching) views were rarely if ever obscured. All the corridors are on the same side of the train, and each car has a half-dozen fold-down seats that let you sit by a window and watch the world go by (there's just enough room for someone else to squeeze past). At the junction areas between cars, windows open to either side. A few windows in each car theoretically folded down a little, but seemed locked, so at first I thought that I'd only be able to take pictures through the windows. However, it turned out that the windows in the bathrooms do fold open a little—in fact, *just* enough to permit the egress of a Canon PowerShot A620 and a pair of hands. Good thing I never got that SLR.

By the time I woke up and drank my Nescafé we were almost in Xi'an. We stopped there only briefly and weren't allowed off the train. As far as I could tell, of the half-dozen stops the train makes en route to Lhasa, you can get out at only two of them: Xining, which is midway, and Naqu, four and a half hours before Lhasa. Westwards through furrowed green highlands, steep river gorges, and loads of tunnels, making a couple of stops whose names escape me, before we reached the mighty Yellow River and followed its wide flow for some time. We arrived in Xining at about 9:00 p.m., after an unusually scenic but otherwise typical train ride across China, endless fields of green carved up by roads and cities.

Day two was anything but typical. At first, as we climbed gradually through the Kunlun mountains, there was absolutely nothing around the train but stark, ragged rock, not even lichen, it was like riding a train across the moon except for the snow-dusted mountains visible in the distance.

There was also a road. There would be for most of the journey; the tracks were largely built alongside the Xinjiang–Tibet Highway. Cargo trucks, a few passenger cars, and a bizarre convoy of more than fifty empty military trucks passed us as we continued through the Kunlun and emerged onto the Tibetan Plateau, which, although higher, is more bountiful than the mountains. Though not much. Only lichens and a few hardy grasses can survive this high. Amazingly, that's enough to support human habitation. Tibetan nomads wander with their herds of sheep and yaks throughout the entire plateau, usually by motorcycle, with modern tents, though I saw a few on horseback and on foot, and some yak-hair tents.

The terrain doesn't vary much: vast fields of furrowed hills of permafrost, barren but for clumps of brown grass and dark lichen, sometimes with a few snow-capped mountains in the distance, but it's beautiful, in the way a desert is beautiful. I was happy to spend hours sitting and staring out the window. (Mind you I also read two books on the train.) Mostly the train rides on a huge raised embankment walled by green metal fences, though the fence isn't yet complete, and workers constructing it were visible in some places.

At about 1:00 p.m. we reached our maximum altitude, the 5,072-metre-high Tanggula Pass. There was no announcement, and no real sign in the landscape, but I felt it coming. Even with the extra oxygen they pipe in, the altitude was hitting everyone on the train. I'm pretty good with heights, and even I felt dizzy, headachey, full of malaise. I forced myself to get up and walk through the train. Everywhere people were slumped on their bunks or their seats, staring dully and miserably out at nothing. Many were breathing through their cannulae, and one of the staff was administering medicine to an old Chinese woman. It felt a little like we were all fleeing some disastrous battle, or like the entire train had been poisoned. A couple hours later we were back down to 4,600 metres (according to my Japanese compartment-mate's altimeter) and life had returned; people were drinking beer and cracking jokes in the dining car, until the staff kicked them out.

There were occasional towns en route, if you can call them that: a few low barracks huddled slovenly on the steppe, maybe with a PetroChina gas station. There were enormous numbers of rivers and watercourses, mostly very wide and shallow. In some places water snaked through a few creases in those beds; in others, it was frozen solid. Birds flew past, black kites, and I saw some kind of crane next to the huge lake we hit at about 3:20. At about 5:20 we reached the first outcrops of the Himalayas proper; an hour later, we hit the outer ring of the towns that the surround Lhasa, and the traffic on the road beside us began to grow livelier. The sun set at 7:30, and then there was nothing to do but wait and watch *House of Flying Daggers* before we rode into Lhasa.

October 2006: Seventy Hours in Tibet
Lhasa, Tibet
Of course Tibet was never the idyllic Shangri-La of myth. Fourteen hundred years ago, its armies conquered half of China. Seven hundred years ago, when Tibetan Buddhism was the state religion of Kublai Khan, the monks were bitterly resented by the Chinese, who were forced to feed, shelter, and convey them at their own expense, and who were executed if they so much as raised a hand against a man in a saffron robe. And if you'd come here before the Chinese invasion seeking a land of spiritual bliss and meditative detachment from the material world, you'd have been barking a long way up the wrong mountain.

In 1943, Austrian mountaineers Heinrich Harrer and Peter Aufschnaiter escaped from a British POW camp in India and made an amazing journey across the Himalayas and into Tibet, where they stayed for seven years. Harrer describes a charming, friendly, welcoming country, but also one ruled by a corrupt theocracy that wasn't above using howitzers on rogue monasteries, and that viewed all kinds of progress and innovation as an attack on the absolute power of the monks. I'm certainly not trying to justify the Chinese invasion, and by all accounts the current Dalai Lama is an amazing human being, but if you were imagining pre-invasion Tibet as a land of peaceful enlightenment, guess again. (And frankly I found the Nepalis of six years ago a hell of a lot nicer than today's Tibetans; then again, to quote Matthew Hogan's classic essay, 'oppressed people suck'.)

Modern Lhasa is only about half Tibetan; the other half is a fairly modern (and fairly boring) Chinese city. In the streets you pass roughly equal numbers of Han Chinese and Tibetan faces (they're pretty easy to distinguish), large numbers of them wearing breathing masks against the city's acrid smog. Many of the Tibetans are poor peasants who have come to the big city to make a pilgrimage to the Jokhang Temple and the massive Potala Palace that looms above the heart of the city, surrounded by parks and plazas.

The palace is immense, with literally thousands of rooms. Hundreds of birds swarm above, and the views of Lhasa beneath and the mountains beyond are stunning. The chapels inside are feasts for the eyes; Tibetan Buddhism is all about relentless detail work and repetition, and in most of its rooms every square inch of every wall and ceiling is occupied by painted patterns, etchings, engravings, mandalas, *thangkas*, lacquered wood carvings, drapes, scarves, prayer flags, paintings of Buddhas or Wrathful Protectors, cubbyholes full of bronze Buddhas of Longevity or sacred books (about the size of bread loaves, loose-leaf but wrapped in leather and linen), all of it intricate and colourful. The central features are usually giant Buddha sculptures, or huge three-dimensional mandalas or stupas, or, in several cases, the tombs of Dalai Lamas, all made of metal, sometimes solid gold or silver. The tomb of the fifth Dalai Lama (seventeenth century)— considered one of the two all-time greats, along with the thirteenth (late nineteenth century)—is some twenty feet tall and apparently incorporates almost four tonnes of gold.

The thousands who filed through the Potala Palace today were about 30 percent tourists and 70 percent Tibetan pilgrims, mostly dressed in rough nomad clothing, chanting ceaselessly, wielding handheld prayer wheels or prayer beads, bags full of yak butter* and handfuls of money, which they left at the many offering sites.

---

* Most rooms in the palace boast large metal lantern-vats full of yak butter in which eight or ten candlewicks burn; the pilgrims help replenish the butter.

Occasionally we passed monks who worked there, keeping a stern eye on the treasures, or vacuuming the Buddhas, or just sitting and chatting over tea as if there was no herd of tourists and pilgrims filing past them. Despite the pilgrims and monks the palace felt more like a museum than a place of active worship. Of course, the Dalai Lama hasn't lived here for a good fifty years.

The streets around the Jokhang are a lot more lively. Seething crowds of pilgrims make the circuit around the temple—some on foot, some prostrating themselves all the way—passing walls of stalls selling all sorts of religious paraphernalia when they're not selling trinkets to tourists. (Including the 'Tibet' baseball cap I picked up for 30 yuan. The weather is cool—Lhasa's farther south than Cairo but also two miles up—but the sun at this altitude gets nasty in a hurry.) The local Muslims in their white caps hang out at the nearby mosques, cycle-taxis carry tourists to and fro, incense burns, and generally the whole area, indeed, much of the entire city, is a combination of Major Religious Site and Pedestrian Shopping Mall ... but in a good way.

July 2011: Notes from the Foothills of the Himalayas
Towards Manali, India
Wow. India has gotten positively *mellow*.

Relatively speaking, that is. Once—which is to say, the first two times I came here, in 2000 and 2004—it was a pounding, nonstop, all-out assault on every one of the human senses. For travellers it was a destination of constant hassle, a land of lies and scams (some so elegant that they were almost beautiful). Those moments of transition when I first stepped out of the airport and into India proper—the arena, if you will—remain two of my most searing, powerful travel memories.

This time? I girded my loins, battened my hatches, readied my defences, stepped past the airport barriers, and found myself beset by ... nothing. There was no gauntlet of touts or taxi drivers. Nobody noticed or cared. A twenty-first-century train service took me to New Delhi Railway Station. There was indeed a vast mass of humanity there, waiting to be security-groped before entering the metro—the *metro!* Delhi had no metro ten years ago, nor even any hint of one; now it's five times the size of Toronto's. I bypassed them and found an autorickshaw driver, who hardly tried to rip me off at all. We took a six-lane highway past green parks and the airbrushed Red Fort. And I kept thinking: 'Am I *sure* this is India?'

Don't get me wrong. Delhi and its zillions are still an all-consuming vortex of humanity. Step past the gleaming new shopping malls and five-star hotels and you'll find yourself in a twisting warren of narrow alleys and grinding poverty. Once, though, there was almost nothing *but* those narrow alleys, in which nothing seemed to happen; now they, too, thrum with activity, as men carry, drag, cycle, and drive immense loads through apertures that seem too small for them. Now droplets and pockets and even corridors of a whole new First World city has erupted from that sea of poverty, while brand-new satellite cities like Gurgaon boom on its outskirts. The infrastructure can't keep pace, but no wonder. It's all happening so *fast*.

On Thursday night we went to the offices of the Himachal Pradesh Tourism Development Corporation, and waited only ten minutes past the scheduled departure time, while a family of monkeys frolicked outside. (Cows and monkeys remain common sights in Delhi, but I don't expect to ever again see an elephant right outside the railway station, as I did in 2000.) Then a battered but seaworthy Volvo bus appeared, collected us, and carried us across Delhi's vast cityscape and along a massive under-construction highway to Chandigarh, via a stop at a roadside restaurant/department store that sold nearly-life-sized Indian Elvis statues, six-foot-high gold-plated lamps, and had a surprisingly decent book selection. A wretchedly bad Bollywood comedy played on the flat-screen TV, and M. (my travelling companion) and I took turns taking refuge in my iPod. I think it was about 2:00 a.m. when we finally began to ascend into the mountains, the foothills of the mighty Himalayas, the very roof of the world.

July 2011: Kullu Valley Blues
Manali, India
We felt the mountains long before we saw them, swaying back and forth with every switchback as we passed Tata and Ashok Leyland trucks, some driving by night, many more parked beside the road. The only road to Manali and thence Leh, National Highway 21, is not a route for the faint of heart or the low of skill. It climbs and climbs, paralleling and traversing many a sheer precipice and roaring river, and at its best it's two unmarked lanes. Plus there are all the more usual problems of

driving in India—the endless traffic and the endless chaos and the endless noise as everyone leans on their horn to survive.

Eventually the dark turned to light, though more slowly than normal, as we were driving along a steep gorge with five-hundred-foot walls on either side that kept us in deep shadow well into morning. The road wound past roadside diners and through fair-sized towns overlooking the Beas River. Scattered houses and a few temples somehow perched on the other side of the gorge, reached by bridges that were sometimes real bridges and sometimes little more than a pole laid horizontal and two ropes to hang on to while you walk across it. The gorge was lush, overgrown, intensely green. At first a few palm trees still hung on, down at its base, but as we climbed they vanished.

Then, suddenly, a tunnel—a tunnel a full three kilometres long, no less, dark and cavernous—and we emerged into the wide Kullu Valley, at the other end of which I sit and type. It, too, is a green and fertile land. Apple trees grow everywhere, surrounded by corn. Enormous pines reach a hundred feet or more towards the sky. The road up the valley is bleak and unattractive, and even the attempts at pleasantry by the many hotels and motels (the Kullu Valley received two million tourists last year, 80 percent of them domestic) do little to leaven its oppressive industrial feel; but everywhere else is green and glorious.

And then, finally, Manali; which is to say, its mud-pit of a bus stand, and overpopulated, overtrafficked streets. The first impression is not exactly welcoming. But the touts weren't too bad, and while my overall impression of the town itself has remained stuck at 'dung heap', there are many consolations. There's an absolutely wonderful park at one end of town, a huge and downright mystical cathedral of pines; there's only one official entrance, but I have discovered various other unofficial ones, some of which lead through fields of wild marijuana. Our hotel is a little bit away from the worst of the noise and the chaos. The people here are, by and large, very nice. And Old Manali, at the other end of the park, is a classic hippie-backpacker oasis à la Yangshuo in China, or Caye Caulker in Belize, or (once upon a time) the Vumba in Zimbabwe, albeit largely populated by that distinctly Indian mix of gorgeous Israeli girls and sketchy Israeli guys. (A few months in India after completing one's military service is Israel's gap-year equivalent, so the Israelis here tend to be young, extremely fit, and more than a little surly.)

Also, did I mention that there are mountains? There are

mountains, green and stark in the foreground, snow-capped in the distance. Today we hiked to an enormous and beautiful waterfall—the holy place sign next to it was really quite unnecessary—and (once I caught my breath) back down, and across the Beas River, and through three small villages, all of which are booming: new houses, new cars, new construction, new satellite dishes, the works. Between the cash crops, the tourism, the overall development of the region, and India's more generalized economic boom, Manali seems to be doing quite well.

As further evidence, I give you the ski resort we came across at the very end of today's trek, which in summer is a paragliding/quad-bike/pony-ride park, densely populated with domestic tourists. Near it is a sign that proudly proclaims the US$365-million tunnel that will replace the Rohtang Pass we intend to traverse on Tuesday, which will open up an entire new region to year-round access. I'm kinda glad I got here early enough to do it the old-fashioned altitude-sickness way. Kids today. Sheesh.

October 2012: Burmese Days
Bagan to Rangoon, Myanmar
'Bagan. Shit.'

That dusty land of many temples. And I mean *many*. Eighty percent of them have been razed by various conquerors or devoured by the ravenous mile-wide Irrawadday River, and still nearly three thousand remain, crammed into a mere hundred or so square kilometres of dusty land. More than two thousand pagodas and monasteries, ranging in size from 'chapel' to 'cathedral', all red brick covered by whatever may remain of weather-eaten plaster, occupying the foreground, background, and skyline in every direction, jutting into the sky above rice paddies, bushes, cactus walls, thatched farmhouses, five-star hotels, an eighteen-hole golf course. Some remain original, but most have been reconstructed—unconvincingly—

'What about you, Marlowe? Do you think my reconstruction methods have become ... unsound?'
'I don't see ... any method at all ... sir.'
—*Apocalypse Now*

—but they're still magnificent, eerie, mind-bending. Especially at dusk, when the packs of feral dogs who infest the area appear out of

nowhere and make it look like a land sacred to canine gods rather than human ones. But truth be told, I'm a little templed out, and the sight of just one more gilded Buddha might make me wince, or groan, or even howl with some kind of cumulative fury.

So I take the bus. Easy enough. It comes to pick me up at my guesthouse in the warren of motorcycle-ridden dusty streets called Old Bagan that overlaps the Monument Zone. Almost every establishment on these streets caters to tourists; there is almost no industry other than Bagan, in Bagan.

Only ten minutes out of town it is different. Everything is ragged, hardscrabble, utilitarian. The villages are wooden buildings mostly with thatched roofs, maybe one or two of corrugated metal. Roadside stalls sell gasoline in converted one-litre water bottles. The road is pitted but decent, and mostly empty; motorcycles are ubiquitous in Burma, but gasoline is expensive and intercity transit prohibitive.

Beyond the road's laterite red and the brown villages there is little but green on green. Rice paddies, orchards of spindly trees, tufts and thickets and clusters of bushes, flood plains filled with palm trees, steep hills dark green with thick uncultivated vegetation. Some few are topped by white-and-gold temples.

The bus has room for forty but carries only twenty: fifteen Burmese, dressed in *longyis*, mostly burdened with many bags of cargo carried as errand or favour; two elderly German women; a French couple; and me. The seats are large and comfortable, air conditioning hisses down to every seat, and floral curtains cover the windows against the sun. Music videos and surprisingly well-made Burmese movies play on the television at the front, with the soundtrack turned up to 11. The faces of the women and children are chalked with the by-now-familiar pale tree-bark paste, a combination of sun protection and (mostly) fashion. Here it is not artfully applied, as it is in stylish Mandalay; here it is streaked and smeared.

We stop for lunch at a large roadside restaurant of wooden terraces, where soup and rice and a Coca-Cola cost me a combined 1,500 kyat (US$1.90), a dark cloud of flies buzzes around the block of squat toilets, and women sell small roast chickens and other less identifiable foods from trays balanced on their heads. Back on the bus, and then, suddenly, the highway.

A gleaming, divided four-lane highway connects Yangon and Mandalay. It is almost entirely deserted but for buses. Once we pass a man in a ragged *longyi* with a wicker basket on his back, striding along the path worn into the highway median, carrying a bright C-shaped scythe in his hand, like some Burmese avatar of Death. All around is green, green, green: hills and trees and rivers but mostly an endless almost-indistinguishable green, a sea of life. Rainy season only just ended.

The penumbra of townships that surrounds Rangoon come as a rude shock. As does the smog, which I try to convince myself is fog.

Beyond Rangoon

So. Rangoon.

In a way it's like every Asian city rolled into one, but poorer. Blistering heat, cracked pavements, foot-high curbs, Stalinist towers linked by thick anarchic tangles of electrical wires, occasional colonial buildings whose stains and tarnish cannot conceal their magnificent bones, dense fields of sidewalk stalls hawking food and every cheaply made article under the sun, ancient automobiles of every description converted into taxis.

(Yesterday I rode in a red Volkswagen van, which I think was older than I am, to the Savoy Hotel, a converted colonial mansion, where I ate at Kipling's restaurant and drank at the Captain's Bar while watching Tottenham Hotspur play Chelsea. I suppose I should have quaffed gin-and-tonics rather than Dagon beer to make the colonial kabuki play complete. Note to H.P. Lovecraft fans: Yangon/Rangoon's original name, for some five hundred years, was Dagon.)

Rangoon is located at the confluence of three rivers, not far at all from the ocean, beneath the hill that is allegedly the most sacred spot on Earth. Said hill is now host to the Shwedagon Pagoda, the most colossal temple in all of Myanmar. The main pagoda and the forest of lesser towers and filigreed halls full of colourful Buddhas that surround it are indeed quite impressive; I overheard a guide claim that they were decorated with a full sixty tons of gold. But what I liked most about the place was the vast plaza that surrounded it, and its endless exterior nooks and crannies, and its laid-back feel. People come here to worship, yes, but also just to hang out. I would like churches far more if they were the same.

From the Pagoda you can see Rangoon sprawled out before you like a reeking corpse. That's unflattering, isn't it? But there's no denying it: the city smells. It's a little fresher near its inland lakes, Inya and Kandawgyi, where the upscale suburbs full of embassies can be found. But it's even riper near the rivers, where the jetties are strewn with filth and chaos, where hawkers shielded from the awful sun by parasols sell fruit and other foods of every description and some that threaten to defy any at all. The traffic there, both human and industrial, is churning and constant. (But no motorcycles; they are banned in the city center, as autorickshaws are in downtown Mumbai.) Another pagoda down by the river is all but sealed off by a gigantic wall of shipping containers.

The downtown is divided into occasional wide one-way avenues interspersed with many narrow alleyways thick with life and commerce and dogs. The sheer number of feral dogs in Myanmar must be immense. They find places in the shade to hide during the worst of the day, but in the last hour before dusk they come forth. I saw packs numbering in the dozens in the shadows of the temples of Bagan, and another ranging up the train tracks in central Rangoon this afternoon, beneath the four monumental pagoda-like towers of the central train station, keeping a wary but not fearful distance from the humans doing the same. They are silent and watchful. One could almost get the sense that they are waiting for something.

Not so the human population. What they have been waiting for—freedom—seems at last to be at hand, after fifty years of military tyranny, and the city is erupting with life, action, noise, trade. Department stores and new hotels are under construction all through the downtown. Shirtless labourers pause to stare at flocks of beautiful young women in filigreed cheongsam-like outfits beneath delicately decorated parasols. Elderly taxi drivers regard their new city with some suspicion; they have no longer seen it all. Bald Buddhist monks mingle in the markets, small groups of fresh-faced bespectacled teenagers, or lone burly men with tattoos beneath their saffron robes. Even during the heat of midday hardly anyone lingers. Everyone seems to have a mission. Except for me.

Not far east of my hotel is the Ministers' Building, once the seat of Burma's government: a colossal colonial complex of red brick, occupying an entire city block. Seven years ago the government was moved to a purpose-built city midway between Yangon/Rangoon and Mandalay, and today the complex languishes abandoned, its grounds thickly overgrown, rusted strands of barbed wire green with moss dangling from its outer fence. Aung San and his entire cabinet were assassinated in this building one dark and bloody day more than fifty years ago, before the military took over.

Now there is talk of converting the whole edifice into another four- or five-star hotel. To an outsider that may seem somehow disrespectful of the past; but then, in Burma, and especially Rangoon, the past is not something that anyone wishes to cherish or celebrate. This is a city giving itself with abandon to the future.

October 2012: Notes from the Burma Road
Pyin U Lwin, Myanmar

I write to you from Pyin U Lwin, née Maymya, roughly seventy horizontal kilometres east and a thousand vertical metres up from Mandalay, in Myanmar, aka Burma. It's a town originally built circa 1900 by the British as their summer capital; every year their civil service would move here *en masse* for several months to escape the brutal heat of Rangoon. They left behind a church, a clock tower, a number of magnificent colonial buildings now converted into hotels or government offices, the loveliest botanical gardens I've ever seen, and sizable Indian and Anglo-Burman populations. There's also a railway station, of course, on the line from Mandalay to Lashio, which in turn was one terminus of World War II's famous Burma Road.

But enough of history. If ever a nation has had too much of history, it is this one, and today, at last, it seems finally to be shrugging off history's yoke. Today the streets of Pyin U Lwin bustle with thousands of motorcycles (and scores of horse-carriages) and shake with the passing of Toyota trucks. On the road here, the 'gas station' we stopped at consisted of a few metal barrels from which gasoline was siphoned into large aluminum kettle-like containers, which were then poured into cars via a big aluminum funnel; but that was an aberration. Directly across the divided highway was a modern (albeit Chinese-style, pagoda like, not Western-style) gas station, and I've seen far more of the latter than the former.

Wandering around yesterday, I came upon, to my surprise and delight, a very new and very modern Japanese lakefront restaurant serving Thai, Chinese, and sushi. I hadn't even known there was a lake. Discretion being the better part of inland Burmese sushi, I didn't try it, but still. There was free wi-fi, too, slow but acceptable. I haven't come across any blocked sites at all, although uploads to Flickr seem to be barred in some way. They begin, get to 5 or 10 percent, zero out, begin again, etc., ad infinitum.

Many of the women and children here wear wing-shaped pats of clay smeared artfully upon either cheek (and sometimes chin and forehead, too) allegedly as sunscreen and moisturizer, which gives them the look of going about semi-masked at all times. Girls also start riding motorcycles at a young age, so it's not uncommon to see two teenage clay-faced girls roaring along on a motorbike, one driving and the other riding sidesaddle, in flowing clothes utterly devoid of any road-rash protection … with one or even both in conversation on their mobile phone. It's pleasingly surreal.

On the whole, though, this is no longer the Land That Time Forgot. True, there are no chain stores here, and I've seen no Western brands at all except for Coke, Pepsi, and Apple, but while Burma/Myanmar is much less wealthy than Thailand or even Cambodia, it really doesn't qualify as remote and isolated anymore. Twice now I've been passed, while walking, by gleaming new tour buses full of elderly Europeans. Everyone seems very pleased to see so many tourists—many smile and/or cry out 'Hello!' to me as I pass—but no longer surprised. And this is just the beginning; once ATM and credit-card connections are forged (right now it's a cash-only country) and visas-on-arrival are implemented, the floodgates are *really* going to open. After all, it's only US$200 return from Bangkok to either Mandalay or Yangon.

This whole post-tyrannical phase is deeply weird for the traveller; I can only imagine what it's like for the Burmese. Is it okay to spend money at government-owned establishments now that Aung Sun Suu Kyi has picked up her Nobel Peace Prize and joined the parliament? (Although she's still barred from the presidency because her sons are foreign citizens.) Pyin U Lwin is a resort for wealthy Burmese and Chinese with a golf course and a dozen high-end hotels. Do the worldly, fashionably dressed packs of young rich Burmese I saw laughing and goofing off in the botanical gardens today feel unease about their families' presumed complicity with the military government? Or relief that they're no longer international pariahs? Do they expect amnesty or do they fear prosecution? Do they think about it at all?

While waiting for our Myanmar visas at the Bangkok embassy, the subtext of most discussion was 'I'm so glad I get to go there *now*, before it's *ruined!*' To which I couldn't help but think: *What, ruined by democracy and freedom? Come on!* And yet. I can't say I didn't understand. To the traveller Myanmar always loomed large as another world entirely, one shrouded behind the curtain of tyranny; travelling there, it was said, was like travelling back in time. No longer. I felt far more in-another-world in the global shipping hub of Djibouti last year than I do here. Of course being connected to the world, its wealth, its investors, and its goods and medicines and technologies is inarguably a good thing; and yet, for the travellers who seek places away from not just the madding crowds but also that web of roads and wires called modern society, it's a little bittersweet to see them all being slowly eaten up, one by one, year after year.

Well, not *all.* You can still get really remote and isolated and untouched-by-the-modern-world if you really want to. You can mount an expedition to the Danakil Depression in Ethiopia, or the Irian Jaya jungle of Indonesia, or the remote mountain vastnesses of western Nepal; it just takes a whole lot of time and work and money. And in Burma/Myanmar it's arguably a moot point, as it was already heavily economically influenced by China before the doors were opened to the West.

But as much as I approve of the web of data packets and supertankers and shipping containers that connects us all, I'm glad I commenced my travelling career before it was quite so pervasive. In China in 1997 and West Africa in 1998 I felt—because I *was*—far away, in genuinely alien lands, to which one could venture and return (and make phone calls) but not expect to check your e-mail daily or eat at Pizza Hut in every major city. It seems kind of a shame to me that today's generation of travellers will never have that same experience unless they put a whole lot of time and effort (and money) into it. The changes are for the greater good, of course, but at the same time, I think it's fair to say that something has been lost.

October 2013: On Farming Coral
Moalboal, Philippines
'You know,' I said to Gavin, an old friend and fellow traveller—we first met on a Himalayan trail in Nepal, thirteen years ago—'I've spent ten days around here, that's way more than I've spent almost anywhere else I've travelled to. I thought I'd get a deeper and more nuanced understanding of the place than if I'd just spent a few days.'

'And did you?' he inquired.

'Nope.'

Moalboal may not have hidden depths, but it is not without its intriguing elements. Its geology, for one thing, is striking: the earth for many miles around this peninsula essentially consists of a vast coral atoll that rose above the sea millennia ago. You don't have to dig very far—in fact, half the time you don't have to dig at all—to come across the bedrock of dead coral: jagged, striated, fractally pockmarked, and extremely hard.

The result is a brittle and infertile land. Mamas, don't let your babies grow up to be coral farmers. There are virtually no actual fields within a five-kilometre walk of the mid-scale beachfront resort in which we stayed. In many places crops are planted within the little bowls of topsoil caught within what is essentially an outcrop of solid coral. In several places farmers have built waist-high lattices and grown cucumbers in the air rather than try to sow this coral soil.

As a result Moalboal is quite a poor corner of the Philippines, which otherwise feels reasonably wealthy, albeit with income inequality that makes America look like Sweden. The little rural villages, which dot the white-coral roads winding through the thin greenery, are still to a considerable extent made of wood with thatched roofs, though concrete is making inroads. Coconut palms have successfully colonized the coast (though oddly no one here seems to eat coconuts) and banana plantations have taken root, but almost no real trees of any size grow within ten kilometres.

Everyone has a phone, of course, and cell towers dot the landscape; don't get me wrong, it's not *that* poor. But those phones are almost invariably old candy-bar Nokias.

They do raise livestock here. Chickens squawk across the road, using their wings to accelerate out of the way of oncoming motorbikes. Little tethered goats nibble at everything. Lone cows low mournfully at passersby. One family along my usual running route was raising a flock of turkeys, and on my drive today, in the hills, I saw an ostrich prance through a pasture in which a few cows also grazed contentedly. A 'tricycle'—a motorcycle with a sidecar, usually two tiny passenger seats mounted front-and-back, but sometimes a cage for cargo—once rattled by with two full-size pigs pressed into its cage. Piglets sell for US$25, full-size pigs for $100 and up.

And then there are the semi-feral dogs, small and cautious, with fur patterned faintly like tigers, picking their way along the roads and through the scrub that manages to cling to the coral soil. Many are mangy and ridden by parasites. By night they seem to triple in number. There are a surprising number of frogs, too, which speaks to the general cleanliness of the environment; amphibians are the canaries of the coastal world, almost always the first to be decimated by pollution.

That environment supports two of the region's only three real economic activities: fishing and diving. (The third is transit; Moalboal proper, a town that basically consists of a few dusty and congested roads five kilometres east of the coast, is a minor nexus on the single highway that runs up the west side of Cebu Island.)

We were there in part for the diving, which I think used to be world-class. The reefs start from the beach—in fact, with a couple of exceptions for beaches that I believe to be artificial, the reefs *are* the beach. No frolicking barefoot on the coastline here, not with sharp coral waiting to scar your feet with bloody cuts that take weeks to heal. Only a little ways out the coral drops almost vertically to a depth of fifty metres. The current sweeps along parallel to that cliff, so you don't even need to swim, you just drop down and drift. Better yet, a few kilometres offshore is the island of Pescador, an almost perfect circle of green, essentially a thin cap on a tall cylinder of coral that, again, drops steeply and is perfect for drift dives.

But the reefs are dying. Oh, they're certainly not dead yet, don't get me wrong, and in the one marine reserve in the region they remain quite lively. On my very first dive I found myself in the midst of a dense flickering school of sardines the size of a small shopping mall. One group (not us) dived with a whale shark a few days later. We saw a half-dozen turtles, a sea snake, and an amazingly alien-looking jellyfish.

But, on Pescador in particular, which looked, from the surface, like paradise for divers, and probably once was, there were big holes in the coral that spoke of dynamite, and the reefs were battered and bleached out and dived out and fished out, pale and lifeless, and the clouds of fish that still surround it were all worryingly small. Gavin mentioned that while snorkelling he'd come across a spear fisherman with a stack of recently killed fish, none of which were bigger than his hand.

Panagsama, the dive area west of Moalboal, is a classic dive town: a single coral street lined by a half-dozen dive shops and the lodges, bars, restaurants, convenience stores, and souvenir shops that go along with them. There are places like it in tropical coastal places all over the world, although they usually don't have quite the same thinly veiled undercurrent of prostitution. (Yes, that's right, yet another little town in Southeast Asia where you see a whole lot of relatively wealthy decrepit white dudes with poor, young, temporary girlfriends. Act surprised.) In 'the season', which allegedly begins two weeks from now, all these establishments are allegedly packed. But if the reefs keep dying—and worldwide, there's considerable evidence that *all* coral reefs are dying, as the oceans warm, even without the helping hand lent by the local fishermen here—that whole stretch will turn into a ghost town, and Moalboal will get even poorer.

But, on the other hand, what are you going to do other than overfish, given that the alternatives consist of either farming coral or moving to the desperately squalid shantytowns around Cebu City a hundred kilometres away? (And if you say 'Teach them to code', I will personally drive to your house and slap you with a sea snake.)

It's such a pretty spot. But I don't see how it has a future.

How to drain the sea?

I started wandering around the world way back in 1997, which means, according to *The Economist*, that my globetrotting has more or less corresponded with the most extraordinary period of disruption, growth, and change across the developing world in all of recorded history, one which is now coming to a close. Sheer luck, for me, that I managed to witness so much of this change from the ground level.

It was change that has indisputably been immensely beneficial. China, India, and sub-Saharan Africa, to name three examples I've visited in person two or three times each over that period, are (as a whole) so much better off now than they were then that any comparison is almost comical. But now that great transformation is coming to an end. Is another one coming, propelled by technology? Can the transition from Nokia candy bars to Android smartphones kick-start places like Moalboal?

I used to think maybe, but now, I don't see it. There'll be plenty of benefits, sure, and some will go to Moalboal, too, but more and more I think our economic systems are set up such that most of the benefits of new technologies accrue to those who already have a head start. Capitalism rewards competitive advantages, but some places don't *have* any competitive advantages, or, like Moalboal, are seeing the ones they do have global-warmed and overfished (and/or automated) into extinction.

My ruminations on how development works, a few years back, ended with likening long-term poverty eradication to 'draining the sea'. Sometimes, though, you drain the sea and all you find is infertile coral beneath. Maybe there'll be some way to make it bloom, but right now, I can't imagine what that would be.

This Big Weird, Wonderful World

Like so much else about my travels, my superb timing was dumb luck.

I didn't plan to travel across much of Africa and Asia before the Internet really reached them, but I'm very glad I did. That made it possible to be truly remote, genuinely far away from the world in which I was raised. I feel sorry for travellers who commenced their voyaging only a few years after I did. That haunting, thrilling remoteness has become difficult to attain.

I didn't plan for my travelling career to encompass the extraordinary period during which globalization, mobile phones, and the Internet drew almost all of our far-flung world together into a single interconnected web. It was dumb luck that I was able to spend so many months of my life witnessing that transformation.

I always wanted to be a writer, and I always wanted to travel, but it took me an embarrassingly long time to realize that I might somehow combine those things. It was dumb luck that I wrote a thriller about Western travellers in the developing world at the right time just before I moved to the UK, a ripe market for that kind of thing. It was luckier yet that I then parlayed that book deal into six years spent as a full-time wandering novelist.

Some people like to plan their travels out in detail, in advance. Not me. I believe in turning up with only a few vague goals in mind, always ready—no, eager—to abandon any plans in favour of the unexpected opportunity, the destination with the magical name, the curious side road that catches your eye. Never be shackled to plans you made before you understood what your destination was really like, before you began to know its streets and smells and people. In travel and in life, blind obedience to plans will make you deaf to dumb luck's knocks.

There's a moment of tense trepidation I still experience before I step out of an airport into a new city, or cross a border into a new nation; a moment before I leave the world I understand in favour of consciously giving myself over to the unknown. I've learned to cherish that moment. Because the world is much larger, much weirder, and far more full of wonders than we know.

Photo Captions*

---

* All photographs were taken by the author.

About the Author

Born to an expatriate Rhodesian father and a Canadian mother, Jon Evans grew up in Waterloo, Ontario, and graduated from the University of Waterloo. He has a degree in electrical engineering and over ten years of experience working as a software engineer.

Evans won the 2005 Arthur Ellis Award for Best First Novel from the Crime Writers of Canada for his book *Dark Places* and has been reviewed in such publications as *The Economist* and *The Washington Post*. His graphic novel *The Executor* was named one of the Ten Best of 2010 by Comic Book Resources, and his novel *Beasts of New York* won a 2011 ForeWord Book of the Year medal.

Evans has also written for magazines such as *Maisonneuve, The Times of India, The Walrus,* and *Wired,* and the newspapers *The Globe and Mail* and *The Guardian.* He writes a weekly column for *TechCrunch.* Now based in California, he frequently travels the world to research the locations of his novels.